GLYPH 7

GLYPH

TEXTUAL STUDIES

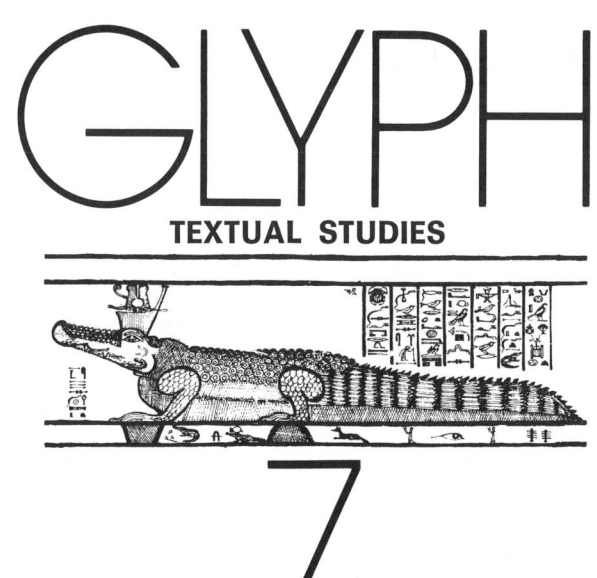

7

The Strasbourg Colloquium: Genre
A Selection of Papers

THE JOHNS HOPKINS UNIVERSITY PRESS
Baltimore and London

The Johns Hopkins University Press, Baltimore, Maryland 21218
The Johns Hopkins Press Ltd., London

STATEMENT TO CONTRIBUTORS

The Editors of *Glyph* welcome submissions concerned with the problems of representation and textuality, and contributing to the confrontation between American and Continental critical scenes. Contributors should send *two* copies of their manuscripts, accompanied by return postage, to Samuel Weber, Editor, *Glyph*, Humanities Center, The Johns Hopkins University, Baltimore, Maryland 21218. In preparing manuscripts, please refer to *A Manual of Style*, published by the University of Chicago Press, and *The Random House Dictionary*. The entire text, including extended citations and notes, should be double-spaced.

Copies of *Glyph*, both hardbound and paperback, may be ordered from The Johns Hopkins University Press, Baltimore, Maryland 21218.

The illustration on the cover and title page, an Egyptian crocodile from the Ptolemaic period, is reproduced through the courtesy of the Walters Art Gallery, Baltimore.

CONTENTS

	Foreword	vii
ONE	Genre PHILIPPE LACOUE-LABARTHE AND JEAN-LUC NANCY	1
TWO	Genus Universum MICHEL BEAUJOUR	15
THREE	Writing into the Wind, Bettina FRIEDRICH KITTLER	32
FOUR	The Infinite Text MANFRED FRANK	70
FIVE	The Mixture of Genres, The Mixture of Styles, and Figural Interpretation: *Sylvie*, by Gérard de Nerval RODOLPHE GASCHE	102
SIX	The Politics of Prose and the Art of Awakening: Walter Benjamin's Version of a German Romantic Motif IRVING WOHLFARTH	131
SEVEN	The Theory of Accidents DENIS KAMBOUCHNER	149
EIGHT	La Loi du genre/The Law of Genre JACQUES DERRIDA	176
APPENDIX	Bulletin of the International Colloquium on Genre	233
	Notes on Contributors	239
	Notes on Translators	240

FOREWORD

THE PAPERS PUBLISHED in this volume of *GLYPH* are among those presented to an International Colloquium on "Genre," held at the University of Strasbourg in July 1979. The colloquium, which was attended by around 150 persons from Europe and North America, was sponsored by the universities of Strasbourg, SUNY Buffalo, and Johns Hopkins.

The papers were distributed in advance of the colloquium and give a general indication of the considerations that led to its organization. Beyond the specific questions addressed, the Strasbourg gathering was meant to serve as a focal point for a variety of research activities situated on the border of literary criticism and philosophy, and engaged in an effort to rethink the relation of "literature" to its conceptualization in those disciplines.

The texts here published can, of course, give only a partial impression of the proceedings in Strasbourg, for obvious reasons. First, they comprise less than half of the papers submitted, presented, and discussed at the conference. The full dossier of the Strasbourg proceedings, including the seminars and discussions as well as all written contributions, can be obtained by sending a check for $10 (US or Canadian) payable to *l'Agent comptable de l'U.S.H.S.* to: Karin Ferreto, Groupe de recherches sur les théories du signe et du texte, Université des Sciences Humaines, 25 rue du Maréchal Juin, 67084 Strasbourg Cedex, France. The second reason why the papers here presented can give only a partial impression of the Strasbourg meeting is the fact that what distinguished this gathering from many others was its "communicative context," one that was not guaranteed, as is frequently the case in large international congresses, by the consensus of an academic discipline or of a strictly defined subject-matter, but rather by the far more elusive contours of a set of problems, addressed but not limited by the preliminary statement on "Genre." The risks involved in such an undertaking were evident from its inception. As an attempt to explore the possibilities of interaction based upon a set of similar concerns, the colloquium was surely only a partial success. But in allowing the problems and obstacles to such interaction to emerge with more clarity than before, in indicating that the "same" problems or questions can yet have such differing aspects depending upon the linguistic and cultural configurations in which they are approached, the Strasbourg Colloquium pointed—mutely, despite the constant flow of discourse throughout its five days—at factors situated beyond or outside of discursive practices, narrowly defined. After all of the assertions and affirmations, this remains, for me at least, the question generated by the colloquium on "Genre."

SAMUEL WEBER

GLYPH 7

ONE

GENRE

Philippe Lacoue-Labarthe
and Jean-Luc Nancy

WHAT THEN, is the question?

Quite simply, it is *the* question: "What is literature?"

In Romanticism's own terms, and especially in those peculiar to the very well-known fragment 116 (on which, from all indications, the *Lessons* and the *Conversation* are, after all, the commentary) a certain question arises: "What is Romantic poetry?" To be more precise: "What is the Romantic genre?" Consequently, this question is nothing less than what, in condensed form, we called the question of the "literary genre."

In any case, the important thing is that the question be precisely *this* question. That is to say that first of all, the question must persist and be maintained—and obviously, that we must wait for the answer. It does not only mean that Romanticism is, strictly speaking, the locus at which this question appears, nor even that Romanticism inaugurates the era of literature. Nor does it only mean that, as a result, Romanticism can find no other definition than that of the perpetual introversion of the question, "what is Romanticism," or "what is literature?" It means rather that Romanticism, as such, dates literature as its constant auto-implication, and as the ever-repeated asking of its own question. It means therefore that there is and can be no answer either to the Romantic question or to the question of Romanticism. Or at least, that the answer could only be interminably deferred, a constantly deceptive

From Philippe Lacoue-Labarthe and Jean-Luc Nancy, *L'Absolu littéraire, Théorie de la littérature du romantisme allemand* (Paris: Seuil, 1978), pp. 265–78.

answer which always recalls the question (if only by denying that it is still necessary to ask the question). This is why Romanticism, which comes into being at a given moment, the moment of its question, will always be more than just an "era," or, on the other hand, why, even now, it has not stopped in-completing the era it began. And this is something of which Romanticism was perfectly conscious: "The genre of Romantic poetry is still in the process of becoming; it is its true essence to be always only becoming and never to be capable of completing itself." (*Ath.* 116: "Die romantische Dichtart ist noch im Werden; ja das ist ihr eigentliches Wesen, daß sie ewig nur werden, nie vollendet sein kann.")[1]

Romanticism finds itself in an impossible situation where it cannot answer the very question with which it is confused, or in which it is entirely caught up. This inherent impossibility within Romanticism is, of course, the reason why the question is actually an empty one, and why, under the rubric of Romanticism or of literature (or of "Poetry," "*Dichtung*," "Art," "Religion," etc.), the question only comes to bear on something indistinct and indeterminate, something that indefinitely recedes as one gets closer to it. It is something susceptible to being called (almost) any name, but not able to tolerate any one of these names: it is an unnameable thing without shape or form—in the end, this something is "nothing." Romanticism (literature) is that which has no essence, not even in its inessentiality. And this, after all, is perhaps the reason why the question is never really asked, or else, why it is asked an incalculable number of times—and why the Romantic texts, in their fragmentation or even in their dispersion, are only the interminable answer (always approximate, neither here nor there) to the question that is really unformable, *i.e.*, always too quickly, too lightly and too easily formulated, just as if the "thing" worked all by itself.

Moveover, neither the fragments (for "form"), nor religion, for example (for "contents"), unless it be *vice versa*, could adequately answer or ask the question of literature (of Romanticism), since, in any case, all of these only came to be by removing what they had sought to enclose; or, to state it another way, they were only the *Darstellung* of what was refused to every presentation in itself, in the exact ratio of its will to appear. "Literature" did not start to devote itself just yesterday to swerving from the truth. If one noticed that the term "mystical" designated the specular itself for Schlegel,[2] it remains nevertheless clear that, quite understandably, he signalled thereby the negative theology of Jacob Boehme. This was necessary then, as it will always be, if one dares to say "another turn." And in many ways, this is what the *Conversation* represents here.[3]

There are two reasons for this, the first one being, of course, the fact that the *Conversation*, once again, seems to attack the question head on. It has to do quite openly with "poetry" (literature); of all the texts that appeared in the *Athenaeum*, it is the only essay of any depth devoted to poetry. Or at least, it is the most ambitious of them. Most importantly, it is auto-referential by its own method of exposition, its *Darstellung*: it is a dialogue, and that fact alone is sufficient to bring to the fore the same question of literature, brought into play here until the time that it becomes witness to its own impossibility. But we know all too well that this question will never be brought into play except by means of the "formalist" inversion, by the endless interreflection (*mise-en-abyme*) that is inseparably specular and speculative. And it is not quite certain that, in this interreflection, the question is always capable of losing that very thing (what thing?) it claimed was the question.

But here it is necessary to de-compose.

And to note, first of all, that the dialogue, no more than the letter or the aphorism, is not a stranger to fragmentation. Moreover, it will be recalled that this was unequivocally announced in *Ath.* 77: "A dialogue is a chain or a crown of fragments. An exchange of letters is a dialogue on a greater scale, and memorabilia are a system of fragments." ("Ein Dialog ist eine Kette, oder ein Kranz von Fragmenten. Ein Briefwechsel ist ein Dialog in vergrössertem Maßstabe, und Memorabilien sind ein System von Fragmente.) We have spoken of the "necessity of fragmentation."[4] The words could not be more appropriate when they refer to the *Ideas* and to the *Letter to Dorothea*.

On the whole, Friedrich never yielded one bit on this early demand of Romanticism. If we may make a conjecture, he would even rather have "increased" its role (—think, for example, of the fact that the *Conversation* itself does not fail to contain a letter). As we shall see momentarily, this is doubtless the explanation for the rather singular fashion in which he conceives and creates dialogue, not at all comparable to that of August (who had strongly encouraged him along this line),[5] nor to that of Novalis (whom Friedrich in turn, with his usual strategy, had more or less encouraged to follow the same path).[6]

The essentially fragmentary nature of the dialogue has at least one consequence (among many others which we cannot examine here): the dialogue, no more than the fragment, does not properly constitute a genre. This is the reason why, in fact, the dialogue, like the fragment, is a privileged battlefield for the question of genre as such. But let us not be too hasty.

The fact that the dialogue is not a genre means first of all (by means of an equivalency to which we are already accustomed) not that the dialogue lacks something vis-à-vis genre, but rather that it can, by definition, contain all genres. The dialogue is the "non-genre," or the "genre" that is a mixture of genres. The dialogue thus takes us back not only to its own origin (*i.e.*, for Schlegel, a Platonic one), but also to the Roman satire, and, in general, to all the late literature of the Alexandrine era in which all the forms of ancient poetry, including philosophy, of course, came together, reflecting each other, thereby fulfilling themselves. From this fact is also issued the very tight link forged between dialogue (and the fragment as well, but in a more immediate manner for the former) and the spirit of society (the social, the urban[e]), the *Witz*, great culture, popularity, lively intellectualism, virtuosity, etc.: in short, all those values and qualities that Romanticism took from the tradition of the Enlightenment and from English or French moral philosophy, qualities which, by the way, the dialogue had not failed preferentially to cultivate.[7]

We are now in well-charted territory. This also explains how the dialogue, by perpetuating the necessity of fragmentation, allows for the appearance of several contradictions, which no genre (or "genre") theretofore used by Schlegel in the *Athenaeum* had permitted. In distinction from the letter in particular, which was based quite emphatically on the opposition between writing and speech (that is to say as well, as we have mentioned, between masculinity and femininity), and which, because of that, carried to its most acute point the problem of popularity.[8] The dialogue (and we are not twisting things around in order to state matters in this fashion) is actually in the position of a relief (*relève*) inasmuch as, in the *Conversation*, it is explicitly given as the transcription (a more or less exact one, to which point we shall return) of real conversations. Moreover, to see women, in fact, oppose the spontaneous practice of simple conversation (though it be brilliant) and call rather for reports, that is, for the reading of written texts, is not one of the lesser paradoxes of this text. This exchange of roles is revealing as well, and we shall soon see, in the most minute fictional creation of the *Conversation*, that the male protagonists' observation of this female injunction allows the dialogue's author to realize the wish he had previously expressed in the *Letter to Dorothea*, and to write, by mixing styles and genres (thus including the "letter" itself) these little essays whose number he hoped to increase. He no longer feared the proliferation of "projects" in which the rapid change of subject inherent in a lively conversation was cause for worry, and which essays were a necessary step to be taken on the road to true popularity. In this way, the dialogue, once and for all, attained the position of what we have called the "moral genre of the fragment," and, if it does not wholly fulfill this (we shall see why), it actually only misses the mark by very little. From this point on, the reader is not astonished when, under the rubric of "didascalic genre," or, what comes to the same thing, under the rubric of the "reciprocal transfers between poetry and philosophy," he finds that one of the reports especially insists on the gnomic aphorisms (and the philosophical dialogues).[9] Nor is he astonished when he finds that one of its substitutes (in this case, the "letter") refers, with the intercalation of Rousseau, to the tradition of the confession, or to that of "subjective literature" in general.[10] The dialogue is, above all, the "genre of the Subject."

And paradoxically, this brings the dialogue back to its origin, that is to say, to Plato. In fact, all the themes that we have briefly outlined above interweave and intersect around what fragment 42 of the *Lyceum* calls "the exalted urbanity of the Socratic muse" ("die erhabne Urbanität der sokratischen Muse"). For modern metaphysics, it follows once again that Socrates (the person and the character) has always represented the projected incarnation or prototype of the Subject itself. For Schlegel, at least, the reason is that Socrates (*i.e.*, Plato's Socrates; the Socrates in Plato's works) is, in a wholly privileged way, what could be termed the ironic subject; in other words, Socrates is the locus at which the very exchange that defines irony ("logical beauty," ["*logische Schönheit*"] according to *Lyceum* 42) operates both figuratively and in practice. This is the exchange of form and truth, or, in what amounts to the same thing, of poetry and philosophy. Socrates is thus made the subject-"genre" whereby—and wherein—literature begins (and begins with all the power of reflection, because irony is that as well: the very power of infinite reflection or reflexivity, which is another way of saying specularity). In a rigorous argument, Socrates would thus be called the formal or figurative Subject (the exemplary Subject) and would thereby be considered to be the eponymous "genre" of literature, that is, philosophy. Consequently, this is a "genre" beyond all genres, including a theory of this very "beyond": in other words, it is a general theory of genres, and of itself as well.

It is precisely at this point that the novel is called into question.

But it is necessary to be patient a little longer in order to unfold these matters in a methodical fashion, hoping of course that they are in fact unfoldable. There are actually three elements that are put into play; to put it efficaciously: the name, the author, the reflection. This in turn supposes three questions: that of genre, of subject, and finally of theory, questions which are inextricably linked with one another. As is always the case in Romanticism, there is no privileged position that might afford a bird's eye view; there is no fixed point (*ancrage*) beginning at which one might categorize (*arrimer*), and thus arrange, if not organize, a system. This is the reason why fragment 42 of the *Lyceum*, always in the name of irony, proffers the dialogue as a pure and simple substitute for the system. "Wherever people philosophize, not only in a systematic fashion, but also in either oral or written dialogues, irony must be both demanded and used" (". . . denn überall wo in mündlichen oder geschriebenen Gesprächen, und nur nicht ganz systematisch philosophiert, soll man Ironie leisten und fordern . . .").

Philippe Lacoue-Labarthe and Jean-Luc Nancy

However, in order to see a bit more clearly, ironically or not, one must resolutely begin with this platitude: the *Conversation*, deliberately (it re-marks on this at least twice) takes the Platonic dialogue as a model. And it is not just any dialogue, but rather the one which, more than any other, by its agonistic nature, connotes the social: that is to say, the *Symposium*. This does not mean, of course, that the *Conversation* presupposes a fictional symposium. Unlike Hemsterhuis, for example, who pushed the cult of genre (or of "genre") to the point at which he claimed to have been able to retranscribe a Platonic dialogue that he had miraculously "discovered," Schlegel only copied the model's structure, that of a dialogue with intercalated reports or "discourses," in an appropriate format. More precisely, as we shall soon understand, the only thing that interests him is the complexity of the structure of something like the *Symposium*: that is to say, that, the question is not at all of a dialogue, but rather of a story including, or recalling, a dialogue, which in turn, contains intercalated discourses.

We know that, since antiquity, this type of structure has been the reason for the true originality of the Platonic mode of writing. It is this structure as well that we in fact find in varying degrees of complexity in most of the major dialogues of Plato, from the *Republic* to the *Sophist*, and including the *Theaetetus*. We know too that this very structure was not only "reflected" on and condemned by Plato in the *Republic* (in the light of the epic structure, and under the name, if name it be, of a mixed diegesis, that is to say, of a mixture of pure story and of "mimetic" or dramatic form).[11] But also it is this structure which proved to be of great consternation to Aristotle in his attempt at creating a taxonomy in the *Poetics*. This was so much the case that he was forced to yield and leave a blank, or anonymous space (ἀνώνυμος)—for lack of a common term (κοίνον ὄνομα), a concept lacking for a single genre (between prose and poetry, according to Diogenes Laertius), in which he could have placed the mimes of Sophon and Xenarch, the *Sokratikoi Logoi*, and didactic poems, such as those of Empedocles.[12] Added to that and thereby giving justice to the inventor of this "art without a name" is the fact that Plato's condemnation of "genre" (or the "self-criticism," as it were, of Plato) devolved upon the general putting into question (*mise-en-cause*) of mimesis, that is to say, as far as writing is concerned, the putting into question of "apocryptia," of the dissimulation and the dispersion of the author (or of the subject of discourse) behind the figures (characters or narrators) of dialogical narration. For Schlegel, this mimetic power had always been the lot (or appanage) of the genius, and particularly, of the great writer.[13] We therefore understand that, in the aftermath of the Greeks that Romanticism would wish itself to be, the Platonic dialogue appears as the very model of the union of the poetic and of the philosophical, and consequently, as the original matrix of the *novel*, that is, of that thing for which the Moderns had finally found a name.[14]

Lyceum 26: "Novels are the Socratic dialogues of our time." ("Die Romane sind die sokratischen Dialoge unserer Zeit.")

Athenaeum 252: "A philosophy of poetry in general . . . would hover between a unification and separation of philosophy and poetry, of praxis and poetry, of poetry in general and the various genres and species. . . . A philosophy of the novel, whose first foundations are seen in Plato's political theory, would be the keystone . . ." ("Eine Philosophie der Poesie überhaupt . . . würde zwischen Vereinigung und Trennung der Philosophie und der Poesie, der Praxis und der Poesie, der Poesie überhaupt und der Gattungen und Arten schweben. . . . Eine Philosophie des Romans, deren erste Grundlinien Platos politische Kunstlehre enthält, wäre der Schlußstein.")

This is actually what the *Conversation* proposes.

Or at least, it is what allows for the explanation of its own *Darstellung*, or, in other words, its own method of fictional creation.

Irony, of course, is both its rule and its principle.

First of all, that which constitutes order in the *Conversation*, or, in other terms, the fiction-making (*mise-en-fiction*)—in order not to say incorrectly, the staging (*mise-en-scène*)—is ironic in a strict sense, and down to the smallest detail. Here it would be necessary to take the time to dissect carefully the "fabrication" of the text. Failing that, we shall be satisfied to point out two major characteristics, which are, by the way, practically inseparable.

The first one is obviously (if we do not forget that we are still in the realm of the "necessity of fragmentation") the reunion, as if "through the looking glass," of the group itself, and, as if by mere chance, in its most "critical" phase—that is to say, the phase that, in the fall of 1799, began with the last great meeting at Jena, where all the members of the "alliance," except Schleiermacher,[15] had a reunion. In fact, many people have spoken a bit too rashly about the *Conversation*, for it is not very difficult to illuminate the identities of the protagonists of the *Conversation*: the whole *Athenaeum* is there, everyone with his own preoccupations (from the "new mythology" to the "characteristic of Goethe"), his quirks of tongue and mind (particularly evident in the "reports" where Friedrich gives free rein to his genius at pastiche and to his virtuosity). There are the salient features of each one's character or personality (from good humor to guarded caution, from playfulness to rivalry or to quick retorts). And the simple interrelations of everyone within the group show, like an open book, the seeds of the group's impending dissolution. It is doubtless correct to emphasize the fact that, whatever the "realism" of the *Conversation*, it is basically only the author of the text who speaks or gives his theoretical views.[16] That, by the way, is the second major characteristic of

Philippe Lacoue-Labarthe and Jean-Luc Nancy

this "fiction-making" to which we shall return momentarily. But it is obvious that the latter characteristic does not preclude the former; on the contrary, that is precisely the logic of mimetic behavior where the more the differences (that is to say, the dissimulation) are accentuated, the more the identity is reinforced, and *vice versa*. Schlegel was less aware than any other member of the group of this fact, Schlegel, who had made a career as a virtuoso, and who recognized in this principle (which is, from at least one point of view, the principle of the self-constitution of the Subject) the basis of the power of the novel, and as we shall see further on, of characterization.[17] That is why it is hardly valid not to see in the two women's roles in the *Conversation*—Amalia and Camilla—Caroline and Dorothea[18] respectively. As for the men's roles, one can see the philosopher of the meeting, and the author of the *Discourse on Mythology*, Schelling, in Ludoviko; in Lothario, whose pseudonym is borrowed from Goethe[19] and who, in this case, represents the poet who always announces a work to come, we see Novalis. In Marcus, the Goethe "specialist" obsessed by the problems of the theater, is Tieck; in Andrea, the philologist who begins the series of reports with his recapitulation of the history of literature (the *Eras of Poetry*), can be seen August. Finally, giving every man his due, in Antonio (which, in *Lucinde*, was Schleiermacher's pseudonym, for he was the one who knew about sailing), we see Friedrich himself, or "himself," whose prestation is at the center of the *Conversation* (this *Letter on the Novel*, which is precisely not a report, which was not even supposed to have been divulged, and which actually re-marks, this time on the literary level, all that is at stake in the *Letter to Dorothea*).[20] This prestation, which is a proposition for a "theory of the novel," is actually the keystone of this "philosophy of poetry" that actually determines the extent of the former.

Nevertheless, the *Letter on the Novel* does not occupy the center of the text. For that to be the case, it would be necessary, at least if we follow the series of reports,[21] for Marcus's essay on Goethe's styles to have been followed by Lothario's reading of the work, which, from the beginning, he has attempted to create, and for which, at the end, he settles for a repeated promise.

The "theory of the novel" would be the center of the *Conversation*, were it not for the absence of the work—the "poem," the "*Dichtung*" (for at the moment, the genre matters little). In which case, again as a result of irony, the re-mark would be doubly impeccable: first, by the author, or "novelist," insofar as he projects himself and disperses himself in the multiplicity of characters or "personalities" he creates (and we know he does this in order to reassure himself of his power); that would be the second characteristic of the "fiction-making" of which we spoke earlier. But it would also be the re-mark (and this time a new step is taken, marking a greater degree of complexity in the *Darstellung*, in the broadest sense) of the "fiction-making" itself—that is to say the Platonizing, if not really Platonic, re-mark of the infinite power of introversion that is characteristic of "literary" mimesis.

This, however, is not the case. Certainly, there are allusions to the "fabrication" of the *Conversation* which subtly "reflects" itself (Schlegel is a master in underhanded manipulation, and in any case the Platonic model is the *law*). Just as the *Conversation* would be the transcription of real conversations, in the beginning of the text there is a short passage on the division between truth and fiction; in the same way, the first discussion, during which the rules of play for this modern "symposium" are adopted, is concerned with—and this comes as no surprise—the theater, and precisely with the *theater* (which, according to Plato, was the purely mimetic genre) and not with the *novel*. Similarly, Lothario's missing work, which places the *Conversation* in a state of disequilibrium, or more precisely, puts it off-center, should have been a tragedy. Here, the power of irony is at a disadvantage. That is to say as well that it is reinforced. For there is nothing in the whole work left to chance or to quick improvisation; for you can't judge a book by its cover.

That nothing is left to chance means exactly that the *Letter on the Novel* cannot be at the center of the *Conversation* because the *Conversation is not itself a novel*. To put it another way, borrowing a formula from the self-same *Letter on the Novel*, with the proviso that the terms be inverted: only a novel is equal to the task of containing its own reflection and of including the theory of its own "genre." Once more, with the terms in their correct order: there can be no theory of the novel that is not a novel. And neither the *Conversation* nor the *Letter on the Novel* contained in it is a novel. But *Lucinde* could very well be a novel,[22] unless, in this game of funhouse mirrors (*cette fausse mise-en-abyme*) which is the ultimate ironic barb, the incomplete aspect of *Lucinde* (upon which the *Letter* offers much commentary) is sought and reflected; unless the dialogue is the form of renunciation, the *Darstellung* of the impossibility of self-constitution, and that the parody of Plato (or the multiple pastiche, already present, of the Romantic "style") is the admission of the insufficiency and failure of the work; unless, quite possibly, it is the "out of work quotient" (*l'indice du désoeuvrement*). In which case, beyond, (or rather aside from) the question of literature there would be a sort of uncanny writing secretly at work in this apparatus. But where then would the difference go, and would irony still be able to control such an ob-literation of the mark (*un tel démarquage*)?

This is perhaps the basic reason why the *Conversation* is never quite able to define or delimit the Romantic genre, that is to say, the literary genre—and most certainly not, though we often think in this fashion, in (or like) the novel.[23] This does not mean that the novel is not the "genre" that was obstinately sought for by Romantic theory; the contrary is the case. But it means rather that the inability to be defined or delimited is probably part of the essential nature of this genre. Without a doubt, genre is the completed, differentiated, and identifiable product of an engenderment or of a generation; even in German, where the etymology of the word is completely different,[24] *Gattung* is not unrelated to congregation in general, indeed, to marriage. However, the process of generation or of assembly obviously presupposes interpenetration and confusion; that is to say, a *mixture* (*gattieren*, in German, means "to mix"). This would seem to be precisely what the Romantics sought as the very essence of literature: union, in the satire (another name for mixture) or in the novel (or even in the Platonic dialogue), the union of poetry and philosophy, the confusion of all the genres that had previously been delimited by ancient poetics, the interpenetration of the old and the new, etc. But is that sufficient to define the nature of the mixture? What is, in fact, the nature of the fusion or union? And, all told, what is a genre? Or to be more precise, Genre?

The answer is quite simple and well-known to us besides. Simple and unfathomable: Genre is "more than a genre" ("Die romantische Dichtart ist die einzige, die mehr als Art . . ." *Ath.* 116). It is an Individual and an organic Whole capable of self-engenderment (*Ath.* 426); it is a World, the absolute *Organon*. In other words: generation is dissolution (*Auflösung*) in the sense of Kant's intussusception,[25] that is to say, that the idealist step in the properly speculative sense of the term, has in fact been taken. Not only is there dissolution like decomposition or resolution, but also, beyond a simple chemism (again, *Ath.* 426), there is a dissolution like organicism itself or like the process of auto-formation. This is actually a far cry from being able to delimit a genre, but is completely equivalent to Genre *in toto* (in the absolute), in the dissolution of all limits and the making absolute of all individuality. The literary Genre is Literature itself, the *Literary Absolute* (*L'Absolu littéraire*); it is "true literature," Schlegel would say several years later,[26] that is to say, literature that is not "one genre or another, willing to content itself, as if by whimsy, with a specific formation, but rather that literature is a great totality, with complex connections and organization, which encompasses in its unity many worlds of art—it is a unitary work of art" (". . . so daß nicht etwa nur diese oder jene Gattung, wie es das Glück will, zu einiger Bildung gelangen, sondern daß vielmehr die Literatur selbst ein Großes durchaus zusammenhängendes und gleich organisiertes, in ihrer Einheit viele Kunstwelten umfassendes Ganzes und einiges Kunstwerk sei . . ."). Reread fragment 116, or look at the *Essence of Criticism*:[27]

Genre

Romantic poetry . . . should not only unite the divers genres of poetry and make poetry, philosophy and rhetoric join together. It intends to, and has to, both mix and meld poetry and prose, genius and criticism, artistic and natural poetry, poetic life and society, poeticize the *Witz*, fill to the brim all the various forms of art with basic cultural materials, and inspire them with flashes of humor. Romantic poetry includes everything poetic from the largest system of art, itself containing other systems, down to the breath or kiss that the child-poet exhales in an artless song. . . . It is more than adequate to the greatest and most universal formation . . . ; for each whole that its products should form, it adopts a similar organization of its parts, and is thereby given to a perspective that allows for a limitless classificatory system. . . . Other poetic genres are complete and can now be fully dissected. . . . Only Romantic poetry is infinite as only it is free. . . . The genre of Romantic poetry is the only one that is more than a genre: it is, in a way, the very art of poetry: in a certain sense, all poetry is or should be Romantic.

Just as one must look to mythology for the origin and common source of all poetic genres, it is equally true that . . . poetry is the tallest cyme of all, found in the flower from which, once perfect (*sich vollendet*), the spirit of all the arts and sciences is resolved (*sich auflöst*).

It is understandable then, how in this situation, Literature, or Poetry, the "Romantic genre," insofar as the thing exists at all, is always sought for as a kind of "beyond" of literature itself. In actuality, this is what prohibits the *Conversation* from producing the promised concept. The process as such of absolutization or infinitization *exceeds*, in all senses of the word, the theoretical or philosophical power in general of which it is, after all, the fulfillment. The "auto" movement, if it can be called that—auto-formation, auto-organization, auto-dissolution, etc.—is always in a state of excess with itself. In a certain way, this is also what fragment 116 marks: "The genre of Romantic poetry is still in the process of becoming, and it is its proper essence that it is always only becoming, and that it is never capable of completing itself. No theory can exhaust it, and only a clairvoyant sort of criticism could dare to characterize its ideal." ("Die romantische Dichtart ist noch im Werden; ja das ist ihr eigentliches Wesen daß sie ewig nur werden, nie vollendet sein kann. Sie kann durch keine Theorie erschöpft werden, und nur eine divinatorische Kritik dürfte es wagen, ihr Ideal charakterisieren zu wollen.").

Translated by Lawrence R. Schehr

NOTES

1. Friedrich Schlegel, *Athenäums Fragmente*, in *Kritische Friedrich-Schlegel-Ausgabe*, vol. II, ed. Hans Eichner (Munich: Verlag Ferdinand Schöningh). (Translator's note)
2. Cf. *Ath.* 121.

3. *Conversation* refers to *Gespräch über die Poesie*, Schlegel, *Kritische Ausgabe* (trans.)

4. Cf. the authors' *L'Absolu littéraire* (Paris: Seuil, 1978), pp. 198ff. (trans.)

5. Cf. in the *Athenaeum* the two dialogues signed by August, with the collaboration on the second of Caroline: *Languages: A dialogue on the grammatical dialogue of Klopstock*, and *Paintings*. Both of them, notwithstanding the fact that the second is interspersed with long reading passages, are simple dialogues, that is to say, without a story. This is why, in reference to them, we use the term "dialogue" (*dialogue*) and not "conversation" (*entretien*) even though the same German word is used in both cases: *Gespräch*.

6. Cf. *The Dialogues* (1 to 5) which Novalis intended for the *Athenaeum*. In the last section of *L'Absolu littéraire*, pp. 428–33, the first two can be found. Here again, these are simple dialogues.

7. We refer the reader here to our "Dialogue des genres," in *Poétique* 21 for the historical analyses that we cannot develop here. Insofar as the relationship between the dialogue and Roman satire, and consequently the novel, is concerned, see *Lyceum* 42, and *Ath.* 146, 148, 239, and 448, among others, as well as the *Eras of Poetry* in the *Conversation*.

8. Cf. *On Philosophy* and the analyses developed in *L'Absolu littéraire*, pp. 181–205. One can also refer to *Lucinde* (*Kritische Fr.-Schlegel-Ausgabe*, vol. V), pp. 74–78 (also, in the French translation by J. J. Anstett [Paris: Aubier-Flammarion, 1971], p. 221ff. [Julius to Antonio]).

9. Cf. *The Eras of Poetry.*

10. That is to say, to the tradition which we have followed back to Montaigne, and which the Romantics knew essentially by English "literature" or that of eighteenth-century France.

11. Cf. Gérard Genette's "Frontières du récit," in *Figures II* (Paris: Seuil, 1966).

12. *Poetics*, 1447b—Since these pages were written we have been made aware of Gérard Genette's essential study, "Genres, 'types,' modes," in *Poétique* 32. In a decisive manner, from the point of view of the history of poetics, this study illuminates the process whereby Romanticism, while completing a movement begun at the least by the Abbé Batteux, tended to project on ancient poetics (Plato and Aristotle) a distinction of *genres* (lyric, epic, dramatic) which: (1) does not appear as such either in the *Republic* or in the *Poetics* (nothing is in fact determined for the lyric); (2) actually conceals a distinction between the modes of enunciation (direct, or in the first person: *diegesis*; indirect, or by an interposed person: *mimesis*).

It is thus understandable that that which Romanticism calls, or desires, under the name of "genre" is actually the result of this double distortion. It is also understandable that, as we mention at the end of *L'Absolu littéraire*, Romanticism's "generic speculation" bumps up against the problem of the lyric. In the following discussion it is taken for granted that the word "genre" is used with the meaning the Romantics gave it.

13. Cf. in the *Conversation*, for example, the developments concerning Goethe's *Wilhelm Meister* (*Essay on Goethe's Various Styles . . .*): the first quality of *Wilhelm Meister* is that "the individuality that appears there is divided among different rays of light and distributed among several persons." ("Erstlich daß die Individualität, welche darin erscheint, in verschiedne Strahlen gebrochen, unter mehrere Personen verteilt ist.")

14. Cf. Nietzsche, *The Birth of Tragedy*: Plato is the inventor of the novel in antiquity (chapter 14).

15. Cf. Roger Ayrault, *Genèse du romantisme allemand*, 4 vols. (Paris: Aubier-Montaigne, 1961–76), III, p. 74ff.

16. *Ibid.*, IV, 294ff.

17. Cf. *Ath.* 22 and 418, as well as "The Formation of Character," in *L'Absolu littéraire*, pp. 371–93.

18. Amalia was already used as Caroline's pseudonym in August Schlegel's *Four Letters on Poetry, Metrics and Language*.

19. As Ayrault (IV, p. 290) reminds us, Lothario in *Wilhelm Meister* is the figure who symbolizes the problems of economic activity, and who is, for Schlegel, "the most interesting character in the entire work."

20. At least it re-marks some of its important themes, beginning with that of the "erotic" pedagogy. It is clear that the relation with Catherine is not at all the same as the one glimpsed in *On Philosophy* or in *Lucinde* (where, by the way, the "Platonic" love of Friedrich for Caroline is recalled in the chapter, "The Learning-Years of Masculinity" (*Kr. Aus.*, V, 35–59); this is why there is no trace here of the theme of initiation. Curiously, the *Conversation* is a *Symposium* without Diotima.

21. Herewith, for expediency, is the plan of the *Conversation*, the first pagination being that of *L'Absolu littéraire*, the second referring to vol. II of the *Kritische Ausgabe*:
   1) Prologue: pp. 289–91; pp. 284–87.
   2) Story; Play production: pp. 291–94; pp. 287–90.
   3) Andrea's report; *Eras of Poetry*: pp. 294–306; pp. 290–303.
   4) First Discussion: pp. 306–11; pp. 303–11.
   5) Ludviko's report; *Discourse on Mythology*: pp. 311–17; pp. 311–22.
   6) Second Discussion: pp. 317–21; pp. 321–28.
   7) Antonio's text; *Letter on the Novel*: pp. 321–30; pp. 329–38.
   8) Third Discussion (Summary): p. 330; pp. 338–39.
   9) Marcus's Report; *Essay on Goethe's Various Styles in his Earlier and Later Works*: pp. 331–37; pp. 339–47.
   10) Fourth Discussion: pp. 337–40; pp. 348–51.

22. *Lucinde* actually does contain a chapter entitled "Allegory of Impudence," and in the form of a "waking dream" there is a sort of theory of the novel. It would not be difficult to show that the whole text of *Lucinde* is built on the principle of self-engenderment; however, this important point still remains: the book was never completed, or, as it were, was aborted.

23. It is best to refer the reader here to Szondi's seminal study, "La Théorie des genres poétiques chez Friedrich Schlegel," in *Poésie et poétique de l'idéalisme allemand*, trans. Jean Bollack (Paris: Minuit, 1975), pp. 117ff. By concentrating on the posthumous "fragments" in particular, collected in the *Kritische Friedrich-Schlegel-Ausgabe*, and the *Literary Notebooks*, edited by Eichner, Szondi attempts to recreate a "system" of Schlegel's poetics, which wavers between a "critique of poetic reason" and a sort of pre-Hegelian synthesis which, both in and like the novel, would reconcile subjective and objective poetry. In light of the above, it remains true that Szondi's analysis stops at a recognition of Schlegel's contradictions and a paraphrase of fragment 116. Moreover, the editor of the French edition notes, on p. 120, that "Peter Szondi was not indifferent to the objections made to him about the validity of placing the category of the novel in the genre that Schlegel had

defined as objective/subjective, as well as on his imposition of the oppositions: poetry of nature/poetry of art, and antiquity/modernity." On the other
hand, Walter Benjamin, in his *Der Begriff der Kunstkritik in der deutschen
Romantik* (Bern: Francke, 1920), pp. 94ff., demonstrated that the novel is
not an ideal, insofar as it permits poetry to fulfill itself as prose ("The idea
of poetry is prose."), that is to say, poetry, which for Novalis was that which
should define "the Romantic rhythm." In addition, this theme will be found
quite explicitly in A. Schlegel's *Lessons* (published in *L'Absolu littéraire*, pp.
341–68): "In Romantic poetry, a genre blossomed which not only can do
without verse, but also, in many situations, actually prohibits versification:
this is the novel." One must attach this ideal for prose of the *oratio soluta*
to what we have called "the necessity of fragmentation," that is to say as
well, to everything seen to devolve on the speculative theme of the Ab-solute
(cf., on the Ab-solute, Heidegger, *Schelling*, trans. J. F. Courtine (Paris:
Gallimard, 1977), pp. 82–83).

24. The root *ghedh-* is found in *gatten* (to join, to assemble) and in
the pair *Gatte/Gattin* (husband/wife), which refers as well to the idea of
joining or connecting. Perhaps to the idea of system?

25. Cf. "L'Exigence fragmentaire," in *L'Absolu littéraire*, pp. 57–80.

26. In "Of the Combinative Spirit" ("Vom kombinatorischen Geist") in
the introduction to the second part of *Lessing's Thoughts and Beliefs* (1804),
Kr. Aus. III, p. 83.

27. Friedrich Schlegel, *Schriften und Fragmente*, ed. Ernst Behler
(Stuttgart: A. Kröner, 1956). For the French translation, see *L'Absolu littéraire*, pp. 407–16. (trans.)

GENUS UNIVERSUM
Michel Beaujour

ROMANTICISM HATED above all the taxonomic distribution of discourses and texts into a hierarchical genre system. Yet neo-romantic terrorism —echoing the Schlegels's Jena circle[1]—likes to play with the conceit of one Genre, because the notion is logically self-contradictory and therefore likely to generate arresting strings of oxymoronic utterances. Absolute singularity confers upon the discarded notion of genre an aura of paradox and ambiguity. Reduction of the Many to the One might also help to stem our rampant acquiescence to uncenteredness and multiplicity . . . *Genre,* as opposed to *genres,* intimates what it does not denote: a line must—but can not—be drawn somewhere between *everything,* and *something* that is unnamable. It is therefore necessary to turn the empirical, taxonomic and poetic question of genre into an ontological aporia drawing its verisimilitude from the anti-Aristotelian context of post-Romantic German philosophy. Between *genre* in the empirical, historical, normative sense and *Genre* in an absolute sense, there lies the difference that separates empirical naïveté from (post)philosophical sophistication.

Nevertheless, positive inquiries into genre (in the old Aristotelian sense) are still being carried out. As the normative and academic connotations of genre faded away, a wealth of philological and ethnographic information was being accumulated, well beyond the knowledge available to our predecessors who studied the Western tradition and, more often than not, limited their research to their own national literatures. Within the linguistic, logical and anthropological contexts, the question

Michel Beaujour

of genres has again become rather interesting and complex. As a result, the old (romantic) periodizations, the supposed correspondences between the "ages of man" and dominant genres, have lost much of their credibility, and crises of the World Spirit have turned into local *coups*. As our former ideas of human beginnings fell apart, we also observed more attentively what other cultures had been up to: our dogmatic belief in an imminent, in an already consummated End, was shaken. Indeed it is likely that there have been, are, and will be genres, despite the Romantic belief that History and the World Spirit made an about-face inside someone's backyard in 1800 or thereabouts. The sense of belatedness experienced by some of us may arise from our commenting on exclusively those texts that recapitulate History and predict the ultimate whimper with eager anticipation. But there is still much work to be done in order to understand the phenomena not accounted for within one philosophical tradition, our own. The work of general poetics is merely beginning; the ethnography of speaking and genres is still awaiting its anthropological synthesis. And even our understanding of genre within the Western literatures calls for important revisions in the light of socio-linguistics and pragmatics. Many poeticians have undertaken the task. Some of them, such as Todorov, are also taking into account the terroristic denial of genre in post-romantic modernism, while Genette attempts to dispel the most common misconceptions.

In his criticism of Maurice Blanchot, whose paradoxes have attained more than authoritative status in France, Todorov dared to point out the unstable coexistence of two incompatible lines of argument in the master's works. Blanchot's romantic challenge to the legitimacy of genres and other taxonomic systems and his claims in favor of an "essence of literature" associated with Mallarmé's *Book* (an essence which is not to be defined empirically), are self-contradictory. On the one hand, Blanchot typically would assert that:

The book, such as it is, only matters, at a distance from genres, outside such headings as prose, poetry, the novel, non-fiction, under which it refuses to be classified and to which it denies any power to assign a place, or determine a form for it.

On the other hand, it is easy to find passages where Blanchot himself "uses categories that undeniably resemble generic categories." Furthermore, the transgression of genre demanded by the Blanchotian Book does not do away with *norms*. On the contrary, the transgressive work will become a norm or a generic paradigm in its turn, thus establishing a new taxonomy of kinds. In the course of his argument, Todorov was necessarily led to evoke "the German romantics and Friedrich Schlegel in particular" in whose theoretical work two divergent tendencies are visible. One produces "Crocean assertions: 'each poem, a genre in itself,'" while the other proposes "an equation between poetry and genres": poetry exists only *in* and *as a result of* the mutual opposition of various genres.[2]

Without further examining the vast corpus of contradictory statements about the existence, power, demands and refusals of Book, *Dichtung*, and Genre in Romantic and post-Romantic literature, one feels justified in asserting that this very contradiction—perhaps an insurmountable one—characterizes modern Western thinking about kind and genericity. The perplexity we experience when faced with the concept of genre may well result from the incompatible claims of two compelling modes of thought. According to the first one, linguistics, semiotics, ethnography and poetics are producing ever more accurate and pertinent descriptions of the specific genre systems found in pre-literate, scribal, typographical and post-typographical cultures. For the other one, an unprecedented ontological situation demands the overcoming of genres, which trivialize the Essence of writing and desacralize its End, glimpsed at the extremity of a *via negativa*.

It is easy enough to choose rationally between empirical poetics and the mysticism of the Book. But the arguments of Blanchot and his disciples are so manifestly allergic to the principle of contradiction that one must assume their undeniable appeal and imperviousness to commonsense criticism to be grounded in something beyond—or beside—Aristotelian logic. Or it may be that their ideological construct does account adequately for the "essence" of certain important modernist works (or nonworks) such as Mallarmé's mythical *Book*. The cut-and-dried categories of poetics, they say, merely anatomize these writings, but they cannot account for their powerful hold over the modern reader/writer, nor for their radical differences from other works that were produced within less problematic ontological and generic contexts. In any case such ideological constructs as an immanent poetics always contain a plethora of nonconceptual components that remain unanalyzable during their productive phase. A discourse that juggles persuasively with All and Nothing and the theological attributes of the Book, but refuses to countenance such relative matters as *genre*, obviously serves a nondescriptive purpose: it is meant to sacralize a handful of extraordinary texts through which post-romantic paradoxes hold on to a literary status they otherwise challenge and undermine. There is an immeasurable, ontological, difference between the fragments of a Book-yet-to-come and the given totality of extant texts; this difference is all that remains of the age-old distinction between the Sacred and the Profane.

Is it possible to choose between a *hieropoetics* and a *sociopoetics*? The function of a hieropoetics is to shore up the fading powers of the poets/philosophers who are the priests and interpreters of canonical texts (*interprêtres* in Derrida's clever portmantese). For such hierocritics, *genres* are mundane, because the only Genre that matters is their own, which must remain nameless or go by the name of *The Book*, in order to suggest an unmediated essence of writing. *Sociopoetics*, meanwhile, seeks to describe systems of discursive functions and speech acts embodied in all kinds of utterances. Now devoid of any normative power, profane poetics sets no *a priori* limits to the multiplicity of genres, and confers upon none of them an exorbitant status. Unlike hieropoetics, descriptive poetics does not speak the language of power, nor does it harbor any nostalgia for the hierarchical order within which the mysterious Egyptian hieroglyphs were endowed with a numinous aura: the notion of a *hierogenre*, favored by Renaissance *magi* and their modern descendants is alien to a poetics that is lamely egalitarian and rather boringly allergic to obscurity.

Yet the history of Western poetics teaches that a few texts have habitually enjoyed exceptional status because they were reputed to contain—or to transcend—all known and possible genres. In Greco-Roman cultures the Homeric poems were said to encompass *in nuce* all the canonical genres. Inversely, the Bible transcended all actual genres, since divine revelation could not be generic in any logical sense of the word. Descriptive poetics therefore had to explode the myth of an original text harboring virtually all later specific kinds, as well as the tenacious belief in a nongeneric privilege of Revelation.

Leaving aside the Homeric myth, which does not categorically forbid generic analyses of the poems, we must acknowledge that the generic profanation of Revelation is on a par with the sacrilege perpetrated by philological and historical criticism. Those who wished to retain a belief in some sort of ontological revelation were forced thereafter to reaffirm that the Book *denies* to generic headings "the power to assign its place and determine its form." Whereas descriptive poetics operates within a homogeneous Aristotelian space (where all *genres* and *books* merely are books and genres), older poeticians, for many centuries, were forced to defer to a transcendental and heterogeneous imperative. They shared the fate of the philosophers, who prospered nevertheless so long as they acknowledged the irrelevance of reason and the impotence of logic in the domain of faith and revelation. And we have thus become atavistically accustomed to a Judaic segregation between Scripture and those other writings that are subjected to a mundane division into several genres roughly corresponding to social *status*, while the Bible stands above the hierarchy. If this segregation corresponds but imperfectly to the distinction between the uses of Latin and the Vulgar tongues in medieval culture, it seems clear that co-existence of a priestly tongue and various lay languages resulted in the institutionalization of a dichotomy: it is no accident therefore that the post-Romantic period attempted to reinstate this duality within the various vulgar literatures in order to counteract the tendency to homogenization and equality that accompanies the removal of a sacred hierarchical principle, and the fading away of a hieratic language formerly used at the top (and beyond the top) of the scale. The purpose of this reinstatement has become obvious: an extraterritorial space had to be marked off as a refuge for hieroglyphic writing and interpretations. This explains the illogical attempt to create an extrasystemic Genre, obscurely but firmly kept apart from the demotic genre-system which Mallarmé dismissed as "universal journalism." Such a gambit appears most visibly within French culture: it may be rooted in the peculiar status enjoyed by "intellectuals" and "poets" in France since Baudelaire's time.

This dichotomy is so manifest and generally accepted that it causes little puzzlement and hardly any serious opposition in France—one has to be bloody minded to suggest that such a radical distinction between "prose" and "verse" on the one hand, and "poetry" or "the text" on the other, or between *communication* and *production/consummation*, may well be a surreptitious return to the old model that made sense in quite a different cultural context. The dream of an ultimate *Gesamtkunstwerk*, divorced from mere dramatic literature, fits the same hierarchical scheme. So does the hypervaluation of marginal texts flaunting the stigmata of martyrdom. Such texts stand outside "art," and in their obsession with writing itself, they elevate it to the hieratic status of Sacrament and Passion. Meanwhile, any work conforming to generic criteria excludes itself from the nonclass of writerly texts— hieroglyphic status cannot be achieved inside normal art. The nongeneric Genre has sucked all prophetic and generative energies into the black hole of a Book-yet-to-come. But one could entertain a different view of this evolution.

In the past, every major cultural-literary crisis has been bound up with a radical shift of the writer's position in the communicational and power networks, embodied in rhetoric and a symbolic system. There is no reason to think that the current, post-Romantic crisis is fundamentally different. Western writers have not yet come to terms with all the consequences of the Renaissance typographical-rhetorical revolution. They are still desperately clutching to the residues of oral culture, and trying to confer upon an idealized typographic Book the aura that surrounds the *letter of Revelation* in the Scribal context. No wonder then that the more recent upheavals wrought by tele-phony and television have deepened a crisis where *presence* is at stake, but keeps on being understood in an archaic and basically *philological* fashion, while the momentous consequences of the *media* are downgraded to the trivial level of technical innovations. The writer's consciousness is deeply split when a semiotician of the media can also be a pre-typographic scribe, and a neo-textualist, a Platonist at heart. Screen ideologies featuring Revolution, Desire, Transgression, and Deconstruction have often served to mask this deep-seated contradiction. This is not tantamount to saying that it is easy, or even desirable, for the writer to be completely at home in the dominant communicational setting of his own culture.

But it follows from this that the Crisis—which is here symbolized by the question of Genre—does not jibe with Romanticism, even in its most radical form, i.e., German Romanticism. For the year 1800 or thereabout does not call any *decisive* upheaval in the structures of rhetoric, symbolization and communication to mind. What it does conjure up, however, is the *promise* (and, perhaps more frequently, the *threat*) of democracy. Writers were faced with a choice between, on the one hand, protective obscurity, stylistic opaqueness, difficult disjointedness, and a conceptual slipperiness which could keep the democratic (bourgeois) masses at a distance and, on the other, an open-handed eloquence and esoteric simplicity responding to the inchoate expectations of a vast new audience that had grown outside the main philosophic and literary traditions.

This relationship between writers and democratic "masses" (which entailed in some countries a reassessment of "folklore") indeed caused a notable upset in the classical generic institution. But I find it difficult to relate causally the Schlegels' speculations about fragments and encyclopedias to the social changes heralded by the French revolution, since such preoccupations may be considered a radicalized version of Enlightenment *"philosophie"* and *"idéologie."* Besides, the German Romantic innovations can also be perceived as a delayed replay of the Renaissance encyclopedia mutation, and as an anticipation of the Symbolist dream of a virtual Book orienting the production of fragments. The question of an ultimate or unique Genre above all kinds of writing is not securely anchored in the period of Hegel's proclamation of the end of Art.

One might be well advised therefore in taking a look at the Crisis from the vantage point of the Renaissance, where the rhetorical system of communication was transformed by typography.

As we have seen, our mythical discourse on the critical emergencies of Genre implies two distinct phases: the profane and the sacred, the many and the one, clarity and obscureness, genres and Genre, systemic works and numinous extrasystemic texts, etc. Usually, however, this sort of crisis is seen as a struggle in the course of which a new system of genres, presumably demanded by a new cultural situation, supplants an obsolete institutionalized system. Such changeovers are accompanied by much theoretical and philosophical bluster, and characterized by abrupt assertions. Compromise or a dialectical synthesis are beyond the reach of participants who feel their very existence is at stake.

France experienced the Renaissance crisis in poetics more vividly than other major European cultures, perhaps because France itself had been the cradle and home of medieval literary and philosophical forms while it was not the birthplace of humanism. No doubt, French literary history has turned the Renaissance break into an etiological myth of neo-classicism. But this myth does not really betray the stated intentions of the young poets who surrounded Du Bellay when he was writing his *Défense et illustration* in 1550, at least insofar as genres are concerned. Before the manifesto, the obsolescent late medieval genre-system still prevailed (despite the "weird excesses" caused by its "childish senility," and the scattered efforts of various "precursors"); after the manifesto, there came into being a generic system which would eventually evolve into the classical model. The sharpness of this break is remarkable, even if we acknowledge that the actual situation was more complex than its legend. It is not necessary to recount in detail the mutation that took place between 1500 and the triumph of Pléiade poetics. Let us merely note that the new, neo-classical poetics did not radically modify the standing relationship between rhetoric and literature, although it was manifestly bent on eliminating the "rhetorical" (i.e., tropical and metrical) aspects of poetry-writing that had been prescribed by the old *Artes of Second Rhetorick*. Moreover, the Pléiade's neo-classicism emphasized the ancient relationship between music and poetry (which it often called *song*), and disregarded—at least theoretically—the advent of typography which the *Grands Rhétoriqueurs* had missed so completely that most of their production has come down to us in scribal codices.

This capital oversight is understandable: all these writers were to some degree court poets and musicians, who produced their work in the context of a *face to face* relationship with their primary audience. Besides, the prevalent Platonic ideology did not favor any theoretical awareness of print. The reactionary modernism of Renaissance poetic theory (as opposed to the modernist conservatism of late "Gothic" poetics) insured that the import of typography, seen as a merely technical innovation, would be overlooked. Humanist pedagogy trained *orators* as if speech-making were still a powerful social tool, and it tended to consider writing a mere representation of speech, as the Ancients had done. Persuasive rhetoric therefore conserved the values of an outdated, predominantly oral, culture. This is particularly visible in the Renaissance's appreciation of a coded redundancy (*copia*) that had been a requisite of oral/aural persuasion, and in its emphasis on metrics as a distinguishing feature of both poetry and *Kunstprosa*. Humanism, which depended on the printing press for its work and livelihood, conferred a paradoxical privilege upon orality, eloquence and Ciceronianism in its struggle against the scribal, medieval culture it equated with manuscript tomes full of mnemonic *sigla* and discordant Latin style.

Especially when dealing with *genre*, Renaissance literary theory kept obscuring differences between the classical and modern vulgar literatures: one of these differences was that the moderns produced (mainly) vulgar poems, although they had only studied classical poems in school. Modern vulgar productions were often treated as if they were additions to the classical corpus, while traditional French poetry could not be fitted into the classical "genres," as they were understood by Renaissance theoreticians. Adopting classical (or pseudo-classical) models in vulgar French poetry entailed a thorough transformation of the poetic idiom, in order to escape the attraction of late medieval modes. The emphasis on linguistic change led in its turn to a theoretical emphasis on speaking and singing. As a result, poetry was placed in an increasingly fictitious context of oral communication, while the printed book, in which most readers would encounter the poem (and in which the poets themselves had read their classical models), was overlooked as if it were immaterial and irrelevant to a poetic experience anachronistically symbolized by ancient musical instruments and lost musical modes.

These facts are, in principle, common knowledge. Yet, even such an excellent historian as Graham Castor tends to minimize the contradictions imbedded in the Renaissance generic shift.[3] Blindness to actual, contemporary conditions and fantasies about the return of archaic ones facilitated the victory of Pléiade poetics which simplified the issues radically, and covered up with patriotic braggadocio its liquidation of French national traditions in the name of a mythical neo-classicism.

The Pléiade poets thought they had achieved a *tabula rasa*, upon which they could start imitating ancient poetry in a rejuvenated national tongue, which would soon match Latin, Italian and even Greek in greatness. Their campaign in favor of the Ode, especially of the Pindaric sort, symbolized this break and their deliberate estrangement from "real life." *Enthusiasm* was their utopia.

No need to say that the neo-classical genre system, promulgated around 1550, did not account for all the genres or forms actually produced in France at the time. On the contrary, the Pléiade program deliberately widened the gap between ordinary "popular" productions related to traditional festive occasions, and serious poetry. The new poetics also separated verse from prose, and did away with the *versi-prosa* that had been a characteristic kind of late medieval writing, since it combined the arts of first rhetoric (prose) and second rhetoric (verse). With the Pléiade, verse poetry was divorced from prose *poeterie* (where meaning had been ingeniously concealed by means of allegorical figures and mythological stories). Furthermore, the Pléiade insisted on a distinction between mere *versifying* and a *poetry* that was ontologically higher in origin and status. As the seamless cloak of rhetorical writing was ripped apart, *poetry* could not find its self-justification in superior craftsmanship (which well-wrought prose could also display), or even in the mystery of dark, allegorical, conceits: it found its rationale in an ideology purporting to account for poetry's incomparable mode of production, and its uncanny insights into cosmic order.

The idea of an "inspired" poet rising to visionary intuitiveness through Platonic *furor* had one purpose: limiting the class of those who might rightfully claim poetic status. The old poets used to be verbal artisans. The new poet was the medium of a revelation. Poetry, ontologically superior to any other linguistic art, had become a Genre above all ordinary genres and verbal practices: it had been restored to the status of *genus universum*.

What was this once and future universal genre, the loss of which Crassus could already deplore in Cicero's *De oratore*? In some sense, *genus universum* is the whole of Culture, the sum of the arts and sciences in their essence, the entire domain ruled over by the Muses, under the authority of their mother Mnemosyne. *Genus universum* is the total Museion: a flawless encyclopedia of knowledge, as well as the ideal *paideia* which puts it to work and hands it down from one generation to the next. Particular arts are its fragments (or *species*). Thus poetry stands above all the arts, it is closer to Mnemosyne herself than to her subordinate daughters. Poetry is the full potential of cultural memory embodied in myth and language.

Belief in a forgotten, ancient science obsessed Renaissance humanists, especially those who were Platonically and magically inclined. They set themselves the task of discovering the *clavis universalis* of memory, that would unlock the secrets of the lost *genus universum*.[4] The superior Renaissance man is often thought to have been "universal" in his knowledge, and there is a tendency to confuse Pico's, or Ficino's universality with that of a Leonardo. But the esoteric knowledge implied in such notions as *genus universum* and *clavis universalis* is quite distinct from the inductive, empirical know-how of a brilliant engineer. It is, rather, the result achieved through a dual anamnesis: cultural anamnesis attempts to recover the lore enigmatically inscribed in the texts and monuments of the Ancients, especially the Egyptians; individual pneumatic anamnesis brings the seeker close to an intemporal

Michel Beaujour

source of inspiration, to which some exceptionally fortunate men may have direct access. In short, the Renaissance *magus* and poet had to be *inspired* scholars.

The idea of a *genus universum* exacerbated rivalries for access to esoteric knowledge among various claimants: along with poets and *magi*, there were cabbalists, and all sorts of neo-Platonists. In its higher reaches (Pindaric Odes and Ronsard's Hymns, for instance), poetry claimed to be scientific. Conversely, much Renaissance science, clothed in myth, allegory and rhetorical figures, is "poetic." Both offer intuitive access to archetypal images, and, if one follows C. G. Jung, a collective unconscious which is the spitting image of *genus universum*. . . .

Genus universum is bound up with the belief that there existed a forgotten short-cut to knowledge and power, a direct access route through signs and numbers that could be manipulated efficiently. Renaissance poetry imitated ancient poetry especially in order to find the latch hidden by the mythological veil of classical texts. Imitation, beyond its esthetic function, was an esoteric apprenticeship.

Ritual praise for Homer and Hesiod, the original and complete poets, and J.-C. Scaliger's anti-Aristotelian reinstatement of the "pre-Socratics" among poets, were part of an attempt to flesh-out a myth of the poet whose intuitive semiology transcended the empirical and technical knowledge of specialists. The poet was a kind of philosopher, whose philosophical vision, unimpaired by logical discourse or argumentative lucidity and raised by *furor* to a higher plane of intellection, was expressed through the obscure images of myth which he brought to life and perspicuity by means of tropes, numbers, and musical harmony. *Furores* and anamnesis were integral modalities of an enlightenment leading to Mnemosyne, the keeper of living memory. To this conception was evidently tied a widespread belief in *prisca theologia*, an original, continuous and continuing revelation that had first been bestowed upon the ancient Egyptians and obscurely inscribed in the books attributed to "Hermes Trismegistus" (Thoth), and "Horopollo." Those Egyptian *magi* were the inventors and interpreters of the hieroglyphs, which concealed their divine knowledge. *Prisca theologia* reconciled the higher poetic knowledge of ancient pagans (all in some way indebted to Egypt) with gnostic interpretations of biblical revelation. Mythical knowledge was one, and ultimately recoverable through poetic anamnesis guided by a correct decipherment of the hieroglyphs.

Attempts to elevate poetry to the status of a *genus universum* were tied to a rhetoric of secrecy, enigma and obscurity, the main figures of which were *allegory* (taken in a broad sense), mythology, and emblems, considered to be the modern versions of ancient hieroglyphs or ideograms. *Genus universum* brought about a vision of visual figura-tion and poetic tropes, which more recent oneirocritics still consider to be characteristic of dream work. The semiotically polymorphous *genus universum*, on this score also, may be considered an earlier variant of what would later be rediscovered and named the "unconscious."

Humanistic Orphism was epitomized in Marsilio Ficino, the main Renaissance translator of Plato into Latin. In France, traces of this Orphic Platonism are visible in the works of most major poets of the seventeenth century: Scève, Pontius de Tyard, Ronsard himself, as well as in the poetic Academies (Baëf's, in particular) according to Frances Yates' persuasive studies. These academies had a function analogous to that of journals like *Athenaeum* and its editorial group in German Romanticism, which would serve as a model throughout the post-Romantic period.

The claim that poetry was *genus universum* set the poet apart from the frivolous, courtly milieu upon which he depended for his livelihood. This was a dangerous moment for the poet, owing to the vulgarization through print and translations of the mythological lore and interpretations which, in a former period, were the poets' own special knowledge or *poeterie*. The poet had to reclaim a specific, exceptional science: this visionary understanding of the ancient gods' meanings was qualitatively incommensurable with the inferior knowledge which any reader could now acquire through easily available books. This was the poet's first attempt to rise above the unhappy choices that now faced him in the age of print culture: he might become a refiner of the commonplaces that passed for truths in his milieu, or he might emblematize the "secrets" of his own pysche. By equating poetry with *genus universum* and, to some degree, with hieroglyphic gnosis, the poet claimed a transcendant power for the kind of "singing" that is attuned to cosmic harmony, *animus mundi* and the spiritual world. The state of the natural sciences had not yet turned such an aspiration into nonsense. In the following centuries, the Western poet's status became increasingly problematic, at least when he attempted to assert some sort of *vatic* superiority for himself, and some kind of *noetic* function for his poems. Take, for example, A. W. Schlegel's fancy that the "three genres" (lyric, epic and dramatic) were modes of the Hegelian dialectical triad, thesis, antithesis and synthesis: the Epic is objective, the lyric subjective, and the Drama an interpenetration of both (*Lectures* of 1801–2). The discrepancy between claims and actuality would perhaps reach a limit in Mallarmé's idea of the *Book*: an absolute, individual and impersonal reaching for *genus universum*, that proved in effect to be a mere insubstantial gesture toward nothing.

Poetry's claim to *universal genrehood* was not universally accepted, nor universally applicable, even in the Renaissance when much poetry was merely pretty, lyrical, narrative or satirical. Christian orthodoxy (both Catholic and Protestant) looked askance at *prisca theologia,* despite its tolerance of learned neo-Platonic syncretism.[5] The main— but largely unvoiced—challenge came from within humanism itself, which was developing a rival *Genre* as a by-product of its scholarly work, and as a weapon against the logic of the school.

Humanism had two distinct faces. On one side, it was very firmly committed to the social here and now: its sophistic pedagogy prepared "orators" and princes to achieve or retain power in a world clearly motivated by self-interest and the passions; on the other, humanism was turned toward classical and Christian antiquity, whose secrets it sought to unravel. Out of this bipolarity there arose the need to elaborate a new encyclopedia that would combine the concrete problems of the *hic et nunc* with the powerful Ancient commonplaces. In this up-to-date *speculum,* mankind's increasing diversity *and* the individual would be problematized, while a space would be arranged for the inquisitive mind that was now raising the questions of a new encyclopedia, and its epistemology, usually by means of sceptical strategies. In short, the new encyclopedia would prepare, at least virtually, a place for the questioning *ego* or *subject.* The *textual subject* came into being as a side-product of the humanist's gathering, deciphering and classifying of ancient textual fragments in order to make them operative in the new culture of print.

We are now aware that this vast, piecemeal process, which was eventually synthesized and systematized by individual writers, gave birth to another *genus universum* directly challenging the poets' exclusive claim. We also know that the humanists' encyclopedic *genus universum* was a metamorphic product of the rhetorical revolution that took place in the Renaissance, when rhetoric assumed an imperialistic posture in order to do away with (school) philosophy. Finally, it is clear that the very structure of the new *genus* was intimately affected by typography.

The names of five writers may be summoned in order to flesh out these abrupt assertions: Ramus, Montaigne, Bacon, Descartes, and Vico. Their works all attempted to make rhetoric responsive to an unprecedented communicational situation, and to re-orient it toward the discovery of new topics. Rhetoric, which had traditionally been a compendium of practical advice to orators, rather than a systematic description of linguistic and dialectical operations, was forceably turned into a reasoned *taxonomy* (an encyclopedia of commonplaces) and a *method* (of thinking). In the process, memory (the treasure house of eloquence) was de-emphasized, while the means of discovering new "things" were developed well beyond those of traditional *Inventio*. Memory became the feedback device of discovery itself. The text thus turned into a repository of written traces, a model for future invention, and a regulating system for ulterior additions and modifications to the printed encyclopedia. Moreover, the reader was invited to imitate in his own solitude (thus mirroring the author's self-presentation as a solitary writer) the procedure of discovery featured in the text. The new Genre was a program for the reader's own dialectical operations (including self-discovery) rather than a *summa* of authoritative data to be memorized and fitted into a preexisting structure. Rhetoric, which had been a powerful instrument for social and moral conservatism, was turned into a machine capable of producing unprecedented idiosyncrasy.

Thus were the various Renaissance *methods* developed. Ramus's *method* was taken up and developed beyond recognition by Bacon's new *organon* which Descartes discarded as he centered his own method around his *ego*, thereby systematizing and normalizing Montaigne's sceptical invention of a subjective method.

The *methodical* expectations of Renaissance epistemology were embodied in texts whose novel generic features were caused by the withdrawal of such transformational operations as would normally take place between the "invention" of a text and its completion. A generative shortcut between the parts of rhetoric and the printed text imparted to the books in question an unwhelped appearance according to Renaissance artistic criteria, which did not normally admit sketches or drafts to the status of works. The deliberate and functional primitiveness of the new books might be called *neoteny*: they would be brought to completion *after* their publication.

These nonnarrative, nonmimetic texts were, so to speak, the disconnected entries (or fragments) of a virtual encyclopedia-to-be. Or else they were raw taxonomies and tentative dialectical exercises gathered into commonplace books and topical collections. The titles under which these texts were published imply an apologia for their shapelessness: essays, *sylva*, timber, *bocage*, *bigarrures*, anatomy, meditations, etc. These collections, along with other gatherings of unprocessed philological data such as Erasmus's *Adagia* and *Apophtegmata* could be considered raw materials for a future literature. Yet they were not mere source books. They could be read for pleasure, as well as consulted when the need arose in the process of composing a rhetorically well-favored discourse. Moreover, most of these texts were works-in-progress, simplified and reshuffled from one edition to the next, so that their fragmentariness became a permanent, functional feature of books that would never end evolving until the writer's death.

Michel Beaujour

The endless process of revision and addition was evidently made possible by the advent of print. An open-ended form with an encyclopedic and methodical orientation: such was the challenge to the poet's *genus universum*, which was turned toward the mythical origin of all knowledge.

The anachronistic notion of a "Book-yet-to-come" is a suggestive metaphor for those Renaissance works. But it does not square precisely with a state of culture in which *Book* did not quite mean what it does today. To be sure, when Montaigne wrote *"my* book," stressing the possessive, he was already referring to something we still recognize as a "book." But "book" often meant a part of a volume, a small printed pamphlet, or inversely, a collection of more or less related materials by one or several authors. A book, a material, printed *codex*, was not necessarily isomorphic to the textual entity, endowed with a beginning, a middle, and an end, which has become the usual meaning of "book." In the Renaissance, rhetorical composition was a relatively *local* matter, limited to the length of a discourse or "chapter:" the *neotenous* texts in question were indeed delinquent and aberrant within that narrow scope. Beyond this, if there were some vague compositional principles applicable to the canonical poetic genres and more precise ones applicable to eloquence, no recognized criteria could be used to assess the well-formedness of longer nonmimetic and nonnarrative discourses. No way to tell whether a book was well proportioned. Hence our impression of "disorder" (or of "freedom") when reading such Renaissance texts. Rabelais's "novels," although obviously grotesque, are mere hyperboles of features common to all Renaissance books, especially where they do not tell a story.

It follows from this that the Renaissance idea of a Book-yet-to-come (if such an idea actually oriented the humanists' *genus*) might well be something very close to the philosophical works, intellectual essays and encyclopedic surveys of a topic developed in the ensuing period when they became ruled by the principles of internal coherence, dialectical progression and discursive homogeneity, made available by the advent of *method*. Such exigencies have become normal and generally accepted, although they are often observed in the breach.

The first major step toward modern composition of nonfiction, a step made necessary by the collapse of the scribal *mnemonic order* under the impact of typography, was the Ramist method with its non-syllogistic, synoptic, order and the binary forks which allowed the division and subdivision of topics within a spatial framework. The deliberate disorder of Montaigne's *Essays*, a disorder which disregarded both the accustomed procedures of topical invention and the decorum of composition, might be considered a transitional strategy, the negative and affirmative functions of which are implicit in the very word *essay*. Through the essay, new heuristic pathways and novel judgmental procedures were laid down. This innovation is the dialectical aspect of thematic and discursive novelties which we now call inwardness or subjectivity. The dialectic of self-portrayal thus appears to be one of the variants of the tentative *genus universum* which challenged the claims of poetry in the Renaissance.

The emergence of a new topical and dialectical deal coincided with the dismemberment and reconfiguration of the discursive system: fragmentation, open-endedness, neoteny, and serious playfulness were the symptoms of the cultural upheaval. Rhetoric itself was at stake in this crisis. Rhetoric: that is to say, the traditional encyclopedia of commonplaces and the transformational rules allowing writers to turn those into completed, effective discourse. And beyond this: the status and anthropology of the authors operating the productive machine, their place in the network of communications, and their role in elaborating new commonplaces and new operational rules. In the passage from a memory-oriented to an innovative culture, the criteria of truth were thrown into jeopardy: Pilate's question dominated the period. Rhetoric had not been meant to answer such a question, it was not competent to do so, yet philosophy itself was helpless. Rhetoric merely names *what is*, and tells how to use it to the best practical effect: in order to come to grips with the question of truth in a time of uncertain commonplaces, rhetoric turned itself inside out, questioned its own cultural foundations, challenged the validity of its topics and tested the limits of its competency in a world of print. In order to give birth to *method*, to the discourse of subject and *ego* (in the *essay* and *meditation*), rhetoric gave up the philosophical innocence of forensic persuasion— with Descartes, it eventually produced the *discourse* of a *method* grounded in *meditation*. An antirhetorical method purporting to be self-assured, universally valid, inexhaustibly productive of knowledge, yet able to persuade, and to stir up the passions. When it reached this point, the method, born of the suicidal travails of Renaissance rhetoric, had become strong enough to stop taunting the old philosophy, for it had indeed become the new philosophy itself: Descartes had succeeded —where Bacon had failed—in converting rhetorical procedures to the pursuit of Truth.

Before the new, and rather forgetful, philosophy could justify its claim to being *genus universum* and *clavis universalis*, Renaissance writing had had to suffer fragmentation, disintegration and disorder; it had failed to reconstruct knowledge in the *image of man* and in the *image of the world*. A new space had been cleared for a *Book of the World* and for a *Book of the Subject*, each being in most respects an

Michel Beaujour

enchanted glass for the other, and an outgrowth of the old rhetoric. In actuality: a collection of generically aberrant texts, ranging from Erasmus's didactic compilations to Descartes's *Meditations* and including Montaigne's and Bacon's works. These books were all paradoxical and, in some sense impossible: they fed on their own impossibility as they mediated a passage from medieval dogmatic and logical certainties to the self-assured epistemological hubris of the classical age.

It has been my contention, then, that the Renaissance produced two rival claims to *genus universum*. One too many—at least—for sound logic. Yet, oddly enough, both managed to survive into the present. Their variants keep cropping up in the dreams of poets and philosophers, and we still experience in our own writings their incompatible (and unwarranted) claims. They have even attempted reconciliations with their natural, and implacable enemy: the exact sciences. Meditative philosophy and gnostic poetry grope for one another as they hold on to a hieroglyphic secret that has already sunk.

In describing the two divergent paths to *genus universum*, the ordinary meanings of *genre* were left aside. *Genus* has meant to us something akin to Heidegger's *Dichtung*: the Language of our *Volk*, with all its etymological and mythological freight. Consequently, *genre* did not denote speech acts and discourses originating in important and recurrent real-life situations. It may well be that the main symptom of a Crisis is a widening gap between ordinary, real practices and utopian speculations that have little regard for empirical observation. For, in critical times, empirical observation gives no encouragement to those who, so understandably, are nostalgic for the past: a past in which men (readers and writers alike) would enjoy the seclusion of a library and communicate silently through books where self and world were at once conjured up and negated. We thus rehearse, in the area of the book to be and interlinked computers, the Renaissance man's nostalgia for Socratic dialogue, and the song of rustic pipes. *Genus universalis*, and the question of Genre, tell us that despite his fancies to the contrary, the poet must live by a law he did not make, or else cease writing.

NOTES

1. This essay refers implicitly, but constantly, to the contents of *L'Absolu littéraire, Théorie de la littérature du romantisme allemand* by Philippe Lacoue-Labarthe and Jean-Luc Nancy (Paris: Seuil, 1978). The term *genus universum* was borrowed, along with much else, from Rosalie Colie's inexhaustible little book, *The Resources of Kind: Genre Theory in the Renaissance* (Berkeley: University of California Press, 1973). See particularly pp. 20–21. Readers will notice the pervasive influence of Walter J. Ong's work on this article.

2. Todorov's article, "La Réflexion sur la littérature dans la France

contemporaine," *Poétique* 38 (April 1979), in which Blanchot is abundantly quoted, came as a welcome reinforcement as I was writing the present piece.

3. Graham Castor, *Pléiade Poetics* (Cambridge: Cambridge University Press, 1964).

4. Paolo Rossi, *Clavis Universalis: Arti mnemoniche e logica combinatoria da Lullo a Leibniz* (Milan-Naples: Ricciardi, 1960).

5. Hiram Haydn, *The Counter-Renaissance* (New York: Harcourt Brace and World, a Harbinger Book, n.d.), chap. 6, pp. 325–79.

THREE

WRITING INTO THE WIND, BETTINA
Friedrich Kittler

LET'S SAY that I say something. There is a way that does not turn back, because the spirits of the night direct it. The woman for whom I write here has dreamt of it, the woman about whom I write has written of it.

B II 357

To all who do not suspect that they must renounce pleasure to pursue fortune and to keep it within sight.

S I 325

The way begins where Ofterdingen's way wound up. "Where are we going?" "Always homeward," Romanticism had informed its children. So now they sit at home, the many wits at Brentano's, for example. They enjoy being to-

B II 91

gether, attend to their education, and along with other mental gymnastics also make up riddles. Except that when it comes to Bettina, she doesn't know any. She looks around, embarrassed, she sees the faces, friendly and intelligible features on none, and she asks why people do not see spirits. No one can solve her riddle, although it is really quite simple: "Because they are afraid of ghosts." "Who—people?" "No, the spirits."

It is so uncanny at home. Not because spirits haunt families, but on the contrary: because they have abandoned them, ever since families were pronounced the goal of all ways. Children with second sight are still just a "where to?": onward, forever onward.

B II 351-57

The Brentanos enjoy their family gathering at Christ-

mas. The walk to church in the grey dawn led past a place
of ancient powers (*Machtplatz*), a ruined cloister haunted
by spirits of the night. The lantern carrier whispered this
to the Brentanos. But now, in the evening, they have long
been together again at the home of Grandmother La Roche.
Cards are given up, the players' gestures are unintelligible,
horrifying, their talk like curses and spells. And because
the spirits are afraid of such ghosts, they come to Bettina:
she is to come in the night. It is to no avail that for once she
does not wish to see the spirits herself and tries to hide in
the curtain: the spirits are more powerful. Already Bettina
is out the door and at the gate of the yard, her dress thrown
up over her head so as not to be recognized by the people
of Frankfort, or so as to be recognized by the spirits, no
difference. She is following the call.

Over snow in fugitive leaps, through snow-covered
rocks up a mountain to the ruined cloister. Listen to the
wind and the spirits of the winter night. Climb on the
churchyard wall and look down into the deep where the ice
floes go on the Main. And while fear and vertigo still grow,
have already climbed over with hands and feet, on the way
down to the river, to the poet who never, never ends.[1] Look
at the ice float, and when a piece buffets into the shore,
spring onto it, and when it breaks, onto the next one. Thus
from piece to piece, into the middle of the river, and pick
up speed. Float and be floated, where the way does not turn
back, pass over the point of no return, where water and ice
and wind cast their great die. Thus did the *Wetterau* get its
name.

And as with the ice floes, so too the letters. They float
along, without stop or return—once again, the adventure
that they describe. If the friend can not tell that already,
she gets it in writing.

G I 479f.
One thing I want to tell you about my letters, I never reread
them—I must let them flutter away like sounds that the wind
carries along, I write them away, understand it as you will, they
are a deep sign of how my spirit steps through yours and is
penetrated again by it, and nothing more.

The letter carrier wind does not like thoughts. It only de-
livers letters that weigh nothing and are nothing. Fortunately, Bettina can not write any other kind.

G I 279
I am so happy that I am insignificant, because I don't have to dig
up clever thoughts when I write you, I have only to tell stories,
otherwise I would think that I dare not write without a little

moral or something else intelligent to weigh down the content of the letter a bit, now I don't ever think about it, sculpting a thought right or pasting it together, others will have to do that, when I am to write something I myself don't think anymore.

A sign is a sign only if it can be repeated, the wise men say. But no, that is just their excuse, so that they might install paperweight-ers everywhere. One does not let one's letters simply float away, one reads them again, one rewrites them, one loads them with the morality of obstinate persistence (*Sitzfleisch*), that sin against the spirit[2] or against the spirits of the night—only then can they be called thoughts and not merely paper. Bettina is familiar with the pertinent chapter of letter writers.

G I 355   I have already written three days on this letter and today I want to send it, oh, I don't like to read it over, it's written, it's truthful, too, if you appreciate the instantaneous mood of truth the way I appreciate it, and it alone, although the philistines say that that isn't truth, that only what is admitted after thorough consideration, fully examined by the human spirit, is truth.

The wise men must have a lot of time to spend at their desks if they read everything over first before it goes to the mailbox or to the press.[3] What they call thorough consideration is merely a restraint they impose on their fingers, itching to write. Bettina's fingers in contrast dance as rapidly over the paper as her feet from floe to floe. Not because she is afraid of death, which shortens the time for talk and hurries many a conversation, but because it is so sweet to float, to write away, and it can never go fast enough. There are moments when even writing without thoughts is much too slow.

B II 34   I myself am not always in the mood, sometimes I think so quickly that I can't even write, and the thoughts are so sweet that I can't even break off to write.

Thus writing would sometimes stem the tide of thoughts. Thoughts at other times would stem the tide of writing. Bettina says both, and if it is a contradiction, then only to people who read her letters twice. She herself lets it go as it comes, if only they do not break off, those thoughts without writing or this writing without thoughts. In any case, G I 319   don't be sedentary. Do nothing but leap on table and chairs, seek places to hide, huddle in a tiny corner, walk in moonlight down the long corridors of the Brentano house, across its old floors, and climb around on the glacis of the fortress G I 319   of the even older imperial city, until the sister confirms

F I 115   a predisposition to St. Vitus's dance. After all, origin (*Ursprung*), as the word says, as Bettina says, as Benjamin will say again, origin means to spring from (*entspringen*, to escape from, or to arise—T.N.).

G I 378-80   When someone like brother Clemens demands that she write down her thoughts, that is, that she think and write simultaneously, then it too becomes only a springing away. She would like to obey, of course, and runs immediately into the garden. There thoughts flutter in the air as merrily as butterflies, but they notice how she wants to impale them, and spring away. The writing finger wipes off their beautiful colors. So it only remains to be faster than the thoughts themselves. Hardly has one been caught than Bettina springs into the house, up three flights, and writes it down before it is forgotten again. There it is, the one thought, period, but that is still not what Clemens wanted. All the stories that Bettina always wants to write down because she likes them fail to produce a book, since they are immediately over and done with. Well, she thinks, running back into the garden, climbing back up in the poplar, up there, amidst the swaying and rocking, the new thoughts that stay away from her desk will come. And indeed, barely half way up, the next one occurs to her. So climb right back down, again up the three steps of the house, write it down again, again period, back to the poplar, again a thought arises, again Bettina springs away. And so on, back and forth, until out of writing and rocking a dance is formed, until poplar, garden, stairs, table, and quill become a crazy and unique writing-machine.

     In this writing-machine the book is only wastepaper. It is simply not completed, as Clemens would like to have it.

G I 380   Bettina has been chasing thoughts for four weeks now and is still not even past the cover. The book, written by a dancing machine, can not write down the dancing machine itself. That is why thoughts which are brought to paper seem so ridiculous or mocking, why only those letters work that again throw everything in a jumble and write everything in a jumble: the dance and the rocking, the thoughts and the thinking of thoughts and the writing of thoughts and the writing without thoughts.

G I 324   Surely, melodies are God-created beings that go on living in themselves, every thought brought forth from the soul alive, man doesn't generate thoughts, they generate man.—Oh! Oh! Oh!—A little linden flower just fell on my nose—and now it's raining a bit; what am I writing rubbish here, and can hardly read it anymore, it's getting quite dark—how beautifully though nature spreads her veil—so luminous, so transparent—now the souls of the plants are starting to roam about, and the oranges in the shrub. And the fragrance of the linden—it comes flowing over, wave after wave—it's already getting dark—

A thought, then a strange thought about thoughts, then a sigh over them all, and finally a writing without rereading, that is, without thoughts—the writing machine runs most beautifully when it is disturbed, when falling linden flowers or raindrops intrude, when a fragrance flows into the room, above all, when the light fades and Bettina can still write but no longer read. Her wish-machine is most happily disturbed or even driven by blindness and dark.

G I 254 Do I understand myself?—Even I don't know.—My eyes have fallen shut with sleep so suddenly while meditating, I must give the letter to the courier tomorrow morning, besides, my light is burning low, it will go out soon, good night, letter! The moon is shining so brightly in my room that it looks completely resonant—the mountains opposite are so splendid, they steam off mist in the moon. All this time the light wants to bid farewell, but I want to see if I can't write by moonlight.

G I 255 Today is the Day of the Assumption, and not Sunday, as I mistakenly said, I have written this page by moonlight. You won't be able to read anything now, it doesn't matter, there's nothing there that you absolutely have to know.

F I 204 You must know that I've already been writing a while by moonlight because my light went out. The moon is swimming among the clouds, and the grey mountains yonder are sunning themselves in its rays, I wanted to say: *mooning* themselves, and mutually accompany themselves with shadows, and the small springs rustle as softly as ghosts.

When the light bids farewell, writing fingers escape from reading eyes. What they then perform is as remote from the languages of Central Europe as the beautiful ur-language of Tlön, which has no noun for the moon, but only a verb that would correspond to the Spanish *lunecer* or *lunar*. "The moon went up over the river" is said in Tlön, "hlör u fang axaxaxas mlö," or, after the translation of Xul Solar, "upa tras perfluye lunó. Upward, behind the onstreaming it mooned."[4] Thus in the dark flow river and moon and ink. Sentence after sentence go the way that does not turn back and cannot be read.

The culture of Central Europe, where everyone reads and writes, lives in contrast by the subdued light of its sun and lamps; the blinding dazzle of the yellow sunshine and the dark of the surrealistic night constitute its beyond.[5] Bettina has ventured into this world, but did not discover it. In a culture where the rationality of rational men consists of perceptual feedback, of hearing oneself speak and seeing oneself write, those exceptional ones known as poets have long been free to prove the rules and regulations by means of exceptions. Petrarch scribbled verses on his leather doublet by night. Awakened in the night, Goethe reached for his quill, or preferably for his pencil, in order to fix in the darkness that which had unexpectedly surged forth. Except that the morning after, with the rereading, a strange shame and a singular awe befell him. Shame at the outpouring that had occurred there, awe of the unconscious that had spoken. And with good reason. Goethe's autobiography itself tells whom he had to thank for those gifts of blind writing and invention: a mother. It is her desire for her son to which the nocturnal outpourings reply; it is her unconscious that speaks as The Poet. For this reason, his or her narcissism abhors exchanging the verses, evoked and concealed by wish-fulfillment and the veil of the night, for gold on the market of literature.

JA XXV 10

JA XXIII 280

JA XXV 10

Bettina's relations with the spirits of the night are different. She does not cover shame with a veil, but, just the reverse, throws her dress up over her head. For this reason she also does not write lightless poems that will become works by the next morning's light. For this reason she does not like to reread anything, but instead wants only to see if she can not write by the light of the moon. While The Poet faces the workings of the unconscious with shame and awe, as if at the boundary of incest, Bettina tests them out. Women, who exist in the plural and perhaps do not at all have the unconscious that Man has, are much more talented than the average man at speaking It in an effective way.[6]

This requires someone who uses his ears for hearing and not understanding, who uses his mouth for keeping quiet and not for explaining. Such bodies are rare; perhaps only Günderode, also a woman, makes unconscious speech a possibility.

G I 277

I can't speak in front of anyone but you, I also don't feel the desire and fire to do it except with you, and whatever I say to you and however it comes out, I sense something stirring in me, as if my soul were growing, and even if I don't understand it myself, yet I'm strengthened by your calm and intelligent eyes that look at me, waiting, as if they knew what will come next. With them you charm thoughts out of me that I wasn't aware of beforehand, that astonish even me, other people have no patience with me, Voigt included, who says: "I already know what you want," and says something that I didn't want at all.

Günderode does not say she understands: she merely looks at Bettina as though she understood. She is or becomes a recipient (*Empfängerin*) who accepts unreadable letters, too. Except that sometimes she thinks it is Bettina who means what is written or what is spoken. Günderode grows alarmed when a philosopher's text is exploded by the efficiency of the unconscious, and when a face-to-face conversation gets carried away by the whispering of the spirits of the night.

G I 300

I feel as if I could give birth to the whole world with my mouth. . . . On the green fortress in the red of evening, where we lay in the trenches, I was happy there with my tongue, there it was always as if someone were behind me, whispering to me. You asked why I turned around so often.—I said, "there's dancing behind me"—for I didn't want to say, there's *speaking*, since it was more like dancing, a quick swinging in circles, nymphs who came out from behind the three big cypresses, holding hands, snuggled sweetly together, their tiny feet together and their tiny hands, you looked at me and said: "Don't be a fool!"—ha ha, I have to laugh—it was too late, of course I'm a fool!—because what I blabbed there is a tune to which there's dancing behind me, and thus our philosopher's text was exploded.

Bettina's speech comes from somewhere else. She speaks into the wind that speaks to her when she merely turns her head. Spirits dwell and dance in the wind, spirits who might

G I 318

G I 317

be called Greek nymphs or simply imps (*Kobolde*)—Bettina's name with the Brentanos. And Günderode finds imps even more careless than Icarus, who at least buckled on wings, while Bettina does not require her feet in order to stride, her understanding to comprehend, her memory to experience, and the latter to infer and to conclude. Poor Günderode, she would like to get together for conversation, but is exposed to the workings of the unconscious instead.

G I 318

I'm intimidated by your assertions, on fire with your effusiveness. Here at my desk I lose patience with the colorlessness of my poetic efforts. You can't write poetry, because you're what poets call poetic, matter doesn't shape itself alone (*bildet sich nicht selber*), it has to be shaped. I think of you as the clay that a god, shaping, tramples underfoot, and what I'm becoming aware of in you is that seething fire that his supersensuous touch

kneads vigorously into you.—I must shape (*bilden*, also educate—T.N.) and make myself alone, as well as I can.

She sits at the desk, that is, there, where she wrote and
composed, for no poplar or spirit brings inspiration to
Günderode. She sits at the desk and reads over her poetic
efforts. As if that could help, as if then they would grow less

G I 458   colorless. In vain has Bettina warned her that composing
poetry is not enough, that it meditates on itself too much.
Just as Günderode thinks that Bettina means something,
so too she thinks that meditation, rereading, shaping are
all necessary. She does not want to get carried away, as

G I 449   Koboldin suggests, and abandon the colonnades before which
the myrtle of her poems shyly blossoms. For Günderode,
abandoned by a mythic or mythological lover, writes in
place of a dreamed-of and frustrated speech.

G I 360   Writing poetry with every heartbeat has always revived me; I was
no longer depressed when I could let my dumbness resound.

The hostile world that prohibits a love, the lonely self, silenced by love's pain but reaching towards a written language—such tedious things are designated by the sentence
"I must shape and make myself alone, as well as I can."

G I 225   Günderode's verses are not music but colonnades: grave-
stones to a self that has no substance, only the form of its
sorrow. Yet precisely for that reason it is not willing to disappear, get carried away, and not despair. Günderode's
writing of poetry is an exercise in dying. It gives her no
pleasure; she calls her education a must. And really, those
forsaken by men are easily tempted into imitating their
living, or rather, their dying. This shaping and writing,

JA XII 220   which grows so eloquent when a person is silenced by his
pain, has been practiced by men at least since the time of
Tasso. Günderode is one of the first women to have followed
them.

No wonder that she would sometimes like to initiate
Bettina into dying. It is enough that her letters apply to
Bettina such philosophical terms as "formative form"
(*bildende Form*) and "formed matter" (*gebildete Stoff*).
For thereby emerges something her letters do not know: a
malignant god who tramples girls' bodies underfoot, and a
clay that is waiting to be trampled and kneaded. Strange,
the crassness that is supposed to replace love. But that is
the way it is with philosophers and their terms.

Let's have a look at the concepts active and passive, which dominate all that has ever been thought about the relation between substance and form. It is evident, obvious, that these assertions are merely based on a phantasma, by means of which they would seek to replace that which can never, in any way, be said: namely, the relation between the sexes.[7]

F I 203

Bettina noticed this right away. She gives in a single time and reads Schelling aloud to Günderode. Judging from her request, the latter had hoped for symphilosophical fusions; however, there arises in Bettina no feminine philosophy,

G I 267

but instead, a physical horror. Her overwrought aversion to philosophy leads to intense vomiting, bilious neuritis, and a vertigo that is the inversion of all her splendid giddiness.

G I 229

I mean, one can't read a book, understand it or assimilate its spirit, when the inborn melody doesn't sustain it. Indeed, because I conceive it that way, I wonder whether everything, if it's not melodious, might also not yet be true. To me your *Schelling* and your *Fichte* and your *Kant* are wholly impossible fellows. What efforts have I made, and have actually only run away from them here because I wanted to take a break. Repulsion, attraction, the highest potency (*Potenz*).

Do you know what's becoming of me?—Dizzy—my head swims, and then, you know what else?—I'm ashamed,—yes, I'm ashamed, to venture into language this way, with jimmies and hoes in order to bore something out, and that a person, born sound, should imagine actual lumps on his head and concoct all sorts of physical illnesses.

Because Bettina can distinguish between singing and trampling, between organs of love and a tinsmith's tools, Günderode with her philosophical fellows and their highest potency is not well-received. She recommends therefore that totally different fellows be introduced. Bettina is advised

G I 294

not to run away from her history teacher if rulers and peoples, shaping forces and shaped matters, are not to remain a stagnant swamp in her imagination.

G I 297

In the letter that for my benefit was so lengthy, you said that history is necessary if I am to acquire reflection, self-knowledge; I don't want to contradict!—yet if you could perceive the teasing, terrifying ghosts that pursue me in this wasteland of history. . . . When the teacher opens his mouth, then I look down into it as into an immense abyss that spews out the mammouth bones of the past and all sorts of petrified rubbish that won't germinate, won't bloom, and for which the sun and rain are worthless.— Meanwhile, concerning the present, I can't wait to get up and go, I would like to woo it, but without first having to lie on the anvil and let myself be hammered flat by the past.

No matter how much she would like to get up and go, Bettina obeys the request of her friend. The heroes or ghosts of the past are permitted to climb out of the abysmal mouth of the instructor. Only sometimes, or between the lines of history, the girl who would like to woo the present asks him, in vain, about it.

G I 290 "In its earliest phases the history of Egypt is dark and uncertain."—That's lucky, otherwise we'd have to worry about them, too.—"*Menes* is the first king known to us."—That's all right with me, too, if we only get something worthwhile from knowing him. "He built Memphis and rerouted the Nile into a secure bed. *Möres* dug Lake Möres in order to prevent destructive flooding by the Nile.—Then came *Sesostris* the Conqueror, who destroyed himself." Why?—Was he handsome?—Was he in love?—Was he young?—Was he melancholy?—About all these things the instructor gives no answer, only the remark that he should be thought of as old. I demonstrated to him that he was young merely to set the wheel of time into motion, which always gets stuck in the mire of boredom.—There was also some rumbling about *Busiris*, who built Thebes, *Psamtichus*, who took the divided states under his wing, then the wars with Babylon, *Nebachadnezzar*, from whom *Cambyses*, *Cyrus's* son, takes it away again. The Egyptians unite with Lybia, liberate themselves again, war with the Persians, until Alexander puts an end to the fighting and thank goodness to this history, too.

The few questions with which Bettina sets the wheel of history into motion mark an end to the great men of action who brought rivers and swamps into shape. Self-destruction, for the poet Günderode as well as the Pharaoh Sesostris, is the finale of that sort of formation. When there is no more matter, it is the only thing that remains. Hence Bettina has no desire to be shaped or hammered flat by the form of these forms, by the history of these histories. Her only wish: that the Alexanders eradicate their predecessors, that the dead bury their dead, and that things of the past pass away.

This wish is fulfilled by writing itself. Bettina's letters to her older friend, who suggested the lessons and would now like to read their fruits, abolish history instead through straight, word-for-word repetition. One hundred and fifty years later a writer *On the Theme of History* would simply open the *Kleinen Ploetz* and, deleting all names, copy what had happened in the year 1849—someone is deposed, someone becomes governor, someone is appointed head, someone arranges something, several jointly ascertain something, someone transgresses something, someone lays something down, and so on and so on.[8] Bettina conversely underlines the great men's names that her teacher pulls from the history book until they turn into paper again.

G I 298f. *Astyages* (where does he come from?) marries his daughter to the Persian king *Cambyses*, whose son *Cyrus* pushed his grandfather off the throne (who had thus sat there too long)—, he unites Media, Assyria, and Persia and *founds* the great Medopersian empire, the Jew *Hirsch* of the line of Esau sticks out his rough hand to claim it, he'll keep it subjugated in his old sack until you free it, if you chuck it in the whole in the oven with the old paper, you'll relieve me of some past that's hard to conquer.

All history finds an end in the mailbag of the old Jew who carries the letters of the two friends back and forth. It is

G I 452 so sly to mail letters without reopening or even rereading them. The transcribed lessons can contribute nothing to Bettina's knowledge and education, for like hot potatoes they are immediately passed on to Günderode and there, in the oven, are freed into fire and smoke. If continuous history is the indispensible correlative of the founding function of the subject,[9] then the only escape from becoming a subject, or rather, from becoming subjugated, is to write into the wind.

With one breath a forgetful girl does away with the great men who rule in and by virtue of history, and with the philosophers who rule in and by virtue of understanding. This disturbs not only Günderode, but also Bettina's Grandmother La Roche, who was the first female German author of light fiction.

G I 372 Hearing the opinions of witty men, which is my grandmama's passion, seems to me a waste of time, dear grandmama.—"You can't deny it, dear child, that they understand the world and are summoned to lead it?" she said yesterday. "No, dear grandmama, it seems to me rather, that I'm summoned to do it." "Go on, sleep it off, you're a silly little chit."[10]

With Bettina that curious game comes to an end, in which women first listen to the opinion of witty men, then attribute it to other women, and finally let it be delivered again by witty men, as in the case of La Roche and Wieland. It was in the course of this malicious copulation that the genre of light fiction arose.[11] All of La Roche's novels could like one of her last books be entitled *The Beautiful Image of Resignation*, even when they elevate a Fräulein von Sternheim or a Miss Long to the status of heroine. A woman who was free, according to Günderode, became for her the

matter which she had to imprint with a form that she had
acquired from men and then in all friendliness imprinted
on less-cultivated female readers. This would not be possible
without memory and fidelity, without the widow's veil of
La Roche and the heartaches of Günderode. Enlightened

G I 295   and educating women are the tradition in which Günderode
sees all the seeds of development so loyally and so devotedly

G I 424   sown that questions of power never occur to them. Only
Bettina, who wants to become a great statesman and have
the whole world at her feet, believes that the holiest poli-

G I 380f.   tics—and the mightiest, too—are found in fairy tales. Only
Bettina climbs onto her forgetting as onto a throne of power.
Only Bettina, who retains neither words nor past, seizes
hold of the simple thought forcibly to make true all the
thoughts she writes down without knowing why.

This short circuit pulsates through knowledge and education and constitutes Bettina's freedom.

F I 51   And so what do I gain from all those who consider themselves
witty enough to guide and to bridle me? They talk about things
to which my soul pays no heed, they merely talk into the wind.
I make you a solemn vow, I don't want to let myself be bridled,
I want to trust in that something so jubilant in myself, for in
the end it's nothing other than a sense of my own power (*Eigen-
macht*), it's called a bad side, this sense of power. But of course
just such an arbitrary power is entailed by life itself!

G I 297   You speak of my perceptiveness with respect; whether I've received it from the past, as you surmise—that is, if I understand
you correctly, then I don't know how it came about. Is it a
genius who has come gliding over from there?—That's what you
want me to think!—Clever rascal!—My genius, the blonde
whose beard hasn't sprouted yet!—supposedly grown forth from
the mold like a toadstool?—Truly, there are spirits that turn
around themselves like suns; they come from nowhere and are
going nowhere, they dance in place, giddiness is their delight,
mine is thoroughly intoxicated by it, I let myself be giddily
carried along.

In dance the spirits bid farewell to yesterday. For anyone
who writes into the wind, pedagogical talk is also only talking into the wind. By her own power Bettina escapes from a
philosophical-historical system of education that is propped

F I 75   against heaven's gate like a miserable chicken roost, up
which girls and women are to hop, from rung to rung, like
a hen struggling up to the perch to sit beside the cock.

No cock likes to hear such things at all. The older

G I 302   brother, who otherwise remains in the background and

F I 47 urges women to take his place in studying with Bettina, who always wants to know from Günderode what and how Bettina is doing, who sends cultivated French women to Frankfort to direct Bettina's spirit and soul towards the sublime, Clemens has to come out from beneath his cover. Talk of personal power cannot be allowed. In order to put a stop to it, there are men.

Therefore Clemens, the vagabond, interrupts his guitar playing from time to time and his fairy tale telling that turns the heads of girls in the Rheingau and the German university towns, steps up to his desk before Bettina's picture and lectures her epistolically. Firstly about education in general and of the general, secondly about literature with respect to A) reading and B) writing. Where the narrow genres philosophy and history break down, there the unlimited genre literature begins.

F I 21 The educated soul is that which makes use of all the knowledge it has, in the same way that a mere human makes use of his senses to perceive and judge everything that surrounds him. The merely healthy human hears, sees, feels, speaks; for the educated, however, hearing changes to music, seeing to painting, feeling to shape, and language to beautiful, educated language, all proclaiming his education and love. For that reason be industrious and cheerful.

F I 25 Thoughtlessness is wretchedness. But you will certainly become truly happy, and I, too, but only when we satisfy the needs of our souls, which we can do solely through education. . . . Man is on earth to educate himself and then also the world.

F I 53 Only in and through the general can each individual strength establish its roots, only within it learn to understand itself, and only *upon* it test itself out.

The program is clear, coherent, categorical. To begin with, mere and educated humanity are differentiated as mortality and immortality. Then the cognitions eternalized in the arts become a need of the soul itself, which incessantly pursues its own education and along with it the betterment of Central Europe. For this reason, the soul is referred thirdly to the universal, which encompasses it, and to escape from which through thoughtlessness would be hell.

Thus a German poet writes his sister pedagogically about education. She has never asked him to. Despite or because of this, he writes her in the same year that Pestalozzi writes for mothers. According to Pestalozzi, his book is necessary *and* unnecessary for mothers because their nature already knows the thoughts it contains and will make the book, as the book of a man, disappear.[12] So, too, Friedrich Schlegel three years previously in *On Philosophy: To Dorothea (Uber die Philosophie. An Dorothea)*. According to Schlegel, philosophy is indispensible to women *and* at the same time as natural for them as prose for the Bourgeois Gentilhomme. (Monsieur Jourdain, as is well known, spoke prose as we all do: without knowing it.) With this story, men can hide the violence of their language from their noble townsladies, sisters, mothers, or beloveds. Whatever they write, and that means, prescribe, sinks again into the sea of unutterable knowledge, which is the Soul, or Woman. The female reader becomes the secret authoress and the author becomes her mouthpiece. As if books were an understanding, and commands, a translation. Friedrich, at the close of the letter that initiated his beloved into philosophy:

KA VIII 61   I have even surprised myself, and am now aware that it was actually *you* who initiated *me* into philosophy.

Clemens, in a letter that teaches Bettina to understand the French Revolution rationally:

F I 64   Forgive me, that I am trying to tell you about things that dwell much more purely in your soul, that I actually perceive in you yourself, in order to articulate them for you. The hope of a precious harvest makes me so impatient, I see everything sprout forth and push onward into bloom in you, and can hardly wait for it to ripen, for the sake of truth and beauty.

The men, like laborers, stop chopping and boring. They have learned from Bettina's loathing for Kant and Fichte and Schelling. Writing, they become innocent and literary: gardeners awaiting a precious harvest from nature herself. Their contribution to the growth of the soul or woman amounts to nothing: articulation. But this nothing, no matter how much forgiveness it requires, has to exist. Therein Romanticism is an endless and ingenious exegesis of the classical table of votives or laws, which says: "When the soul *speaks*, so speaks alas! the *soul* no more."[13]

The exegete Friedrich in *On Philosophy: To Dorothea*:

KA VIII 42   Perhaps you would prefer a conversation. But I am an author through and through. Writing holds I don't know what sort of secret magic for me, perhaps due to the dusk of eternity that hovers around it. Yes, I admit it to you, I am astonished at the secret power that lies hidden in these dead marks; how the simplest expressions, seemingly no more than true and exact, can be so meaningful that they shine as out of bright eyes, or so eloquent as artless accents from the deepest soul. One believes one is listening when one only reads, and indeed, with those truly beautiful passages, one who reads aloud can only endeavor not to destroy them. Silent marks seem to me a much more appropriate cover for the deepest, most immediate utterances of the spirit than the sound of the lips. I would almost say in the rather mystical language of our H.: To live is to write; the unique vocation of humanity is to inscribe the thoughts of the deity on the tablet of nature with the stylus of the educating spirit.

F I 18

Dorothea, the God-given soul, would like to have a chat. In this manner, too, Bettina writes her first letter to Clemens, as when she gossiped with him, and because they can no longer together listen to the whispering of the wind. The Romantic authors reply to this pain with their Vocation of Romantic Authorship.[14] The soul does not speak in speech, they write, for the artless accents of the deepest soul are eloquent only when they are written and precisely not said. The sound of the lips shamelessly and indecently lifts the veil before what is most immediate. It betrays the pure meanings of language through the body: the body that speaks and the body that hears. Therefore Friedrich must disappoint Dorothea's desires for once: in speech the soul would become a desire. Goethe lay the veil of the night over his poetic outpourings, the Romantic authors, the veil of writing over lips that are not there only to speak. The modern practices of soundless writing and inaudible reading[15] are the expedients used to avoid women. Friedrich dances at two weddings: one with Dorothea, whom five years after her philosophical initiation he would also religiously convert and marry, and another with the eternity that hovers around him as author.

The wedding preparations of this *nuptiae philologiae et philosophiae* are made by inaudible reading, because it dismisses the eve-of-the-wedding party (*Polterabend*) and its spirits. But the wedding itself takes place soundlessly on paper. Friedrich says it in the mystic language that pertains to a *hieros gamos*. His Romantic authorship swells up to the unique vocation of humanity. For a life-time, that is, a writing-time, humanity inscribes on the writing-surface of nature with the stylus of the educating spirit. In the name of the father (the thoughts do belong to the godhead), the phallus sinks into a matter that is *virgo et mater*. Thus mankind—as Lacoue-Labarthe and Nancy have noticed in translating *On Philosophy* into their own double-edged language[16]—is Man.

KA VIII 45

For this reason, it is of no avail to the Romantic author again to degrade, in the name of an original androgeny, sexual differentiation or heterosexuality—which the letter to Dorothea in fact substitutes for a symphilosophical homosexuality—to a mere formality of human existence that one of course dare not eradicate or pervert, but may by all means subordinate to reason and cultivate according to its highest laws. For the stylus that guides his stylus knows better. Precisely this subordination and degradation is the substitute for an impossible sexual relation. Dorothea learns that.

KA VIII 42

Indeed, as for you, I think that you will perform your share of this vocation of the human race quite adequately if you sing as much as you have until now, inwardly and outwardly, in the usual and the symbolic sense, if you are less quiet, and now and then also read the holy scriptures with devotion, not merely let others read for and describe to you. But you must especially keep the words holier than before now. Otherwise I would be in bad shape. For of course I can not give you anything, and must expressly stipulate to myself that you expect no more from me than *words*, expressions for that which you have long felt and known, only not so clearly and ordered.

Under the stipulations of a Vocation of Man, Woman makes the exception. She remains soul, singing in order to remain soul and not speaking or even writing. Thus she sings most beautifully when she does it inwardly and symbolically. And really: if Women were to write, the Romantic phallus would be in bad shape. It would have no writing-surface nature that it could deflower and mate *and*, because the whole remains paper or the hymen remains whole, could conceive to be a virgin. In this Holy Marriage originates the genre of all genres, literature. Insofar as Woman is mother, the writer and his literary texts become a child that incestuously caresses its mother[17] and that as her phallus cannot give anything that she would not always already be; insofar as Woman is virgin, she is sworn to keep the gifts of words holy, because and although they are not gifts at all. For the soul itself speaks and sings, only wordlessly; that which it knows and feels make its first written and first read words clear and ordered, *clare et distincte*. And really: if Woman were not to read, the Romantic phallus would be in bad shape. It could no longer subordinate to reason that mere formality of human existence, which it holds the differentiation of sexes to be, and educate it according to reason's highest laws. In plain German: the writing stylus would find no more conceivers (*Empfängerinnen*).

Therefore, in the second part of his epistolary lecture, Clemens starts to train his little sister to be a reader.

F I 62   I have given the book dealer *Guilhomman* an order to send you *Homer*. In addition, you should next read the journey of young Anarchasis, and very alertly, for that will instruct and amuse you. Yet you must not compel yourself to do this reading, you must honor it because you love it.

F I 112   It would please me if you were to read some history, and further-more mostly Goethe, and always Goethe, above all the seventh volume of the new Works, his poems are a real antidote to sentimentality. . . . On the whole it is very annoying to me that you write me nothing of your inner development, never ask me what you should read, and the like. What good is all your phantisizing about this and that, which just is the way it is. It would be better if you made such use of your trust in me as to permit me an influence in your education—as to ask me for ad-vice concerning all your reading—and the like.

Friedrich's unique Vocation of Man here becomes an event. The classical authors are deities, and above all, the One who invented modern authorship: God Goethe. Stylus is the elder brother who governs as his deities' priest. Tablet of nature is Bettina, into which literature sinks down, copu-lating. And if Clemens's wishes come true, nature will im-mediately yield a precious harvest: she will herself begin to write. Modestly at first—with inquiries about reading lists; then more self-sufficiently—with discussions of books.

F I 62   Write down, whenever possible, your sensations during or after reading, and send it to me; in general talk in your letters more about the entire scope of your sensations, that is, how they radiate out into the world, rather than about their concentration.

Bettina is to be initiated into the culture of writing and reading. Writing one's own reading is already a step for-ward. Woman starts off as a reviewer. The next step will be to read one's own writing, too. Clemens can only shake his head over Bettina's stupid questions.

F I 19   Whether you can write me disjointed thoughts as though we were talking together?—Dear child, just as from here I cannot interrupt your words before you have even found them, so, too, from such a distance I would not understand you as well. And then, of course, it is also in the interest of art to learn to express oneself completely and concisely. The writer must at the same time write to himself, since through the letter he must become acquainted with himself, you say, the world seems unendingly wide to you, and within it you are as if lost to yourself.

Not merely to the recipient but at the same time to the sender, not merely out of love but at the same time out of an interest in art, writing means rereading all that is written, means polishing until it completely and concisely expresses the unutterable soul. In this way Woman becomes an artist. She no longer swims lost in the Main or the universe, she no longer writes into the wind. The words stop stopping. Letters that become literature compensate for everything that writing subordinates to speech as mere surrogate. Ever since Herder and Schiller, a discourse that bridges and compensates for the two absences of the speaker and hearer is called: a literary work.[18] However unendingly wide the world may be, however wide the distance between Clemens and Bettina may be—in the work absence absents itself. In plain German: the sexual difference disappears.

KA V 68   Friedrich believes that if he were to stay away from his beloved for several months, her style would fully develop itself, hence Woman too would grow a stylus. Bettina should learn to express herself completely and concisely and to procure knowledge of the soul and the world. That is what Clemens then calls education in general and of the general. When women, that striking-out of the general, create literature, they are thus also within the universal and the phallic. From the homosexuality of Romantic symphilosophy via the heterosexuality of writing and reading to the homosexuality of literature.

That is the trick of the multipurpose letters that go to recipient and sender simultaneously. Bettina confirms to Clemens that he himself obviously follows his own prescriptions for writing.

F I 109   I feel that such profoundly pondered throughts (in your earlier letter about art) as you address to me appertain indeed much more to the world.

Friedrich himself writes the same thing to Dorothea.

KA VIII 48   I at least could not love without, at the risk of chivalrousness, revering something; and I do not know whether I could love the universe with my whole soul if I had never loved a woman. But of course the universe is and remains my watchword.

The author is so in love with the universe that all his love for women amounts to bigamy. Friedrich's love letter to Dorothea is at the same time dedicated to eternity and to the world. For this reason, and because he has also, as Clemens demands, informed his beloved *and* to a certain extent himself about philosophy, Friedrich can conclude:

KA VIII 61 In gratitude, I will also, if you have no objections, have this letter published right away.

And multipurpose letters work wonderfully. There result whole journals and entire literatures. The Schlegel brothers, not satisfied with selling their own letters as works of literature, also set their women to writing literary works in the form of letters. And the women, those emancipated beings so celebrated today, agree and start in dutifully at their desks. When they have finished, the brothers return, read, and find the text not quite universal enough. So they strike out the designations of addresser and addressee that make the review a letter and edit this early piece of *écriture féminine*. Out of a would-be letter emerges a proper text that has neither speaker nor hearer.

F I 67 Bettina alone does not play along. In an age whose watchword is the universe, her watchword remains: assist the ice floes in the Main. And assisting means that Bettina writes into the wind, not because to her misfortune or as a woman she can not do any better, but rather, because that is what she wants. In an age whose Romantic men seek a New Mythology to reconcile all the traditions of Europe, Bettina prefers to found a new religion. Rule one: no edu-

G I 340 cation allowed. Rule two: expunge the error of friends of
G I 345 wisdom and church fathers that God is wisdom; *for God is passion.*

In vain Clemens writes and urges her to organize the
G I 204 many tangled stories which overflow from her letters into a unity and a work. In vain he implores her to separate her phantasies more thoroughly from herself—like the church from the village, the sacred from the profane. In vain he
F I 83 invites her to busy herself with, if not universal history,
F I 80 at least the history of her course of education, and to become a biographical person. The answer, as always, is no.

G I 340 Shape my intellect!—I have no intellect— I don't want my own intellect.

F I 57 You've often said to me, I should write out my memories of the time at the convent, which is already three years behind me. It's all still living within me, but I can't break off branches of flowers from the tree that I myself am.

F I 51   Account for it as you like, I can't explain it any further, I can only say that no matter what kind of police of the soul prevail in the world, I pay no heed to them, I throw myself as a roaring stream of life into the deep, wherever it draws me.

And to give the police of the soul their name, or Klaus Theweleit the catchword, the disobedient one writes Günderode:

G I 288   Clemens, who just doesn't let me be the way that I am, he's afraid and can't bear it that I pour myself out.

Thus, Romantic literature meets up with its truth and limit. To dream of a genre of all genres—that is, of one genre—that transcends the difference between sexes instead of fashioning, as before, a republic of learned men, is wish and anxiety at once. On the one hand, literature is

KA II 182   to encompass for the first time everything that is poetic, from the largest, innumerable systems-within-systems of art, to the sigh, the kiss, that a poetizing child exhales in an artless song; on the other hand, it cannot tolerate the outpourings of children. To be sure, ever since the days of Wilhelm Meister and Mignon, the new command is to eavesdrop on, that is, to evoke, those words from the mouths of babes held to be as unthinking as they are significant.[19] But the command turns against its authors as soon as one of the summoned children of the spirits exploits and proclaims

F I 19   it himself. Clemens has assured Bettina that what is significant in her talk is precisely that which she considers insignificant—and now Bettina to Günderode.

G I 271   You must acknowledge to everyone that I'm no big deal, it will pass soon; actually, the guilty one is Clemens, out of great love for me he always takes pleasure in what I've done, and has found my thoughtless talk exquisite.

Now they stream along, those admired and evoked talks, and do not stop again. Now they do not stop not stopping in works. And already they create anxiety. Günderode is alarmed at Bettina's exuberance, but then one of Friedrich's

KA II 269   *Ideas* occurs to her, to the effect that women have no need of poetry because their innermost being is poetry. So the

G I 318   fact that Bettina cannot make up poems becomes excusable. In the end or dilemma of a being that for Romantic literature springs from an artless song, the following century would find consolation for Bettina's writing-away.[20] It is otherwise with the brother, however, who is serious about the need for an all-encompassing literature. If Bettina does not write a work, then he has only one choice. His education, the police of the soul, becomes the police of the body, too.

G I 414 And when he had investigated everything, he then proceeded to lock me up and said I should make a poem out of it, exactly as I had related it, and just write it down in short sentences, and if it doesn't rhyme, why, he wants to teach me to rhyme, and so he went out and locked the door, and through the door he called: "You can't come out until you have finished a poem!"—I stood there—utter nonsense in my head.—I didn't even think about writing down.

Clemens Brentano or *fiat litteratura, pereat infans.*

F I 223 Such locking up is not especially smart, if only because inspiration comes to Bettina solely in running and rocking. And it is not especially modern, either, since the children's crusades have long begun. One does not lock up bodies any more, one has words that record the soul's derangements. Therefore Clemens switches to psychological diagnosis.

I implore you, for the sake of the Kaiser's beard, do not be so sentimental and do not let yourself get so worked up over a cat's song. . . . It's a miserable life for a sentimental person in the world, in fact, precisely because the world is no less than sentimental. . . . If you knew how one can acquire all those peculiarly tender sentiments through blockages in the bowels, and that the possessed and witches of past ages were nothing other than such constipated persons, then you would be more wary of falling into such sentimentality; often helpful in this regard is a lot of physical exercise, activity, avoidance of all thoughts of love and the like. Sentimental people are never productive, because they are unable to master a single thing but are overwhelmed by everything. . . .
It would please me if you were to read some history and furthermore mostly Goethe, and always Goethe, above all the seventh volume of the new Works, his poems are a real antidote to sentimentality. On the whole it is very annoying to me that you write me nothing of your inner development, never ask me what you should read and the like. What does and should your anxious love want of me, when it just forever repeats the way things already are, namely, that we care for each other, and this is how it should be between siblings.[21]

F I 111f. This is clear-text—so much so, that Bettina in copying replaced constipation with sickliness and abdominal problems with hypochondria. What is merely love and not a work is written by a sterile womb, by an hysteric in the literal sense. Thus the good people of the era of Freud and Charcot were not the first who sought to trace mystic things back to tales of screwing, rather, the creators-creatures of classical-romantic education already had.[22] They write as connoisseurs and historians of women's bodies.

And in so doing write nonsense. The constipated belly, which throughout centuries has united and tormented witches and hysterics, the possessed and the sentimental, cannot plug up the gap between the eloquent girls of Romanticism and the wise women of old Europe. Bettina noticed this right away: the sentimental do not tread in the tracks of witches, but rather, their brothers in those of the F I 145   Inquisition. They grow anxious and afraid of desire. Bettina's sentimental letters are supposed to become literature merely so they are no longer the endless repetition of love. For the love that Clemens loves and does not want to cure with a ban on all thoughts of love is something other than hysteric and more silent.

F I 141   Perhaps, and it is to be hoped, God will help you find a darling husband and me a darling wife.

Marriage versus hysteria, norm versus deviation—the hippocritic *Nubat illa et morbum effugiet* has apparently returned.[23] Yet it is not that simple. The darling wife whom Clemens opportunely wishes for himself has little to do with a woman. His fear of Bettina, of her writing and pouring, implicates himself as well. He prescribes that she read the classics, above all, the antidote to sentimentality, so that she too will learn to write closed works; at the same time he himself writes on *Godwi*, that *unruly novel* about *The Petrified Image of the Mother (Das steinerne Bild der Mutter)*. Bettina is to marry a darling husband; Clemens loves girls behind whom Bettina is concealed and eventually marries F I 121   the mother of a child. Therefore the opposition that men's phantasies set up and traverse is not hysteria and marriage, but hysteria and motherhood.[24] The conjugal norm merely serves as an empty standard to distinguish beloved mothers from hysterically loving wombs. Clemens, who would himself like to be a *génie enfant*, the child of a mother,[25] and hence signs his novel Maria, does not like it that other children do not get their wishes from mothers and instead of homeward prefer to go onward forever.

Bettina, however, does not fear the possession of witches but the being possessed of married women.

G I 376   Can I know, then, whether I'm not perhaps possessed by a spirit (*Geist*)?—And isn't possession perhaps a giving up of individuality, and aren't the shrews who resist the intellect (*Geist*) perhaps even stronger individually than those who are permeated with intellect?—Oh, does strength really lie in resignation?

F I 146   I will give myself, but I won't give myself up. . . . You declare: "God will hopefully help me find a darling husband and you a darling wife." These are your words to me! And that is a key into which I can't translate at all. And—I just can't dwell on it, let the darling wife, the darling husband come together however they like, I'm not going to disturb them!

Thus the girl who because of sheer floating simply can not dwell on tales of screwing, discovers the Babylonian confusion of tongues between women and men. The ancient nominalists had written about individual words that in different languages have the same sound but different meanings.[26] Bettina writes the same thing about languages as a whole.

F I 146   Oh, would it be possible that a language so exactly corresponded to another language in its sounds and its sorts of words that someone could write a novel in the one language, and some one else, thinking it was in the other, read what was written in the former in the latter?—And in so doing get a story, no trace of which was ever suspected or intended? That's how it is with you, and I must totally dash your hopes that I will endeavor "to become generally lovable and loved." You haven't read me in my language.

Love is no longer love after its translation. Clemens's language makes a suffering out of a deed, and out of a desire, a desire to be desired. Although other women may love this masculine image of women, Bettina stands by her other language and her other longing. *Clemens Brentano's Garland of Spring (Clemens Brentanos Frühlingskranz)*, the correspondence between the brother and sister, draws to a close, and Bettina, instead of awaiting a beloved husband for whom she would be lovable, continues along the way that does not turn back. The other longing, one that is felt and unconscious, guides her along it. And is not an aspect of the Other, the aspect of God, sustained by the longing of women?[27]

The God is none other than Goethe. Left alone after Clemens has married a mother and Günderode has committed suicide because a married man did not marry her, Bettina crosses over the bridge of the Main to old Frau

Rat. And so begins *Goethe's Correspondence with a Child (Goethes Briefwechsel mit einem Kinde).*

On its stool at the mother's feet, the twenty year old child learns to love Goethe—Goethe, as his mother saw him.[28] Sometimes Clemens was right, after all: as his mother's darling, Goethe is the antidote to sentimentality, and his mother, the opposite of hysteria. A child who never had a mother encounters its God as it is sustained by a mother's longing. For what Bettina hears from the mouth of Frau Rat is the secret of classical authorship.

B II 278 She said to me, she's not only there for her son's sake, but her son for hers, too; and she could rest well assured of her share in his works and deeds.

And because this is so, because the narcissism of the author arises from the narcissim of the mother, because the poetizing soul is always already homebound, towards Frankfort, Goethe's body can remain in Weimar. There, where he was born, another child represents him better in a devouring origin:

B II 38 He has said to me, I should represent him for you and should show all the love that he can't, and should act towards you as if all the love were shown to me by you, whom he never forgets.—When I was with him, I was so stupid and asked whether he loved you, then he took me in his arms and pressed me to his heart and said, "Pluck a string and it sounds, even if it has not produced a note in a long time." Then we were silent and spoke no more about it.

The string produces no note, the mouth no sound, so that the quill may produce that many more works. About love, which was His inspiration, a classical author is silent. He encloses it within that symbolic and unconscious content that gives his works closure. But after he has mutely presented his mother with the gift of a child in return, everything is put into words, pouring out uninhibitedly—through the mouthpiece of Bettina. To be sure, she speaks of it no more, but she writes it, sentence for sentence, letter for letter. For in order to slip with her other desire through the net of mother-and-son love, Bettina is only left with the ruse of divulging all ruses and all loves. In this way she learns to write.

Bettina to the mother:

B II 38 I don't want to lie: if you weren't the mother you are, I wouldn't learn writing from you either.

Bettina to the son:

B II 67 "Dear, dear daughter! everyday, in all the days to come, call me by the one name that includes my good fortune; my son is your friend, your brother, who surely loves you, etc." (Your) mother writes such words to me; what do they entitle me to?

Such cunning honesty and such rhetorical inquiries conjure up the mother-love of the author in Frankfort and the author-love of the mother in Weimar. Bettina's desire becomes one that is not returned, but is indisputable. After she has plucked the string of mother-love in Goethe, something is left over for her, too. The stupid questions elicit a declaration of love for the mother and a substitute embrace for Bettina herself. Thus mother and son make or let little Koboldin dance back and forth between Frankfort and Weimar. So close yet seeing each other so seldom, they both have found a *postillon d'amour* whose endless outpouring of letters speaks to them of themselves. Cunning and

B II 21 motherless, Bettina even coaxes a letter of recommendation from Wieland that introduces her to Goethe as the grand-

JA XIII 3 daughter of La Roche and the daughter of his adolescent sweetheart, Maximiliane, thus conjuring up for him half-faded legends of young love. The mother, however, after the ruse has worked and Goethe has just received Bettina for the first time:

B II 18 Do write what took place. Just think, that I haven't seen him for eight years and will perhaps never see him again, if you don't tell me about him, then who will? Haven't I listened to your silly stories a hundred times so that I know them by heart, and now, when you've learned something new, something unique, when you know you could give me the greatest pleasure, you write nothing. Is something wrong with you?

And Goethe, just after he has lost his mother and has decided upon his autobiography as her replacement:

B II 264 Now you have lived a good while with dear mother, have heard her tales and anecdotes time and again and carry and cherish everything in recent, enlivening memory. So set yourself down and write out what pertains to me and my affairs, and you will thereby make me very happy and indebted. Send me something from time to time and tell me about yourself and your surroundings, too. Love me till we meet again.

The one endures Bettina's silly stories when they are interspersed with stories of her son. The other reads about Bettina when it is interspersed with anecdotes of dear mother and is thus of service to his work. In this way the dispersed desire finds a gap, a way in. Goethe's permission to be loved and written to makes a single thing out of the night's spirits of all the ways that do not turn back and all of Bettina's letters:

B II 35 He said to me: "Write every day, and should it be folios full, it is not too much for me." . . . The life I'm leading now, no one could understand, by the hand the spirit leads me through lonely streets, he sits down with me at the water's edge; he rests with me there, then he leads me up high mountains; then it's night, then we look into the misty valley where one can hardly see the path before one's feet, but I go along, I feel that he's there even when he disappears before my bodily eyes, and wherever I go and stand, I sense his secret roving about me, and in the night he is the cover in which I wrap myself, and in the morning he is what I cover myself from when I get dressed, I am never alone anymore, in my solitary room I feel myself understood and known by this spirit.

Known and understood: the promise with which individuals
B II 354 are enticed by the new genre literature is fulfilled. Goethe's loving understanding makes Bettina's every mood more individual and more delightful. Except that unlike many other female readers whose longing sustains the classical deities, she does not lock up her awakened desire in her lonely
S I 287 room and her reading. She reverses the roles. In *Ofterdingen*, a Goethe named Klingsohr says of a Henrich named Poetry and a Mathilde named love, that love is mute and only poetry, hence, a man, can speak for her. As Bettina, conversely, love speaks and writes for itself. As the *Correspondence of a Child*, the Persian verse comes true, that only love can write the story of love.

And Goethe allows it, even if it be folios full. The sixty-year-old, who does not write unruly novels like Clemens, takes Bettina's unruly letters as they come. He does not demand that she write to him and to herself simultaneously, that she reread what is written, translate it into a work. For he does that himself. To his own and to Bettina's
B II 11f. writings. Bettina, when she asked for her letters back after Goethe's death, found most of them corrected in his own hand, not only spelling but also occasional word position, much underlined in red, elsewhere again in pencil, much
JA XXIII 157 set in brackets, elsewhere crossed out. Such had Goethe himself learned from his father when he was young. In order to make literature of his son's letters and fragments, the old man had come forward as corrector and collector. The success is well-known: the German classic. Thus a

B II 227 life-time later, the son, too, collected a child's stream of
words. Bettina's plea that her letters not be burned or shown
around is more than complied with. Goethe lays the count-
B II 235 less leaves (*Blätter*, i.e. sheets of paper—T.N.) in a secret
place between the blossoms of his exotic window plants and
hardly lets a day pass without leafing through them. Flowers
and leaves—from talking into the wind there grows an
organic work.

And because collecting and rereading devolve on the
Other, Bettina can write what Clemens had begged her for
in vain. That which she was, became, is, everything is
brought to paper. Memories of the convent in Fritzlar, diaries
B II 326 of her travels, events as ordinary as a breath expanding the
breast, anecdotes like the one about the tanned Rhine sailor
who fetched a lost Bettina down from a cliff on the river,
who told of his adventures in India and the frightful blaze
B II 111 of the sun in Spain, and to the question of where he would
like to be most, answered: Spain. Entire epistolary novels
arise, like the one about the three kisses in Bettina's pre-
Goethian life. But the recollected and conjured up biography
does not draw its unity from the writer herself. Nothing
comes of the continuous life story, and nothing of the
founding function of the subject, because all the stories,
like the one about the three kisses in Bettina's life, end and
are extinguished in the love that makes her write.

B II 371 Thus time passed between the ages of sixteen and eighteen,
then I came to your mother, with whom I spoke of you as if
you sat between us, then I came to you and since then you well
know that I have never ceased to dwell with you in this circle
that a powerful magic draws around us. And from then on
you have known everything that passes in my heart and spirit,
for that reason I can say nothing more to you than to draw me
to your heart and keep me there your entire life.

What more can I say? That it is the same story even
today? That it does not stop stopping. . . . Certainly it is
always the same. Bettina's first surviving letter, written on
her eighth birthday from the boarding school in Fritzlar:

G I 309 Dear Papa! Nothing—the left (a hand drawn here with a pen)
slid in his vest on Papa's heart, the right (another hand painted
in) around Papa's neck. If I don't have hands I can't write.

Friedrich Schlegel called writing the unique vocation of
man. An eight year old child could have told him that it is
an activity of the hands which excludes all others. To
forget them one must already love either the world or

G I 370 Sophia, hence, no one. All the mouths that read no further that day; all the hands that embrace a neck; all the hearts that have been spoken about and have spoken out and are empty now, pure Now of desire. How indeed can a person not refrain from wishing himself something other than one who loves?

Bettina asks stupid questions. If the person is a man and an author, then it is all right. Goethe, founder of a League of Renouncers, always writes the same conclusion to his letters.

B II 268 Go on (*fahre fort*) being so dear and charming.

B II 257 Farewell, dearest child, go on living with me and do not let me miss your detailed letters.

B II 215 Write me what you like, it will always be most affectionately received. Your candid chatter is a true entertainment for me, and your intimate divulgences surpass everything for me. Farewell, stay close to me and go on giving me pleasure.

B II 204 Writing and loving me from day to day, stay true to your engaging manner.

B II 133 One thing I ask of you: do not stop liking to write me, I will never stop reading you with delight.

B II 75 I am writing with haste; for I fear to tarry where I am stirred by so much that overflows. Go on making your home with mother; it has come to mean too much to her for her to do without you, and do count on my love and gratitude.

B II 68 "Such fruit, ripe and sweet, one would gladly enjoy on each day that one might be entitled to count among the very finest." Dear mother, give this sealed note to *Bettine* and ask that she write me still more.

And so on. Rather than answering, Goethe answers that Bettina should answer still further. His letters are as ambiguous as his chancellory style and his favorite expression *go on*. She is to write further *and* keep her distance (*vom Leib bleiben*), as if Goethe has read not Bettina, but his mother via Bettina.

B II 69 Your mother wrote as if about me: that I make no claim to answers; that I don't want to steal any time that could bring forth the eternal; but that's not the way it is: my soul cries like a thirsty child; I would like to drink all time, future and past, into myself, and my conscience would bother me less if from now on the world were to get less to learn from you, and I more.

The author remains true to the universe. World and eternity go on learning more from him than the loving one whom he bids to go on. At least with words. For his eyes say something else.

B II 352f. You know, I never freed myself from your arms that way; you were always the first and let your arms fall and said: "Now go!"—and I obeyed your lips' command. If I had obeyed that of your eyes, I would have stayed with you; for they said: "Come here!"

B II 100 They are not at one, lips, hands, and eyes. To the simplest request, the linguistically most gifted of Germans has no answer. Bettina's wish that he "write me the one thing that you have to say, and nothing else" goes unfulfilled, because it involves an author. Her unheard of and idiosyncratic salutation "you (Du), Goethe," that short circuit between an author's name (without Johann and Wolfgang) and a body, again falls apart. The salutation is meant to awaken a body in the author's name, just as Bettina kisses a Goethe

B II 399 made of marble until the Goethe made of flesh grows jealous. But because even that gains him marble verses once again,

JA II 5 Goethe persists in the separation. Eyes entice and read

B II 71 Bettina, hands are at work in the evasion of answers. Instead of answering, he can rhyme her unrhymed letters and

JA II 7 weave from them a garland of sonnets. Under such titles as *The Lover Writes (Die Liebende schreibt)* Bettina's versified letters appear in Goethe's works.

That she writes and speaks her desire makes it at once translatable and unrequitable. There is evidence of this. In order to answer for once, after all, Goethe sends her the sonnet *Charade*, from which Bettina is supposed to extract

B II 156 sufficient advice. But she who knows such beautiful riddles

B II 163 about ghosts and spirits does not succeed. Luckily for her. Since the solution of the charade is Minna Herzlieb: that girl whom Goethe loved as he otherwise loved only the Ottilie of his novel, and for the same reason: on account of her muteness.[29] Bettina is called "forward" in her last appearance in Goethe's diary on the seventh of August, 1830. Perhaps for that reason a Goethe named Klingsohr calls love mute and poetry its only mouthpiece. For when love speaks, it would come to light that the poet will not endure it. His love needs a speechless sweetheart (*Herzlieb*).

Because they are possessed by a reckless language,[30] speaking women appear in literature only as sources. If literature were to answer them, they would no longer be such. Whether Brentano or Goethe, the author makes translations, associations, that in the works, and that means in the writer's absence, become as ambiguous as they are successful. The classic game between Bettina and Minna goes romantically on, as Clemens himself reveals to his sister:

F I 40   Walpurgis has several of your features, and perhaps they attract me the most. . . . These features always make me think of your soul, and I am saying pretty things to that girl when I write to you, and am talking to you when I make her pretty speeches.

F I 38   To be sure Walpurgis is obviously a girl who does not understand her poet. For this reason, Goethe also grows so happy and eloquent when, one day in spring on the banks of the Ilm, first a lucky coincidence and then he himself lay a veil over speaking Bettina.

B II 202   Then I wished to be with you for just one spring, you laughed at me; then I asked whether that was too long for you; "Why no," you said, "but here comes someone who will put an end to our fun"; it was the Duke who was just coming up to us, I wanted to hide, you threw your overcoat over me, I saw through the long sleeves how the Duke came closer and closer, I could tell from his face that he noticed something, he remained standing on the loggia, I didn't understand what he said, I was so afraid under your overcoat, my heart pounded, you waved your hand, then I saw through your coat sleeves how the Duke laughed and stood still; he took little pebbles of sand and threw them at me, and then he went on. Then afterwards we chatted a long time with each other—what was it again?—nothing very wise, for you compared me to the Greek woman full of wisdom who taught Socrates about love, and you said: "No dreaded word do you pronounce, but your foolishness teaches better than her wisdom,"—and you demanded of me with the simple words "Love me forever," and I said "Yes,"—And then a while later you took a spider's web off the railing of the loggia and hung it over my face and said: "Stay veiled before everyone and show no one what you are to me."

The veil that The Poet lays over a woman reverses Goethe's entire work. For in the texts the Woman, and that means a mother, repeatedly spreads veils or even overcoats over a poet whose nakedness could otherwise reveal who arouses her so.[31] On the Ilm, in contrast, the veil of a spider's web allows no one, thus not even its donor, to learn of Bettina's desire. Goethe only chats about Diotima and the veil of the priestess so as not to talk about Diotima's pupil. For despite his years and wrinkles, the latter managed to reverse the rules of the game of Greek pederasty and set himself up as the beloved rather than lover of beautiful children.[32] Socrates, too, could have commanded "Love me forever."

Only once did the veil over Bettina become transparent—so transparent, that she herself has veiled the event. A draft of a letter that was never sent tells about it.

It was in the dusk of evening in the hot month of August, he sat at the open window, I stood before him and held him in an embrace, my glance, pointed sharp as an arrow in his eyes, stayed fixed there. Maybe because he did not want to bear it any longer, he asked me whether I wasn't hot, and whether I didn't want the breeze to fan me; I nodded, so he said: "Then uncover your bosom, so that you can profit from the evening air."—Since I didn't say anything against it, although my face had turned red, he undid my dress and looked at me and said: The red of evening is branded in your cheeks,—and kissed me on the breast, and his forehead sank down upon it.—No wonder, I said, my sun is sinking down in my own bosom.—He looked at me a long time and we were both silent.—He asks: Hasn't anyone ever touched your breast before?—No, I say.[33]

Because Bettina's glance is perhaps unbearable, the veil drops over her bosom. Only a veil of Goethe-words, thin as a spider's web, is left to represent it: out of a body's blush JA XIII 145 of shame and love they make a veil of the red of evening. As if the sun scattered roses over a pair of twins that pastured under roses and aroused Mephisto's envy. As if Bettina's sun sank down on a Madonna in the rose bush who holds her child to her naked breast.

The stylus of literature works on a virgin and mother. Therefore Goethe's speech, when for once it becomes the speech of a lover, encounters a final veil. Therefore the beloved remains untouched in that August night as well. The hymen veils the reason why it does not tear. Indeed, in Goethe's poem the "Journal" it comes to light or to dark that the attempt to lift the veil had nothing to do with desire. The penis denies the phallic function because suddenly, between Goethe and a submissive virgin, there steps an eternally cherished image of Woman whom the author had married in the lust of youth.[34] It cannot, therefore, have been Christiane, whom he married at age fifty-seven.

Only after Goethe's death did the veil-upon-veil fall away. Bettina published *Goethe's Correspondence with a Child*, and she did it to finance a monument to her god that B II 404f. she herself had designed. Goethe sits on a throne, cloak buttoned around his neck, his gaze directed toward the clouds. Next to him Bettina, a graceful childlike menad standing on her little head, and the inscription: "Turn your tiny feet toward heaven only without care!" She who once threw her dress over her head so as not to be recognized by the people of Frankfort, or so as to be recognized by the spirits, remains Bettina in marble, too: a menad with no shame in the presence of shame.

"When the soul *speaks*, so speaks alas! the *soul* no more" had been the decree of Classicism. In other words: women are not to be menads. Before their desire grows audible, there sinks over them the veil of a mother's image. Bettina's love remained unheard and unheard of in every sense of the word. She only found listeners a century later, when another discourse determined that Woman is desired solely *quad matrem*.[35] To be sure, this was merely a supplementary and frivolous universalization of Classical-Romantic literature, but at least it distinguished between women and their image. Literary discourse was the exclusion and thereby the begetting of hysterical discourse. If women no longer spoke when they spoke, all that was left to them was the mute symptom or the witch Baubo's gesture. Thus analytic discourse came about as the offspring and thereby the inclusion of hysterical discourse. It turns around Goethe's "Stay veiled before everyone and show no one what you are to me" to a "Show me, what others are to you." With this cunning restriction, not to have to hear any words addressed directly to him, Freud began to listen to women. Since then, souls or women are eloquent even before they speak: through symptoms. And these do not first arise in the images made by men. The hymen has fallen, the virgin is a woman, the darling man a cover picture.

Thus Bettina's writting-away found readers all at once, precisely because it had never been listened to.

"If you would at least read aloud, bookworm," Abelone said after a while. That no longer sounded so quarrelsome, and since I considered it high time to settle our differences, I immediately read aloud, on and on till the end of the paragraph, and further, up to the next heading: To Bettine. "No, not the replies," Abelone interrupted me. . . . Give it here," she said suddenly, as if she were angry, and took the book out of my hand and opened it right where she wanted. And then she read one of Bettina's letters. . . .

Just now you still *were*, Bettina; I comprehend you. Isn't the earth still warm from you, and the birds still leave room for your voice. The dew is a different one, but the stars are still the stars of your nights. Or isn't all the world of you? . . .

How is it possible that everyone is not still telling of your love? What has happened since then that was more remarkable? What occupies them? You yourself knew the worth of your love, you recited it aloud to your greatest poet. . . . But he dissuaded the people from it when he wrote to you. . . . What does it mean, that he could not have answered? Such love has no need of a reply, it has within itself mating call and answer.[36]

Since then, writing has meant opening one's ears. Rather than works without a wish: letters without a reply. Rather than the universal history that Bettina condemned to the hole in the oven: hysteria, of which the world in any way is. Rather than a philosophy to make her sick: stories about her love. And above all, no books that deal with state and politics in Bettina,[37] or are called *BETTINA. Bettina von Arnim: A Feminine Social Biography of the Nineteenth Century*.[38] For Germany's birds and soil recall her love only because Bettina meant a land and not a state when she conjured up night spirits and ice floes, imps and nooks of the Rhine. Politics does not begin where female social biographers let it, who already in their titles seek feminist familiarity and scientific formality, and who already in their grammar confuse their own life description with the described Baroness von Arnim, and the Baroness with Bettina: with *engagement* for Jews, social cases, weavers. Once again, she who stood on her head is to be set upon universal feet. But love, giddiness, intoxication are the only happening.[39]

That is why it does not matter if they remain unheard and unheard of. All those fine discriminations between the genre letter and the genre literature, between proper and figural meaning, between ephemeral talk and lasting texts or social problems, are indeed only ruses of the universal conspiracy for the misconstruing of desire.[40] But desire does not wait for recognition and responses; it has within itself mating call and answer. A living love, writes Bettina, does not miss its goal, for this lies within itself, like a breath within the breast. And breathing, unlike talking, neither has nor makes cuts and boundaries.

G I 500

Bettina, 1800:

F I 51

My soul is a passionate dancer, she springs around to an inner music that only I hear and others do not. Everyone cries that I should keep still, but caught up in the pleasure of dance my soul doesn't listen to you, and if the dance were over, then it would be over with me.

Janis Joplin, 1970:

I'm here to have a party, man, as best as I can while I'm on this earth. I'm gettin it now, today, I don't even know where I'm gonna be twenty years from now, so I'm just gonna keep on rockin, cause if I start saving up bits and pieces of me like that, man, there ain't gonna be nothing left for Janis.[41]

Again and again, it is the same adventure, breathing and dancing. The adventure of a music. Not the music that Bettina was supposed to learn, and learned to hate, under such rubrics as harmony and basso continuo.

F I 87f.   Basso continuo is also very annoying. I'd like to explode this kinship of tonalities that assert their superiority over each other and detain at customs everyone who navigates the river of harmony. But as sure as these irrevocable laws of ear are only moldy prejudices that genius shoves away with its toe, so, too, these claims of emotions, which I warn to keep their distance: as friendship, generosity, meekness, compassion (that's the most odious), forbearance, honor, and all ethical and moral virtues, will come to a miserable end—they are vampires who with secret pleasure suck out the selfhood of the free will.

G I 245   The other music has nothing to do with family love or rules of exchange. It is unrestrained passion itself. A lover of wisdom could only imagine that, notwithstanding the untruthfulness of what is imagined, his imaginings themselves are beyond all doubt.[42] But love and passion can do more. We would be mistaken to stop at their power to tell lies: they do more than merely imagine. He who loves is more valuable, is stronger. With animals this circumstance elicits new weapons, pigments, colors, and forms, above all, new motions, new rhythms, new mating calls and seductions. With humans it is no different.[43] Bettina's music grows beyond the delicate ringing of the beginning.

B II 51f.   The stars dipped under in a sea of colors; flowers blossomed, they grew upward to the sky; distant golden shadows shielded them from a higher white light, and thus in this inner world there appeared one vision after another; meanwhile I heard a delicate silver ringing in my ears; gradually it became a peal that was greater and mightier the harder I listened, I was glad, for it strengthened me, it strengthened my spirit, to shelter this great sound in my hearing.

B II 126   Such music that tramples incontestable laws of ear underfoot and feeds the sigh of unrequited love back to its fulfillment in the breath of the world, was first achieved, after Bettina's ears, by Wagner. Instead of the moldy holy family of tonalities—a modulatory floating along;[44] instead of poor human voices that musically moan and are bemoaned—the triumph of the wish in sheer resonance and reverberation. Elsa starts off moaning and barely audible; the music swells, grows to mighty tones, ascends to the breezes, and resounds distantly through all space.[45] Thus Wagner's orchestra, that circuit of resonances and feedback, inscribed Bettina's self-fulfilling wish into the real.

For within the symbolic it was always foreign and miserable. Bettina simply could not believe that music had no influence over Goethe and that only those arts are called beautiful that remain, like literature, within the tight boundaries of form. Therefore she never stopped pestering him about music. The child writing away grew evangelical for once, and she stormed the phalanx of experts that Goethe had recruited and stationed so as not to hear anything of another longing this side of the Works. That was something he never forgave. The sacrifice Bettina needed for her music was the death of her God.[46]

So all that was left was for her to set Goethe to music. There is the plan for a Faust overture that would have assigned a predominant role to the drums.[47] There are songs for solo voice and piano. But because Bettina remained true to her resolution, not to pour firebuckets of basso continuo rules over her music, her allegedly *Collected Works* have also not dared to publish her movements for piano. It is indeed a scandal that, however wrong or beautiful the music may be, editor Max Friedlaender reached for the composer's quill and affixed a new accompaniment. The irony of history: even after her death men could not leave unimproved a girl who never wrote a book, or a symphony, but only these letters and bits of music in an extremely small hand.[48] Because even what is written into the wind must become a work, too, they reach like Goethe for red and black pencil, or like Friedlaender into the score—with the fortunate effect, that Bettina's Work does not exist. We will never again hear what happened in the music while a solo voice plays around Goethe's poem about sweet peace.

B II 150
G I 449

B II 127
B II 133

SW IV 258f.

Writing into the Wind, Bettina

But what does it matter? as Salome said. Longing should do nothing. Let's say that I've said it. Let's say I've said nothing.

Translated by Marilyn Wyatt

Abbreviations used in marginal references are as follows:

F   *Clemens Brentanos Frühlingskranz*, in Bettina von Arnim, *Werke und Briefe*, ed. G. Konrad (Frechen, 1959–63), v. I.

G   *Die Günderode*, in Bettina von Arnim, *Werke und Briefe*, v. I.

B   *Goethes Briefwechsel mit einem Kinde*, in Bettina von Arnim, *Werke und Briefe*, v. II.

SW   Bettina von Arnim, *Sämtliche Werke*, ed. W. Oehlke (Berlin, 1920–22).

JA   J. W. von Goethe, *Sämtliche Werke*, Jubiläums-Ausgabe, ed. E. v. d. Hellen (Stuttgart and Berlin, no year).

KA   *Kritische Friedrich Schlegel-Ausgabe*, ed. E. Behler (Munich, Paderborn, and Vienna, 1958ff).

S   Novalis, *Schriften*, ed. P. Kluckhohn and R. Samuel (Stuttgart, 1960ff).

NOTES

1. Kate Bush, *Lionheart*. LP EMI 1C-064-06859.

2. Friedrich Nietzsche, *Ecce Homo*, in *Werke*, ed. Karl Schlechta (Munich: Carl Hanser, 1954–56), v. II, p. 1085.

3. Cf. also my text "Vergessen" in *Texthermeneutik. Geschichte, Aktualität, Kritik*, ed. Ulrich Nassen (Paderborn: Schöningh, 1979), pp. 204–7.

4. Jorge Luis Borges, "Tlön, Ugbar, Orbis tertius," *Obras completas* (Buenos Aires: Eméce, 1964ff), v. V, p. 20f.

5. For the time being see F. A. Kittler, *Der Traum und die Rede. Eine Analyse der Kommunikationssituation Conrad Ferdinand Meyers* (Bern and Munich: Franke, 1977), p. 128f.

6. Jacques Lacan, here in Strassburg, January 1975.

7. Lacan, *Le Séminaire XX: Encore* (Paris: Seuil, 1975), p. 76.

8. Gottfried Benn, *Gesammelte Werke*, ed. Dieter Wellershoff (Wiesbaden: dtv, 1959–61), v. I, p. 383.

9. Michel Foucault, *L'Archéologie de savoir* (Paris: Gallimard, 1969), p. 21f.

10. Cf. in contrast Caroline Schlegel's political and literary belief that men understand these things better, our rationality notwithstanding. *Carolines Leben aus ihren Briefen*, ed. R. Buchwald (Leipzig, n.p., 1923), p. 199.

11. Cf. Silvia Bovenschen, *Die imaginierte Weiblichkeit. Exemplarische Untersuchungen zu kulturgeschichtlichen und literarischen Präsentations formen des Weiblichen* (Frankfort: Suhrkamp, 1979), pp. 190–200. May such exemplary inquiries into the nineteenth century soon follow.

12. *Denkschrift an die Pariser Freunde* (1802), in *Werke*, ed. Gertrude Cepl-Kaufmann and Manfred Windfuhr (Munich: Winkler, 1977), v. II, p. 100.

13. Friedrich Schiller, *Sprache*, in *Sämtliche Werke*, Säkular-Ausgabe, ed. E. v. d. Hellen (Stuttgart and Berlin: J. G. Cotta, n.d.), v. I, p. 149.

14. See the essay of the same name by Norbert W. Bolz in *Urszenen. Literaturwissenschaft als Diskursanalyse und Diskurskritik*, ed. Friedrich A. Kittler and Horst Turk (Frankfort: Suhrkamp, 1977), pp. 44–52.

15. Cf. in this regard my essay "Autorschaft und Liebe," to appear in *Austreibung des Geistes aus den Geisteswissenschaften,* ed. F. A. Kittler (Paderborn: Schöningh, 1980).

16. Cf. *L'Absolu littéraire, Theorie de la littérature du romantisme allemand* (Paris: Seuil, 1978), p. 224.

17. Cf. *Lucinde,* KA, v. V, p. 15: "Cast them off, too, dear friend, all the remnants of false shame, just as I often tear the deadly clothes from you and scatter them in beautiful anarchy. And should this little novel of my life seem too wild to you: then imagine to yourself, it is but a child, and tolerate its wantonness with motherly patience, and let yourself be caressed by it." See F. A. Kittler, "Der Dichter, Die Mutter, Das Kind," in *Romantik in Deutschland,* ed. R. Brinkmann, *DVj,* special issue, 1978, pp. 102–14.

18. According to Heinrich Bosse, *Schiller und der schriftliche Diskurs,* manuscript (Freiburg, 1976).

19. Cf. my study "Uber die Sozialisation Wilhelm Meisters" in Gerhard Kaiser and Freidrich A. Kittler, *Dichtung als Sozialisationsspiel. Studien zu Goethe und Gottfried Keller* (Göttingen: Vandenhoek and Ruprecht, 1978), pp. 52–57.

20. Cf. the quotation in G I 560.

21. Cited by Reinhold Steig, "Bettina," *Deutsche Rundschau* 57 (1892), 264f.

22. Lacan, *Le Séminaire XX,* p. 71.

23. Cf. Lucien Israël, *L'Hystérique, le sexe et le médicine* (Paris: Masson, 1976), pp. 216 and passim.

24. Cf. Foucault, *Histoire de la sexualité* (Paris: Gallimard, 1977), v. I, p. 137.

25. Pertinent observations to be found in Gerhard Schaub, *"Le Génie enfant": Die Kategorie des Kindlichen bei Clemens Brentano* (Berlin: De Gruyter, 1973).

26. S. Wilhelm von Occam, *Summa totius Logicae,* ed. Ph. Boehner (Löwen: n.p., 1951), pp. 39–42.

27. Lacan, *Le Séminaire XX,* p. 71.

28. Werner Milch, *Die junge Bettine* (Heidelberg: L. Stiehm, 1968), p. 111.

29. Cf. Walter Benjamin, *Goethes Wahlverwandtschaften,* in *Gesammelte Schriften* (Frankfort: Suhrkamp, 1972ff), v. I, 1, p. 177.

30. Benjamin, *Metaphysik der Jugend,* in *Gesammelte Schriften,* v. II, 1, p. 95.

31. Cf. "Uber die Sozialisation Wilhelm Meisters," p. 51–59.

32. Alcibiades in *The Symposium,* 222B.

33. Cited by Milch, *Die junge Bettine,* p. 165f.

34. *Das Tagebuch Goethes und Rilkes Sieben Gedichte,* ed. Siegfried Unseld (Frankfort: Insel, 1978), p. 21.

35. Lacan, *Le Séminaire XX,* p. 36.

36. Rainer Marie Rilke, *Die Aufzeichnungen des Malte Laurids Brigge,* in *Sämtliche Werke,* ed. E. Zinn (Wiesbaden: Insel, 1955–56), v. VI, pp. 895–98.

37. Karl-Heinz Hahn, *Bettina von Arnim in ihrem Verhältnis zu Staat und Politik* (Weimar: Hermann Böhlaus, 1959).

38. Gisela Dischner, *BETTINA. Bettina von Arnim: Eine weibliche Sozialbiographie aus dem 19. Jahrhundert* (Berlin: Wagenbach, 1977).

39. I am thinking of Tim Leary and the politics of ecstacy.

40. Moustaf Safouan, *Etudes sur l'Oedipe. Introduction à une théorie du sujet* (Paris: Seuil, 1974), p. 225.

41. *Janis*, ed. David Dalton (New York: Touchstone, 1971), p. 58.

42. René Descartes, *Meditationes*, II.9.24.

43. Nietzsche, *Nachlaß, Werke*, v. III, p. 752.

44. *Oper und Drama. Gesammelte Schriften und Dichtungen* (Leipzig: Breitkopf and Härtel, 1907), v. IV, p. 148f. See also the upcoming essay by Manfred Schneider, *Der Geschleifte Venusberg. Richard Wagners "Tannhäuser" und die neue Ordnung des Eros*.

45. *Lohengrin*, I 2. GS, v. II, p. 197.

46. Cf. Milch, *Die junge Bettine*, p. 197.

47. Cf. Milch, *Die junge Bettine*, p. 142.

48. Pertinent hereafter: Benn, "Chopin," in *Gesammelte Werke*, v. III, p. 190.

FOUR

THE INFINITE TEXT[1]
Manfred Frank

MODERN LITERATURE knows many modes of miscarriage and loss. They supply at the level of content an almost inexhaustible stock of themes and motifs from which recent fiction has repeatedly drawn its inspiration. I call to mind particularly the many adaptations and variations of the Flying Dutchman legend, extending from the work of Luis de Camões to *Bateau ivre* and to *Jäger Gracchus*. The history of this legend is easily traced: it rides the collective fantasy of an aimlessly wandering ship—"sanguine the sails, black the mast"[2]—and draws one back to the advent of the modern era. With the Copernican revolution one frequently encounters in literature the budding and rapid growth of a motivational structure which—independent of its respective contents—develops according to a logic parallel to that of the age. Here a few key remarks may suffice. The cata-strophe (in the sense of an over-turning) which the new cosmo-theological world view of the Middle Ages precipitates, consists, to some degree, in the de-centering of the fixed star earth from her geocentric preeminence and the consequence expulsion of Man from his previous place at the center of creation. A heavily symbolic dis-placement which rends asunder the once stable harmony between the wandering spirit and its proper place; its home. "We have now forged our courage," says Galileo, "and let the heavenly bodies arc freely, without restraint and in great course, as do our ships."[3] Modern man breeches the taboo and transgresses (also

From Manfred Frank, *Die unendliche Fahrt* (Frankfort: Suhrkamp, 1979).

politically, imperially) the limits of the old world. He traverses the uncharted seas and colonizes the wild continents. He will discover the poles and reach the moon.

It is striking that the poets—chroniclers, as it were, of the human soul—never reconciled themselves to the parole of an unchecked progress as promulgated by the secular spirit (*Weltgeist*). Amidst the general celebration of the emancipation from the restraints of a world created and tyrannically ordered by God, whispers of doubt are heard. They grow more pronounced as the age advances, questioning the legitimacy, even the desirability of a self-sustaining secular curiosity. This is not a specifically modern syndrome sprung from some peculiar coalition of poetic word and medieval Christian axiology. Rather, every mythology and every religious world view safeguards, through a continuing act of *sanctio*, the fundamental value judgment which supports the consensus of its adherents. This *sanctio* both consecrates the sacred and punishes infringements of its taboo. It is naïve to believe that one could rechannel the community-building force of a world view legitimated by value judgments into a society struggling to free itself from these axioms. Is it coincidental that the Strait of Gibraltar bears the mythical title "The Pillars of Hercules" and is thus marked as an index of sanction? These are the *columnae fatales* which, according to Seneca's *Medea*, stand apocalyptically open at time's end. For the present they indicate the limits of condoned bravado, the threshold of the familiar, godfearing world. The wise man, writes Pindar in the third *Olympic Ode*, stops here: it would be dreadful to proceed. For the ancients the very building of ships seemed wanton, as the sea itself was sacrosanct. In addition to the posts of Hercules, legend marks other *loci fatales*: in Christian times, for example, the (euphemistically so-called) Cape of Good Hope. Since its circumnavigation—first by the Portuguese and then more decisively by the Dutch—a collective seafarers' fantasy descries the ghost of the Flying Dutchman upon the seas of the New World. Aimless, with helm damaged or lost and only intermittently manned by a living crew, it spirits over the tides of the outer and inner worlds and haunts whomever crosses its path—the curse of goal- and homelessness.

This motif, extraordinarily pervasive in literature, is grounded in ancient traditions: in, for example, the *Odyssey*, the tales of the Argonauts, the *Aeneid*, etc. There is of course a decisive difference: the ancient and the medieval Christian allegories of the *navigatio vitae* obey the economy of successful homecoming. They thus anticipate poetically the modern paradigm of reflection in which point of departure and goal of the course of life, the "Odyssey of the soul," as Schelling says, converge. The goal may be deferred (*différé*) but not altogether lost. This changes upon the threshold of the new era. Here doubts about the "immanence of meaning in life" (*Lebensimmanenz des Sinnes*)[4] disturb the economy of the successful homecoming (*nóstos* implies both journey and return). The points of departure and arrival now coincide as little as the first and third notes of the fool-motif in Wagner's *Parsifal*, signaling that "derangement" which differentiates the "pure" fool Kundry denounces from the fool become "clairvoyant," splitting and temporalizing its identity.

Our historical interest in ideas and motifs encounters the problem of losing one's way only, of course, at the thematic level. In fact, one can observe that modern literature—since Coleridge and Brentano—has identified the aimless passage with the fate of poetic speech. This too follows an old metaphoric tradition which conceives of literature in terms of navigation—as the casting off and venturing forth of an *ingenii barca* into the unexplored regions of interiority. As Derrida has shown for the navigation metaphor, even as it appears in the rhetoric of scholarly discussions of metaphor—which is often held to be the embodiment of poetic language—the figure of carrying over (*Ubertragung*), of translation (*Hinübersetzen*) from one expression to another takes recourse in the linguistic play of navigation: "The figure of the vessel or of the boat . . . was so often the exemplary vehicle of rhetorical pedagogy."[5] As soon as the play of metaphor becomes autonomous—but was it not always so, as the processes of linguistic transformation evidence?—there is no longer any possibility of controlling the transfer: "I can no longer stop the vehicle or anchor the ship, master completely (*sans reste*) the drifting or skidding."[6] The aimlessly drifting ship begins its passage upon the tide of speech itself, and poetic speech makes conscious this process as such. The hunter Gracchus, who sails with the wind that "blows in the deepest regions of the earth," falls, as it were, from his role as actor when he presents himself as author: "No one will read what I write here, no one will come to help me."[7] Does, then, the "mishap" of overshooting the *lieu propre* (the place on which Man is properly at home) suit the process of (literary) writing? The endlessness of the trip clearly becomes a problem in the interminability of writing itself. Literature reflects its own condition when it de-limits (*ent-grenzt*) the metaphor of the journey of life.

It is apparent that the identification of writing with travel presumes a highly abstract concept of "text": writing (*das Schreiben*), literature (*die Literatur*)—titles used as universals only since Romanticism[8]—are no longer exactly situable within a theory of genre. I mean this not (only) in the sense that Romantic literature understood itself as an allegory for the unspeakable, for the infinite or absolute,[9] and therefore strove to overcome the particularism of the various arts and genres, to achieve, for example, a composite work of art (*ein Gesamtkunstwerk*).[10] I am thinking primarily of the concept held by

Fr. Schlegel and Novalis of "transcendental poetry." This coinage is analogous to the expression "transcendental philosophy," with which transcendental poetry shares an interest in the conditions of its very inception; that is, an interest in writing as such. Transcendental poetry, writes Fr. Schlegel, "presents itself as well in each of its representations." It inscribes in each poetic "product" the "mirror" which reflects the movements of "the producing agent" in its pure activity (*poiesis*).[11] Novalis finds this reflective movement also in the domain of (nonliterary) semiology. "The primary signifier (*das erste Bezeichnende*)," he says, referring to the schematizing activity of an originary symbol formation, "will have painted unnoticed its own image before the mirror of reflection, and also the feature will not be forgotten: that the image was painted in this position, that it paints itself."[12]

What consequences such a double designation of the (poetic) symbol might have I wish to discuss in the context of a more fundamental consideration. I believe that the transcendental refraction of meaning has the effect of generalizing every text, regardless of its genre and content. That is to say, that every sign of a symbolic composition which carries within it an indication of the act of its making (its gener-ation) bears an index of its textuality.

Textuality is a general term and characterizes all signifying formations as texts. By text (*textum*: that which is woven) I understand a fabric of sense-expression-unities, of which each acquires its 'local value' (as Schleiermacher calls it) through its differential relationship to all others. An expression does not carry its meaning out in the open (*auf die Stirn geschrieben*: literally, "written on its forehead"—Tr.). This can be ascertained only through recourse to all other expressions. The sense of a poetic (indeed, of any) composition is not revealed directly in the positivity of the "mark,"[13] but rather through a retracing of the relations it entertains to all other "marks." The metaphor "text" refers thus to the *gaps* proper to every fabric which in the final analysis endow its "full and positive terms" with sense and significance. To understand the "complete sense" of a text means, then, to retrace its weaving and to reflect upon it as a generative process.

According to the classical view—still current in the structuralism of A.J. Greimas and the genre theory of E.D. Hirsch—a text reflects the unity of a central *vouloir-dire*, of an intention which determines the sense and arrangement of the expressions and qualifies them as "functions" of a whole. One lays these functions bare by applying a procedure analogous to the analysis practiced by linguists: one begins with the "smaller unities" and climbs towards ever higher levels of systematic conceptualization (morphonological, grammatical, contextual, pragmatic, generic, etc.), until finally, having arrived at the summit of the hierarchical pyramid, one attains the *"sens total"* (as Greimas writes). I will not discuss the hermeneutic or methodological problems raised by this *démarche*. In the present context my concern is rather to shed light on one of its implicit presuppositions: that the systematic, self-contained quality (*clôture*—closure) of the text represents something approaching a transcendental signified (*signifié*) or an expression-founding, originary sense which, as the independent organizational basis of the entire construct, serves like a magnet to hold together the field of all other meaning in a coherent order. The history of widely differing semantic realizations, even the everyday experience of the nonidentity of the two readings of one and the same text, attest to the dubiousness of this supposition which considers reading and understanding to be performances of a fixed, self-identical score. This score—the grammar of a text—would be something like a truism removed from the differentiating play of functions; like a verity which fixes once and for all, from without or from above, the sense of the "marks" and determines them as its "expression" or "realization."

This model (which is incompatible with the arbitrariness of the sign and which has been attacked since Schleiermacher and Humboldt) can elaborate its apparent self-evidence only when closed and discernible declarative unities await interpretation. When, as with the transcendental poetry of Romanticism, the act of writing as such comes into play, the idea of an identifiable "dominant sense" or "principal signified"[14] dissolves and the constructs become—as "*epideíxeis* of infinity"[15]—"inexhaustible," even "all-meaningful."[16] For "infinitely determined is indeterminate in the general sense."[17] The transcendental perspective eradicates the particularity of the text—"the making absolute and universal . . . . of the individual moment, of the individual situation, etc. is the proper essence of *Romanticizing*"[18]—and opens these "*échappées de vue* . . . into the infinite"[19] which allow this particular text to become a paradigm of the "text in general."[20] This does not mean that it escapes the expressive intention of a certain language-play, the "integral meaning" (*Sinnganzen*) of that which E.D. Hirsch calls a "genre."[21] Rather, the poetic manipulation of language lets each sign play on two stages at once: both within the system of this particular text and this particular genre and at the level of writing itself, which cannot be reduced to a single book or library nor controlled "by a referent in the classical sense," "by a thing or a transcendental signified which would regulate all of its movement."[22] The Romantic project for a scientistic bible coverages at this level with "the book" of Mallarmé. Both presuppose the demolition of the economy of the text: what is written is no longer that more or less brief detour which the (undesignated, transcendental) sense must travel in order to achieve self-*expression*. Transcendental reflection de-limits the particular sense of signs by revealing them to be manifestations of writing *in general* (*des Schreibens*), that is, by raising them to the level of an imaginary "text in general." This concept, like that of the subject, presupposes a constitutive deficiency of presence. It designates, as Derrida writes, "an irreducible and *generative* multiplicity. The *supplément* and the turbulence of a certain lack break down the limits of the text; exempt it from exhaustive and enclosing formalization or at least prohibit a saturating taxonomy of its themes, of its signified, of its intended meaning (*vouloir-dire*)."[23]

Thus, what we have seen at the semantic level of the theme of the endless journey repeats itself analogously in the form of the texts which deal with it. The lack of a "transcendental shelter," the "general feeling of dependency" of the subject, has as its counterpart the loss of the fullness of meaning of the text in which it expresses itself. What we earlier called the destruction of the economy of salvation continues in the de-limiting of the text through which the subject mediates its sense-of-self. In both cases we are concerned with—to choose a common title—a *crisis of reflection*. Classical poetics since Aristotle have considered the language of poetry to be an improper, figurative (*uneigentliche*) representation of thought. The metaphor—one of the figures of indirect speech—is a form of *léxis* (discourse) and maintains a right to exist solely in its capacity to serve as a vehicle for nonsensory thought (*diánoia*), which cannot be expressed directly (*Poetics* 1456a). "It is the principle of all of classical literature": Sartre writes, "language is distinct from thought but can express it *adequately*: 'That which one conceives will enunciate itself clearly/ And the words necessary to say it come easily.' "[24] Aristotle does not base the agreement (*homónoia*) of expression with thought upon some overlapping relationship of the two but rather on the teleological orientation of the expression towards its (inexpressible) truth (cf. 1448b and the first chapter, third book of the *Rhetoric*).[25] This orientation upon the axiomatics of the model of reflection, whereby sense, as both the first and final term of the equation, mirrors itself in its expression, reduces the expressive moment of poetic discourse to the dependent and subservient part of the distinction. The metaphoricity of poetic speech will be confined to this mediating status (linking perception to concept, expression to sense, spoken word to thought) until Hegel's poetics. In the background stands always a model of reflection which seeks to reduce difference (indispensable aspect of representation) to unity. This model presupposes in turn a certain determining interpretation of subjectivity as self-presence. Once this hermeneutic presupposition has been shaken; that is, once the perfect transparency and identity of self-consciousness have been called into question, the axiomatics of the text-model alter. When the synthesis of signs can no longer be conceived as an equation of representation (in which meaning re-presents its presence in its expression), the

Manfred Frank

poetic metaphor becomes absolute: it loses the independent criterion according to which its divergence from thought (from transcendental meaning, from truth) might be controlled. That minimal gap which separates one sign from its neighbor in order to give it meaning suffices to destroy its identity forever. Fichte discovered this dilemma in the concept of reflection itself: If one conceives of reflection as an opaque identity of the self with, and only with, itself, one founders on the "law of reflection of all our knowledge," which establishes that the determination of a particular thought presumes its opposition to all other thoughts.[26] But if one introduces this law into the process of self-reference, one jeopardizes the identity, that is the immediacy and irrelativeness of the thought "I." There is no way around it: the relinquishment of the self to its other becomes the condition of its possibility, splitting the self into two aspects—even when it returns to itself and denies its differential structure. The path of the reflected subject to itself as agent of reflection is, however, blocked—namely, by the irreducible exteriority of the signifier. As Derrida writes, "my own presence to myself has been preceded by a language."[27]

Under these circumstances reflection shows itself to be the implicit ideal of metaphor—it *is* metaphor; . . . it transfers (*meta-phérei*) the idea of the observable doubling of a selfsame being to a fundamentally unobserved entity (*Seiendes*). It thus surrenders itself to the structural logic of a peculiar sort of mirror-stage. Consider the horror that seizes literature and literary theory since Romanticism at the thought—realized in a few stories by E.T.A. Hoffmann, in Kleist and especially Mallarmé—that the material mirror could prove to be independent of sight or even imprison the ephemeral glance of the self, insofar as the eye knows itself only through the mirror. The subject of reflection might then conceive of itself as a transformation without origin standing not against an archetypal image, according to which it could correct any deviation, but nightmarishly before a mirror without backing, "a tainless mirror, or at any rate a mirror whose tain lets images and 'persons' through, endowing them with a certain index of transformation and permutation."[28] The reflection anticipated by its own reflex, the thought overtaken by its expression—a structure Novalis called *ordo inversus*[29]—places meaning fully in the shadow of material expression. This effectively destroys both the semiotics of representation and the structuralist view of language as a self-contained taxonomy.

An arrangement of signifiers ultimately disconnected from their signifieds, and therefore from their referents; a system of signs whose meaning is surpassed by their non-significant being—who would deny that this indicates a metaphysical crisis which explodes all restricted economies of systematic thought, as well as of classical hermeneutics/aesthetics? Such an upheaval, which for the first time in Western history produces an object of consideration (*Anschauungsobjekt*) no longer inwardly oriented by meaning, has—in my view—been on the agenda since Romanticism; that is, ever since the word-sign—in consequence of the loss in representation of an "absolute Truth"[30]—receives as its theme "Everything" instead of "something definite." It culminates in the question, so painful to the ear of the semiologist, posed by Beckett's *Endgame*: "Any particular sector you fancy? Or merely the whole thing?"[31]

Meanwhile, "Everything" in the *language-grid* of an absolutely unbound economy seems to have become the fundamental condition of poetic discourse. Poetry evades this condition so much less, the more perceptive it becomes (*je mehr ihr Eidechsenohr geschärft ist*—literally: the more its lizard's ear is sharpened—Trans.) The crisis of literature, of which Mallarmé spoke, takes place in the space delimited by the undiscoverable transcendental *signifié*—of that meaning which, like a central sun, orients the other meanings about itself. It occurs in the situation, then, "when nothing takes place but the place at the point where there is no one to know."[32]

This is the situation of transcendental poetry. It refers each sign to the movement of its production, to the place, that is, not of a given Other but of a missing signifier. The so-called Romantic irony is only one more stylistic device through which the text appeals to the perception of its infinity. Derrida has demonstrated something similar in the functioning of the "re-mark" in Mallarmé: the signs of several of his densest texts contain a superfluous designation, as it were, which refers to that *interstice*, that place between the signifiers—not as to an added sense, but as to a greater-than-the-entirety-of-meaning of a text. "Le blanc" is in this second designation altogether different from a value among values. It is rather an interstitial value or valence itself.[33] It is (in Mallarmé's words) "that which in discourse silences itself," "a silence . . . condition and delight of reading,"[34] namely the precondition inscribed in the text according to which the sign, silhouetted against its emptiness, achieves some sort of meaning only to give it up again, in the recoil of its demarcation, to the "interstice." This "place between" is insensible like the irony of the Romantics: fix the sign, in which one seems to have recognized its presence, and it dissolves like an ethereal watercolor. Irony never shows itself as such, but dis-places the signs on which it works, and reminds language of its integral ability, "to signify *something quite other* than what it says."[35] This is a principle possibility of each "mark" within a system of "types," insofar as the immediate use of words does not lastingly bind meaning to its expression: "We are forced, then, to accept the notion of an incessant sliding of the signified under the signifier."[36] The text owes this open-endedness to that deficiency of an authentic representation of "absolute meaning";

Manfred Frank

to the temporalization of the subject, the phantasm of the aimless
journey and the structure of the endless text.

The endless deferral of the goal which our texts relate thus corresponds to an endless deferral of sense within the structure of the
texts themselves. It is no mere coincidence that specifically the term
"genre" has stood in question since Romanticism. Genres are rule-
systems which make cognizable an aggregate of utterances (they need
not be poetic) as realizations of certain forms of intentionality. One
notices that my remarks stand in the context of a lecture or scholarly
essay, that they develop their meaning within the framework of lyrical
speech, of a dramatic or epic composition, etc. One understands the
corresponding propositions by identifying them as statements of a
certain type of speech-utilization; i.e. by deciphering them according
to the conventions of the genre that governs them.

Yet what happens when saying itself becomes absolute? This
danger surfaces the moment that a text is no longer understood
(merely) as an expression of an intention in some way delimitable, but
rather, for example, as an "allegory" for that which Friedrich Schlegel
called "the Infinite." The first consequence would be that the synthetic
unity of the signs woven into such a (transcendental-poetic) text becomes unstable—if not fully problematic. There is no guarantee that
a particular expression will serve as the vehicle of some conventionally
preassigned meaning. It therefore becomes impossible to speak of a
sign in the strict sense. Language, writes Schlegel, is in its essence
allegorical,[37] and he understands under allegory an "intimation of the
Infinite, a glimpse of it."[38] Language is only indirectly accessible, in so
far as articulated expression effects its significance through stylistic
means: through irony, metaphor and metonomy—such that its "indeterminacy" is shown to be an "intimation of the Infinite."[39] It is like
constructing a bridge which abuts in the "unattainable" or the "ineffable" and which in no way connects with the *terminus a quo* to form
an identity of the reflective dyad. It is "the impossibility of positively
attaining the *Highest* through reflection" that "leads to allegory."[40]
"The Romantic" is the transgression toward the Infinite of all utterances and of the genre which unites them into an intentional whole
aimed at the Infinite.[41] Only the Infinite lends them "meaning." "The
concept of the Infinite" is clearly "transcendent,"[42] that is to say, nothing
extant corresponds to it.[43] The term "Infinite" thus designates a vacant
space, which the finite consciousness futilely—endlessly—yearns to
occupy or to repossess. This is the meaning of the famous "yearning
for the Infinite."[44] It presupposes the loss of an "original meaning" and
feels "driven" to seek it just the same. The self finds itself in a substantially negative relationship to its Other. This negativity nowhere
allows the self to achieve "self-identity." Like the Flying Dutchman, it

suffers through its emancipation from God, a process which, by establishing the self as a free instance, robs it of its substantial identity, of its early acquired goal or sense.

The result is that the "existence" of the self becomes the "greatest secret," the unsolvable "riddle."[45] Determined by the Absolute, i.e. "infinitely determined, (it) is indeterminate in the general sense."[46]

This is an expression of its freedom. This freedom is the originator of the meaning of the self precisely because the "'I' (is) fundamentally nothing";[47] because it is by nature "nothing determinate."[48] It does not arrive in the world already fully equipped with a fixed meaning. The nature—the meaning—of human subjectivity does not shape itself within the frame of reference of some onto-theological economy. Rather, it stands, for that moment of temporal life, upon the brink. Thus "every person (is) variable beyond measure."[49] "*Pluralism* (Novalis uses the English word—Tr.) is our innermost nature."[50] "The principle *I* is, so to speak, the genuine communal and *liberal*, universal principle. To be without limit or determination is to be unified . . . Selfhood is . . . the principle of highest *plurality (Mannigfaltigkeit)*."[51] No wonder that that "philosophy" which teaches the "changeability of character and the relativity of characters in general"[52] aims at a universalization of the Copernican revolution: "Philosophy *unfastens* everything—makes the universal relative. Like the Copernican system it dissolves the fixed points—and sets the static in motion. It teaches the relativity of all fundaments and of all properties."[53] This, of course, has consequences for poetics and genre-theory. In the first case, it means that the poet must aim for "variety in the *representation* of human characters: "No puppets—no so-called 'characters' ('*Karactere*') —a lively, bizarre, inconsequential, multicolored world."[54] "A poem must be fully inexhaustible, like a person."[55] Concerning genre-theory, Novalis asserts: "We are beyond the age of generally valid *forms*." In context it is clear that by "forms" he means genres. Like Friedrich Schlegel he does not reject them outright but rather from the perspective of a discourse become absolute which can no longer control its effects of meaning through the binding conventions of earlier epochs.

The indeterminacy of personality reflects the loss of an absolute meaning of Man. And "when a work has multiple causes, multiple meanings, much interest, and in general many aspects," it signals for Novalis "a genuine outpouring of personality."[56] Precisely the formal and semantic indeterminacy of a work of art strikes the homeless subject as "homey": "On the general *N-language* of music. The spirit is freed, becomes generally *stimulated*—it feels so good—it seems so familiar, so patriarchal."[57] And: "The highest basic science is that which never studies a *determinate* object—but rather treats a pure N. So it is also with art. Manual fabrication is already a specialized, applied construction. The N-making with the N-organ is the subject of this general doctrine and art."[58]

Of course the radicalism of this poetological fantasy extends far beyond what was achieved in the poetry of the day. Even today many of the "aesthetic imperatives" then formulated seem audacious and unfeasible. Yet before I attempt to show, by use of a concrete example, how the Romantic concept of text dissolves under the influence of the experience of the Infinite, I wish to emphasize one characteristic feature of the theses quoted above; that is, the favoring of music among the arts. This privilege is based on the fact that in no other symbolic system is the level of meaning so dominated by the level of expression. Indeed, the intractable gliding of the *signified* under the *signifier* is here the rule. This cannot be true to such an extent in the realm of speech, where each employed symbol has some conventional meaning *as well.* One "romanticizes" the use of symbols by letting precisely that instance which in most communicative situations serves merely to convey meaning begin to resonate. For "symbols" become the "organ of melody" only through their "physical existence . . . in space and time," as Friedrich Schlegel writes in his *Deduction of Rhythm*.[59] The interest of art should be to make symbols musical; that is, to free them from "their allegorical, intellectual existence."[60] Only through their materiality may sequences be said to have "rhythm." The phonic "character of its sound" "individualizes" the tone and at the same time distinguishes it from all other tones of the system.[61] Timbre (*Klangqualität*) has an immediate, quantitative function. It carries with it a certain measure of temporal fulfillment, out of which, when combined with different tones, an accordingly particular rhythmic sequence emerges. Rhythm contributes in no way to the realization or understanding of speaker-intentions. Rather, it is, as an "instrument of poetry," "an organ of music."[62] The poetic function of speech becomes visible when sounds suspend their conventional meanings, when the poet manipulates them according to purely aesthetic criteria. Insignificant speech-utilization does not, of course, preclude the transcendental perspective: it reveals the differential mechanism of articulation, which rhythmically and phonetically distinguishes tones from one another and so allows them to become vehicles of sense. If modulation and rhythm are themselves meaningless, they nevertheless provide a basis for meaning. In their interaction the schematism of symbolic formation becomes perceptible as an unchecked seepage and decay of "absolute meaning," which is, as such, ineffable and only negatively present in the scansion of articulated syllables.

Following this introduction I would like to turn directly to a poem by Ludwig Tieck, the "Mondscheinlied," which was first published in 1798 in the *Sternbald* novel. My choice, of course, is not accidental. It is based on the observance of a formal and functional metamorphosis of lyrical speech during the course of the nineteenth century (a metamorphosis which has shaped the poetry of our century) and further on the hypothesis that Tieck's poem is one of the earliest documents which reveal this change. I will first quote it in its entirety:[63]

MONDSCHEINLIED

1. Träuft vom Himmel der kühle Tau,
   Tun die Blumen die Kelche zu,
   Spätrot sieht scheidend nach der Au,
   Flüstern die Pappeln, sinkt nieder die nächtige Ruh.

2. Kommen und gehn die Schatten,
   Wolken bleiben noch spät auf,
   Und ziehn mit schwerem, unbeholfem Lauf
   Uber die erfrischten Matten.

3. Schimmern die Sterne und schwinden wieder,
   Blicken winkend und flüchtig nieder,
   Wohnt im Wald die Dunkelheit,
   Dehnt sich Finster weit und breit.

4. Hinterm Wasser wie flimmende Flammen,
   Berggipfel oben mit Gold beschienen,
   Neigen rauschend und ernst die grünen
   Gebüsche die blinkenden Häupter zusammen.

5. Welle, rollst du herauf den Schein,
   Des Mondes rund freundlich Angesicht?
   Es merkt's und freudig bewegt sich der Hain,
   Streckt die Zweig entgegen dem Zauberlicht.

6. Fangen die Geister auf den Fluten zu springen,
   Tun sich die Nachtblumen auf mit Klingen,
   Wacht die Nachtigall im dicksten Baum,
   Verkündet dichterisch ihren Traum,
   Wie helle, blendende Strahlen die Töne niederfließen,
   Am Bergeshang den Widerhall zu grüßen.

7. Flimmern die Wellen,
   Funkeln die wandernden Quellen,
   Streifen durchs Gesträuch
   Die Feuerwürmchen bleich.

8. Wie die Wolken wandelt mein Sehnen,
   Mein Gedanke, bald dunkel, bald hell,
   Hüpfen Wünsche um mich wie der Quell,
   Kenne nicht die brennenden Tränen.

9. Bist du nah, bist du weit,
   Glück, das nur für mich erblühte?
   Ach! daß es die Hände biete
   In des Mondes Einsamkeit.

10. Kömmt's aus dem Walde? schleicht's vom Tal?
Steigt es den Berg vielleicht hernieder?
Kommen alte Schmerzen wieder?
Aus Wolken ab die entflohne Qual?

11. Und Zukunft wird Vergangenheit!
Bleibt der Strom nie ruhig stehn.
Ach! ist dein Glück auch noch so weit,
Magst du entgegengehn;
Auch Liebesglück wird einst Vergangenheit.

12.   Wolken schwinden,
Den Morgen finden
Die Blumen wieder:

Doch ist die Jugend einst entschwunden,
Ach! der Frühlingsliebe Stunden
Steigen keiner Sehnsucht nieder.

MOONLIGHT SONG

1. Cool dew drops from heaven, and
The flowers close their chalices.
Twilight departing looks to the green,
The poplars whisper; the peace of night sinks down.

2. The shadows come and go,
While the clouds still linger on,
And draw with heavy, awkward pace
Over the freshened meadows.

3. Stars shine forth and disappear,
Fleeting they glance down and beckon.
Darkness haunts the wood so black,
Gloom spreads deeper, far and wide.

4. Behind the water like glimmering flames,
Mountain-peaks above, sunlit gold,
Stoop rustling and earnest the green,
Bushes their glittering crowns together.

5. Wave, do you carry ashore the sheen,
The rounded friendly form of the moon?
It's seen; and joyfully the wood responds,
To the magic light the branch reaches out.

6. And now the spirits begin to dance upon the tides,
The flowers of the night chime open,
The nightingale wakes deep in its bower,
Announces lyrically her dream:
As bright and dazzling rays the tones flow forth,
To greet their echo at the mountain slope.

7. Waves glimmer,
Wandering springs sparkle,
Glowworms pale glide through
The shrubbery below.—

8. Like the clouds my yearning wanders,
   My thoughts, now gloomy, now bright,
   Desires dance about me fountain-like,
   Forgetful of the burning tears.

9. Are you near, are you far,
   Joy that blossoms only for me?
   Oh! that it offers its hand
   In the solitude of the moon.

10. Does it emerge from the forest? or slip from the valley?
    Does it descend perhaps from the mountain?
    Do the old sorrows return?
    Down from the clouds past anguish?

11. And the future becomes past!
    The current never stands still.
    Oh! is that joy you wish to approach
    Still so distant;
    The joys of love also pass.

12.   Clouds vanish,
        And flowers find
        The morning again:

    Yet youth will soon be past,
    Oh! the hours of spring-love
    Do not descend to the longing.

We are concerned with a poem of twelve strophes, the individual
verses of which show considerable variation in length and metrical
count. The largest verse encompasses 15 syllables (strophe 6, verse 5—
of the German text: all such references will be to the original—Tr.),
the shortest 4 (strophe 12, verse 1). The number of stresses is similarly
inconsistent (a maximum of 6, a minimum of 2). On a first reading
the poem is difficult to scan. Excepting the third and fourth verses of
the third strophe and the final verses, there is not a single pair of lines
constructed according to the same rhetorical rule. This causes the
recital to flow like a prose piece, despite the sustained rhyming and
traditional graphic arrangement in strophic blocks of verse lines. That
is to say that the reader must allow the rhythm of the lines to develop
out of the natural accenting of the words: a rhythm, it is true, hardly
more consistent than the metrical indeterminacy of typical prose. Now
the accented syllables are so frequent that almost every syllable demands to be stressed ("Spätrot sieht scheidend nach der Au"), and now
the intervals dissolve into all sorts of fluidly successive unstressed
syllables ("Schimmern die Sterne und schwinden wieder,/Blicken
winkend und flüchtig nieder"), only to reappear once again with
increasing density ("Wohnt im Wald die Dunkelheit/Dehnt sich Finster
weit und breit"). It is clearly the exception in this poem for one foot to
immediately follow another of the same type. Trochees ("Hinterm

Wasser") alternate with iambs ("Und ziehn"), dactyls ("Flüstern die"), anapests ("Streckt die Zweig", "blicken winkend") and spondees ("Spätrot sieht scheidend"). The only rule which one might recognize in such a combination of metrical types would be a rule of maximum variation.

Tieck's poem reaches here the point at which questions of its form and composition nearly preempt questions concerning its content. To be sure, this was Tieck's declared intention. "Why should the full content of a poem be limited to its mere content?" he has Rudolf ask.[64] Before the reader-listener has a chance to glean just what the "Mondscheinlied" is about, his ear is stamped with the impression of an uncontrollable gliding and flickering of tones, for which he futilely strives to deduce some fundamental metrical order. In the "Aesthetics" of his Berlin lectures of 1801 (*On Beautiful Literature and Art*), A.W. Schlegel defines meter (he writes 'rhythm' but in our time the usage is precisely reversed) as the measure and mode of temporal fulfillment. It demands "an arrangement of the material of temporal fulfillment, in which recognizable relationships occur. There are thus two aspects of rhythm: a common measure of time for the whole series of successions and variation in the duration of the particular. Wherever either of these two is lacking, rhythm does not occur."[65] "Modulation" should be distinguished from meter. Diverging from the strict musical sense of the term, Schlegel understands "modulation" to be the variant timbre of the time fulfilling phases in their succession, exclusively considering the "conditions of their composition, each (of the tones) regarded for itself"—that is, for its height or depth, heaviness or lightness of tone independent of its measure. "Harmony" depends upon "their composition in relationship to each other." And finally "melody" is the "combination of the two concepts of rhythm and modulation."[66]

Utilizing this terminology—carried over to the lyrical from the musical—we must indeed deny the "Mondscheinlied" metrical uniformity, for no steady meter develops "in successions of incommensurably differing duration which do not follow each other according to any rule."[67] Of course the poem has a rhythm (I now use the term in the modern sense) just the same. However, this rhythm becomes—in the absence of an independent and consistent meter—a function of modulation, of the timbre of the tones and syllables. Were there a rule to which the rhythm of the verses could be said to comply, it would be the rule of "a chain of sensations"; that is, of a succession of feelings which find their immediate realization in the musical composition of the sounds.[68] Each tone, as the carrier of a sensation, has a certain quality, according to which it fulfills a certain quantum of time. The feet evolve out of these quanta; and their entirety constitutes finally a meter, which, to be sure, is not fully transparent until the last tone of the chain of sensations has sounded. In short, the meter of this lyrical speech does not develop in accordance with a predetermined metrical rule, but spontaneously formulates its rule according to the force of the various sensations which resound sequentially, each superseding its precursor. In order to adequately represent experienced time, the lyrical language must free itself from the "conventional rules" and follow its own, in the strictest sense unforeseeable "inner rules," "which the nature of art demands." The genuine poet knows only one basic law: "(to) consider that which the nature of perception demands."[69]

It is true that Tieck chooses the language of "the aesthetics of Genius" to make himself understood. Yet he is concerned less with an illustration of the capriciousness of a virtuoso who disregards the prevailing rules than with the insight that no propositional law is capable of determining beforehand how an articulation will shape itself; that speech can recognize and assert what it wishes to say only at the moment of its utterance. Content is for him a function of modulation. The movement of inner temporality must be caught and represented in tones as precisely as possible. Where temperament lingers, so should the flow of language. If it erupts violently, so too the tones, which become fluid and volatile in the extreme. It is also true that Tieck's poetry remains conventional in many respects. His use of metaphor is not particularly original. In the "Mondscheinlied" several tend toward the banal, even the ludicrous. On the other hand, he demonstrates, particularly in the first seven strophes, a degree of syntactical carelessness at the time unheard of in German literature. (In general: parataxes predominate; the logical ties between sentences are opaque; the transitions asyndetic.) The strophes begin almost exclusively with infinitive verb-forms, whereby it is not clear from the context whether conditional clauses implying an "if," elliptical constructions requiring an "it" or an auxiliary verb, or perhaps questions are intended. Certainly, none of these three possibilities could apply equally to all of the sentences—are they sentences? (Particularly not to the fourth strophe with its vibrant dynamic: "Behind the water like glimmering flames,/ Mountain peaks above, sunlit gold,/ Stoop rustling and earnest the green/ Bushes their glittering crowns together.") Elipses also occur in the verb-forms themselves; e.g. "fangen" (instead of "anfangen"), "wachen" (instead of "aufwachen"); at times in conjunction with word transpositions within a syntactical period: "Magst du entgegengehn," "Aus Wolken ab die entflohne Qual," etc. The syntactical vertigo of this speech intensifies the unforeseeable rhythmic turbulence of the lines. And if it is possible, albeit with some effort, to discern a minimum thematic coherence of the poem, the task is certainly made difficult by Tieck's practice of paralyzing the efforts of the understanding to follow it through rapid alternation of contradictory sensations. This, at least, is his declared intention: to prevent, through a relentless "diversion" of the determining intellect, a conclusive penetration of the impressions and to destroy the possibility "of fixing any object in secure and enduring view."[70] The full effect of reading (or hearing) such poetry would be based upon a sequence of contrasting tones or symbols so swift in its succession that the synthetic achievements of the intellect are subverted and a diffuse intuition (in the Kantian sense) arises prior to any understanding. This possibility, Tieck explains revealingly, is due "to the incredible agility of the imagination, which can attach in two successive moments entirely different ideas to one and the same object."[71] This does not mean that Tieck's language lacks sensuous concreteness. Rather, the unsettling vicissitudes make concentration upon a communication impossible. The purpose of the strophically preeminent and grammatically enigmatic verb-forms is now clear: they launch an indeterminate and unpredictably developing movement and force a conceptual fixation upon the *manner* in which this movement proceeds (*kommend und gehend, winkend, flimmend, blickend, blinkend, flimmernd, rollend, springend, blendend, funkelnd, wandelnd, hüpfend, brennend, nie ruhig stehen bleibend*, etc.). The verbs of the poem work more powerfully in their audible than in their semantic aspect. Also at the level of content they emphasize movements ending or just beginning, fleeting visual and acoustic events, barely perceptible transitions and entanglements. Light and dark vowels, plosive and gliding consonants alternate within the briefest span and so intensify the flickering sensation.

To discuss the "content" of the poem under these conditions becomes almost superfluous. The first four strophes celebrate the receding movement of the passing day. The fifth strophe mediates the transition to the world of night: the now dark earth ("below") lives on by the reflected light of the heavens ("above"), the above having been the place of illumination. Now the night rises—the first animated dactyl greets it joyfully. The upward movement of twilight contrasts with the downward movement of the waning daylight. Yet the new state is in no way calmer or less fleeting than its radiant counterpart: the ephemeral quality of the initial rhythms continues beyond the change-of-scene in the vehement modulation of the night strophes. From the eighth strophe on an interpenetration of nature and subject is reflected upon: night and day become ciphers of an inconstant interiority exposing itself in its confusion: "Like the clouds my yearning strays,/ My thoughts, now gloomy, now bright" (strophe 8 lines 1 and 2.) Day and night— and the atmospheric transition which equalizes them before their differences are felt—alternate like "future" and "past," "the current never stands still." (Strophe 11, lines 1 and 2).

The thematics of the river of life and of temporality are thus not missing in Tieck. But the fact that they are made explicit in a belabored movement of reflection detracts from the poem and may be attributed to the bad rationalism of Tieck's muse. Who would have doubted that the "Mondscheinlied" concerns an inner landscape? And, who would not have noticed already in the disruption of the lyrical melody and the emancipation of the modulation from metrical constraints that a decentered subjectivity has chosen this means to express its experience of disintegration? Such an experience seeks a *principle of composition* alien to classical poetics. The homeless soul can no longer securely distinguish substance from accident. Even the constancy of the theme— the transience of life—can realize itself henceforth only as the continuity of change. Adorno has spoken of a "nominalism of musical language inaugurated by Wagner,"[72] which suspends that "paradoxical relationship to time" embodied in the classical sonnet or aria-opera as a theme maintaining its identity through change.[73] The invariance of themes in the flow of time restricts the freedom of subjective reflection and reduces the terrain of "development." For "only as long as the development is not absolute, only as long as it is something not totally subjected to music but rather—in Kantian terms—an *a priori* musical '*Ding an sich*' (thing 'in and for itself'), is music able to hold off the empty force of time."[74]

Translating the esthetic terminology of music into the realm of poetry, we must say that the distinction of themes, motives and their development is no longer tenable. The unity of the text is at stake at every moment, with every expression, with every "tone," and is reconstructed at every point. Each foot constitutes the center of the poem. And yet, when every element can claim with equal right to be the theme and center of the whole, there no longer can, in the strictest sense, be either theme or middle: everything becomes accidental, everything becomes essential. The economy of the poem which would be consistent with its genre, "poetry"—i.e. the organization of a central and dictatorial *vouloir-dire* through the unity of a determining intentionality—becomes unbound, and each individual means of expression suffers what Novalis called the suspension of its distinction relative to all others: "An individuality characterized by all other individualities and thus infinitely is one appendage of an *infinitonomium*."[75] It is, in other words, one element of a differential system lacking fixed limits. Within such an open system individualities can have no permanence, for "the more elaborately something is individualized—the more *variable its frontiers, borders*—and *proximity*."[76]

Adorno demonstrated how the distinction between theme and variation dissolves, using the work of Brahms as an example. In another—and no less anticipatory—way, the same is also true for Wag-

Manfred Frank

ner's "infinite melody" (*unendliche Melodie*). It has been argued with some justification that the only occurrence of this expression in Wagner's *Collected Works*[77] in no way supports the interpretation that Wagner had intended the term to characterize a stylistic technique or a manner of composition. In 1860 (the year in which the expression was coined), the idealistic use of the term "infinite" was still current. The idealists distinguished between an immediate and an extensive, between (as Hegel says) a good and a bad infinity. The former describes eternity, "the Absolute," the totality of "infinite fullness" (re-)suspended in unity. The latter depicts infinity in the sense of a manifold spatiality or an endless temporal extension. Fritz Reckow[78] was able to show that Wagner uses the term in both senses. He maintains that as it is used in the expression "infinite melody" it is synonymous with "timeless," "eternally efficacious" or "eternally comprehensible."[79] Shoud this be the case, the history of its reception nonetheless shows that the expression has been persistently construed as describing a compositional technique. And this on the basis of Wagner's own remarks. On the one hand, he stresses that he has suspended and melodically effaced, through "an uninterrupted musical flux as yet unheard of," the difference between arias and recitative passages.[80] This compositional technique makes it possible to free completely the action "from the necessity of motivation through (external) reflection."[81] "Now it is the music which, by incessantly evoking correlative feeling, empowers us to present this action drastically determined."[82] We have here finally an uninterrupted stream of motivation which makes it impossible to differentiate externally between thematic and developmental passages. As is well-known, Wagner describes that "uninterrupted involvement of the orchestra in the affairs of the singers" as "the 'total composition' " (*Durchkomponieren*)[83] of the musically-spoken work of art which does not generate its unity point by point, in smaller thematically or aria-accentuated passages, but rather realizes that unity "in a fabric of basic themes that pervades the entire work."[84] This is the only compositional form which accommodates the reality of the human self whose essence is marked by temporality; by the want of unfulfilled presence; by boundless yearning; in short: by transcendence:

If this sea (of music) grows turbulent out of its own depths, if it breeds the basis of its movement out of the fundaments of its own element, then its movement is also an endless, never to be calmed, always agitated return to itself, eternally demanding to be exciting anew.[85]

It would be easy to inscribe the symbolism of the endless journey in a reading of this passage, particularly since Wagner himself invokes it a few pages later:

In the realm of harmony there is . . . no beginning or end, like the fervor which, lacking an object, consumes itself, ignorant of its source, and is never more than itself: a demanding, yearning, storming, languishing—a *dying away* (*Ersterben*); ie. a dying without having been fulfilled in an object, thus a dying without death, and a returning always to itself.[86]

—the fate of the Flying Dutchman, the Ancient Mariner, the Hunter Gracchus.

I infer from this quote above all the notion that partial unities no longer suit the yearning subject (*dem Schnenden*). It cannot satisfy itself with any one goal or object. And this impossibility precludes composition according to the stipulations of, say, the sonata movement, with its overly clear differentiation between an insistent theme and its temporally limited subjective reflection, which converges again with the theme during the reprise and, as its development, never escapes its control.

Considerations such as these seem to lead us away from our topic in that they tend to slip from the range of the analogy of music and poetry into the field of music proper. This is, of course, not entirely the case. Wagner's Music-Drama—the result of a fusing and transgression of the boundaries of various art forms (including the verbal)—must ensure that the structure of its texts permits the continued unfolding according to its own rule of an infinite melody freed from the "Procrustean bed" of stereotyped prescriptions. The more so since the metrical uniformity of a poem and the recurrence of its rhyme seem to lead inevitably to a fixation upon a regular period-scheme and a uniform musical syntax. To suspend these conservative elements, the pattern of the text—the rhythm of its verses—must not only be irregular but must provide for a continuous alteration of the metrical pattern immediately following its establishment. When the principle that no syllable or sequence of sounds could be repeated was still valid,[87] it made sense to permit the repetition of even one single foot type purely as an exception. In this regard, Wagner writes in his "Message to my Friends":

Whenever the expression of poetic discourse so shaped my endeavor that I could only justify the melody to my feelings by appealing to poetry, this melody necessarily lost almost all rhythmic (here is meant, as with Schlegel: metrical) character, and so did not stand in a forced relation to the verse; in following this procedure I was infinitely more conscientious and true to my purpose than when I sought on the contrary to enliven the melody by a capricious rhythm. . . . My melody's loss of rhythmic definition, or better: of its striking quality, I now compensated for by an *harmonic* animation of the expression, such as only I could feel the melodic need to be.[88]

This "new *rhythmical* animation of the melody, to be won from its justification *by the verse*, by the *speech* itself"[89] led him to use alliteration, which, through its metrical irregularity and modulative flexibility, is capable of "an infinitely varied manifestation" of spontaneous sensations. The transformation of musical language into prose—expanded to a compositional technique—is the only suitable means of expressing acoustically what Tieck calls a "sequence of sensations." Sensations are not without rules. Rather, by determining through the quality of the successive "tones" a measure for the entire sequence, they create for themselves a rhythm at the very moment of their expression. These sensations cannot be forced into a pattern by some external metrical stereotype—a process which prevailed as long as the musical period-scheme shaped the melodic framework. Conditioned by the regimentation of the musical genre, the "sequence of sensations" was made to conform to some metrical measure, for:

rhythmical regularity—schematism, to express it pejoratively—is, in conjunction with the considerations of harmony and motivation, constitutive. Equally long sections of a melody tend to supplement each other and, when the harmonics and the motivational structure support or at least do not oppose the nexus, to unite into a group. The quantitative factor fulfills a qualitative, syntactical function. And, indeed, the classical musical syntax is hierarchical: two corresponding bars define a phrase, two phrases a half-movement, two half-movements—antecedent and consequent—a period. A group of four bars could, it is true, shrink to three or stretch to five without violating the principle of correspondence. However, in order that the syntax remain comprehensible, such exceptions to the norm of uniform measure must occur only when the rules have firmly impressed themselves upon musical sensibility.[90]

In Wagner's musical syntax—that of the infinite melody—this generic norm is suspended, and it is significant, in the context of our discussion, that this suspension of the rhythm of alliteration is achieved jointly with the emancipation of dissonance. Dahlhaus has convincingly demonstrated that the tonal modulation of the first ten verses of Waltraut's narration ("Seit er von dir geschieden,/ zur Schlacht nicht mehr/ schickte uns Wotan:/ irr und ratlos/ ritten wir ängstlich zu Heer" etc.)[91] and Kundry's formidable response to Parsifal's refusal ("Grausamer!—Ha!—/ Fühlst du im Herzen/ nur anderer Schmerzen,/ so fühle jetzt auch die meinen")[92] in its precipitancy towards prose practically demands the subversion of the musical period-scheme and that the combined effects of the stave- and end rhymes is not capable of halting the dissonant and disintegrating effects of the speech-like, "musical prose."[93] Neither does the sequence of bars follow a rule nor does the coincidence of the periods exhibit a comprehensible logic: the only order which one cannot deny is that of a "sequence of sensations" which spreads itself over the entire drama as an endless fabric—as a text—of leitmotifs and which in no place is governed by a traditional and external economy of genres that would allow for a differentiation of aria and recitative, of thematic and variational or (as Roland Barthes would say) of cardinal and catalytic passages.

If, following our scheme of literary history, we could describe Wagner and Tieck as still belonging to the cultural continuum of "Romanticism," a turn to the lyrical work of the English Jesuit, Gerard Manley Hopkins (1844–1898), would land us directly upon the threshold of modern times. The emancipation of rhythmical modulation from meter reaches a preliminary zenith in his verse, surpassed neither by contemporary nor by subsequent experimental poetry (not by the *Phantasus* of Arno Holz nor by the metrically unbound long-verse of the expressionist Ernst Stadler, for example). In Hopkins' poetological thought, the colloquial distinction between poetry and prose, still maintained particularly in the Latin countries, breaks down conclusively: "The rhythm of common speech and of written prose" becomes the ideal for poetic discourse, as Hopkins writes in the forward to his sonnets.[94] The classically ideal claim that poetry must distinguish itself from the chaotic "totality of language" in such a manner that it—like a heavenly body—"carries its own independent movement and therefore its temporality within itself"—namely "through rhythm and syllabic measure"[95] —is here revoked. Hopkins goes even further: also colloquial prose— such as intentionally rhythmic speech (*oratio*) or the rhetorical emphasis on the desire to persuade (*das Uberreden-Wollen*)—tends on occasion toward "uniformities" which can only be avoided according to the rules of a strictly anti-metrical speech. "Reversed feet" and "counterpoint rhythm"[96] are evidenced already in traditional verse. These are rhythmical licenses lying within the tolerance range of each meter. For example, one's ear can easily accept the insertion through hovering stress of a single trochee into an iambically ascending blank verse (perhaps as the expression of a rhetorical emphasis.)[97] Should such a reversal repeat itself in two successive feet, a second meter would be heard to compete with the first—the two rhythms running beside each other, as often happens in Milton's verse. We thereupon have, according to Hopkins, something like a "Counterpoint Rhythm"[98] dominated, it is true, by the "ground rhythm." Once this last concession to metrical predominance is dismissed, there remains "one rhythm only and probably Sprung Rhythm, of which I now speak."[99] Sprung rhythm describes a totalized counterpoint which fully suspends the fixed metrical scheme maintained through several verses or entire poetic works. In order to prevent even the appearance of a metrical dictatorship, the composition must follow strict maxims.[100] As a rule, no metrical foot should imitate its predecessor. In the Germanic languages the accent should always fall upon the first syllable, which may be followed by as many as three unstressed syllables. Thus, the majority

Manfred Frank

of measures should consist of spondees, trochees, dactyls and paeons. To be sure, this terminology is misleading in that the paeon and the dactyl are integral components of meter, whereas the feet in sprung rhythm stand in an arbitrary sequence and are nevertheless absolutely equivalent.

Enjambment[101] is taken into account rhythmically, so that strophes, rather than lines of verse, become the smallest element of composition. In order to facilitate additional freedoms, allowances are made for rests—the interruption of the flow of tones—and deviant metrical feet —two or three "slack syllables" (marked by a loop beneath the words) "which are not counted in a normal scanning."[102] (Hopkins speaks of "hangers" and "outrides.")[103] Furthermore, several syllables can be united under one stress. Rhythmical inversions are indicated by "twirls." (These, of course, must remain exceptional, for counterpoint must not play any role in a thoroughly anarchized metrical flow: "Counterpoint is excluded by sprung rhythm," and "outriding feet (also reversals) belong to counterpointed verse, which supposes a well-known and unmistakable or unforgettable standard rhythm.")[104]

Sprung rhythm thus emancipates lyrical speech from the schematic periodicities proper to customary meters. Emphasis is placed on the modulation of the verse and becomes its most important aspect. Modulation is governed by the "easily felt principle of *equal strengths.*"[105] Ideally this means that each metrical foot—regardless of whether it consists of one or four syllables—is regarded equally with every other foot.[106] In no way is this a problem that should be placed under the heading of revolutionized lyrical rhythm.[107] As with Wagner and Tieck, the liberation of the foot from the dictates of determinant meter is not intended as a subjugation of language to another master such as an absolutized counterpoint. Rather, the rhythm should develop organically out of the phonic quality of successive syllables; that is, out of the modulation of the "sequence of sensations." Expression had already in Tieck taken recourse to the metaphorics of fabric (text) and interwoven motivation. By "sequence of sensations" he understood a scale of self-engendered intensification and extension of a series of sentiments which augment the initially engaged sensation with "perpetually new prospects."[108] Wagner spoke of a "fabric of principle themes," which extends itself over the entire work and which "can only be engendered through an ever-perceivable development of the suggested moods."[109]

The principle motives of the dramatic action have become exactly distinguishable melodic moments that fully materialize their content; which melodic moments are constituted in their suggestive, always well-conditioned . . . return to a unitary artistic form which does not merely cover certain limited parts of the drama but rather pervades its entirety as a binding coherence in which not only these melodic moments explain each other and so appear at-one, but also the sensuous or imagistic motives—the strongest and weakest elements of the action—are seen to bring each other together according to the nature of the genre and to reveal themselves to the *feelings*. In this alliance a realization of the perfect unitarian form is achieved.[110]

This complicated formulation in *Opera and Drama* demonstrates how difficult it was for Wagner to explain his method of composition in terms of a theory of genre. The long and syntactically opaque sentence attempts to meet the extreme plurality of the sequence of sensations and the subjective factor at play within it at the point where it abruptly changes into the objectivity of a "unitarian form"; that is, where it becomes an infinite fabric, a text not restricted by any economy. The question is not one of a global and synthetic, unifying principle which would govern the mass of individual tones and inflict a law upon them from the outside, but of a textual unity which stands at every moment on the brink and which must be perpetually reestablished.

Precisely on that account freedom becomes the principle of an all-round economy that leaves in music nothing casual, and develops the utmost diversity while adhering to the identical material. Where there is nothing unthematic left, nothing which could not show itself to derive from the same basic material, there one can no longer speak of a 'free style.'[111]

Each tone is what it is through its relationship to all others. It stands within a continual motivational structure which denies it immediate meaning and compels it to travel the detour over all other tones. Hopkins would also have the process seen in this light: "By sequence of feeling I mean a dramatic quality by which what goes before seems to necessitate and beget what comes after, at least after you have heard it it does."[112] Here, too, what is at stake is the paradoxical and abrupt transition from the subjective idiosyncratic freedom (*Willkürfreiheit*), as expressed in terms of the classical esthetics of Genius, to the mode of being of a relational system, the coherence of which cannot be understood as a merely subjective effort. It could be said, continuing the musical metaphors, that the compositional technique of sprung rhythm breaks with the tonality of a keynote or fundamental chord to which the variative development might return at any point as to its *lieu propre*. The result is that the tones are of equal value and that their meaning does not derive from their relationship to some independent and fixed fundamental meaning but from their relationship to each other. This occasions a feeling of a bottomless suspension whose law is deducible only after the fact and applicable only to this particular composition.

I will illustrate this procedure by citing the first nine lines of Hopkins' sonnet "That Nature is a Heraclitean Fire and of the Comfort of the Resurrection" (written in July, 1888):

Manfred Frank

Cloud-Puffball, torn tufts, tossed pillows / flaunt forth, then chevy as an air-
built thoroughfare: heaven-roysterers, in a gay-gangs / they throng; they
glitter in marches.
Down roughcast, down dazzling whitewash, / wherever an elm arches,
Shivelights and shadowtackle in long / lashes lace, lance, and pair.
Delightfully the bright wind boisterous / ropes, wrestles, beats earth bare
Of yestertempest's creases; / in pool and rut peel parches
Squandering ooze to squeezed / dough, crust, dust; stanches, starches
Squadroned masks and manmarks / treadmire toil there
Footfretted in it. Millionfueled, / nature's bonfire burns on.[113]

The similarity of this poem to Tieck's "Mondscheinlied" is perhaps immediately apparent. Both poems are rhymed: in this case we have an
Italian sonnet with three appended codas. In general the lines have six
stresses (more where "outrides" and less where "hurried" feet occur).
The central dieresis recalls the Alexandrine or the classical trimeter
(with a caesura after the third stress). In fact, the number of syllables
in the lines varies between 7 and 20. In contrast to Tieck, not a single
foot in the entire poem repeats its predecessor. Internal rhyme is common; the rhyme-word of one line is occasionally displaced to the second
foot of the following line (from line 1 to 2; cf. line 16ff.); and alliteration is used frequently. However, it is obvious that the connective force
of all of these synthetic devices does not suffice to obviate the sense of
extreme variation in the modulation of tones. Even the phonemic
sequences within the syllables are so chosen as to contrast sharply with
their precursors. Rhythm and lyrical *melos* seem forcibly severed from
each other. Even more than with Tieck the syntax supports this impression: the atomization of the individual stresses corresponds not
only to the continual parataxis but also to the atomization of the
smallest units of meaning, which—at least on first sight—stand practically unconnected next to each other. Singularities stand beside
plural forms "Cloud-Puffball," "torn tufts," "shivelights and shadowtackle"); grammatical elements which belong together are rent asunder
by powerful bars (*hyperbate*); the placement of parts of speech precisely work against the stipulations of grammar and, furthermore, is
in constant flux, frustrating any attempt to deduce a rule even of syntactical contrast. Nor are the morphonological rules observed: audacious
neologisms, ellipses and contaminations (the union of words of differing
grammatical categories, as in "beats level," "yestertempest," "clearest-
selvèd," "disseveral," etc.).

There are occasional grammatical undecidabilities and ambiguities.
For example, it is not clear in the sequence "in pool and rut peel parches
Squandering ooze to squeezed dough, crust, dust" whether one should
interpret "rut" and "peel" as nouns and read them in tandem ("rutpeel"),[114] or whether "peel" functions as a verb form (intransitive?
transitive?) which would join with "parches" in a disturbing (*verfrem-*

dende) combination ("peel-parches")—unquestionably an agrammatical construction, which, however, would not be the only one of its kind: the very next sequence poses similar questions. Is "treadmire toil" a noun formation or is it two audaciously joined verbs? Certainly the grammar of the participial construction provides no conclusive answer. In short: already with semantic deciphering one encounters insurmountable difficulties. The poem complies with perpetually new relational frameworks which cannot be explained in terms of a fundamental and determining unity. This poem, like Tieck's, glows with metaphors of light and darkness. A movement from darkness to light (in the quartets) is reversed in the trios: the light of nature, the spirit of humanity (*Menschengeist*), that which was born out of the chaos darkens (reverts to the darkness, to that which is chaotic, uncontrollably in flux, etc.), and not until the three codas is this downward movement reversed in the victorious certainty of radiant salvation. Nature's beacon, the radiant diamond, that most penetrable yet resistant of minerals, becomes symbolic of the unity of inconstancy and of durability. Like the Heraclitian fire, its everlastingness is guaranteed precisely by its vacillation (its shifting reflectability). This is no longer the everlasting unity opposed to disorder but rather the eternity of a shattered economy as such.

This brings me to the end. I have tried to indicate those traits of modern texts in which the theme of the infinite passage finds its formal or compositional counterpart. The development which I have sketched has seemed to me to be more striking than it would have been had I followed another course, for instance that of the evolution of poetic imagery as described in books dealing with "the Essence of Modern Poetry." Of course, one could also demonstrate the break with the paradigm of reflection by analyzing the emancipation of metaphor from the law of analogy. The two poles of metaphor continue to refer to each other, but they no longer disclose the secret of the law that makes their exchange possible: reflex and reflector remain within the unity of a mirroring-movement, but it is no longer clear whether this unity is one of identity or of its more modest supplement, similarity. I have pointed to this possibility above in the Mallarméan metaphor of the mirror without backing. It too reveals one manner of losing one's way and de-limiting an economy. But this does not involve an originary phenomenon, More rudimentary is the textual quality of being-in-the-world. It teaches that the deferral of meaning (which actualizes itself in the obscure metaphor) is not the dangerous exception to the rule of immediate presence of meaning but rather represents a constitutive possibility of all nonsymbolic (arbitrary, conventional) systems of orientation. In every semantic system, Sartre writes, "what is really involved is a group of relationships between terms which define themselves only through their reciprocal opposition or through a "differential," determining each in terms of the others, such that its sole essence resides in its difference from this or that other term and, hence, from all others."[115]

The non-identity of terms among themselves consequently becomes the condition of the identity of every single term. Herein resides the analogy to the competitive system of bourgeois society, in which man experiences what he is in the reflection of his function as *individu commun*" (as Sartre calls it).[116] Yet this alienation in and through the symbolic "types" is continually at stake, in so far as each significant act enriches the repertoire of the sayable and signifiable by adding countless possibilities of differentiation to the fabric of the social text. The metaphor, never reducible to a fixed identity, is fundamentally only a global expression for this methodologically illimitable possibility of creating, expanding and transforming meaning in the repertoire of what can be said (*des Sagbaren*). This possibility, to be sure, presupposes the inconstancy of language; and the poetological reflections upon the sequence of sensations, infinite melody, and totalized counterpoint are only three different and especially striking accentuations of this insight. Once they have become self-evident to modern consciousness, the "literary Absolute" is born. Yet its absoluteness is no longer founded in absolute knowledge or unshakable faith—but rather in the insurmountability of language. This does not mean that we are sheltered (or perhaps: trapped) in our texts as behind walls (the dream of earlier times: paradise was not—like the New World—conceived of as a land of infinite possibilities but as a preserve, as a restricted ward, as a garden), but rather that the borders of the text, through which we determine our social self-awareness (as that of the *individu commun*), perpetually withdraws before us and affords us those "*échappées de vue* into the Infinite" of which Friedrich Schlegel spoke.[117] The self-disintegration of textual economy (i.e. of its subordination through the idea of an orderly relationship to itself, to its properties and proper place *katà tòn toû oîkou nómon*) becomes the "*epídeixis* of infinity."[118] An infinity, it is true, which, after the loss of a transcendental economy of salvation and return (*Heimkehr*), can manifest itself only in the form of Hegel's *bad infinity*: as the thorn of yearning woven or driven into discourse, and as the boundlessness of being underway, without an absolute goal.

Translated by Michael Schwerin

NOTES

1. "Der unendliche Text"—The English title, which announces its key words in upper case, may be doubly reminiscent of the old order. (Rather than translating such words as "unendlich," "endlos," "unbegrenzbar," "ent-

grenzen," "losmachen," etc.—which appear in key places throughout the text—according to some rigid scheme, I have in each case allowed the context to suggest an approximate English equivalent.)—Translator's Note

2. Richard Wagner, *Der Fliegende Holländer*, in *Gesammelte Schriften und Dichtungen* (Leipzig, 1871), I, p. 271.—Tr. note: All translations are my own unless otherwise noted.

3. Bertolt Brecht, *Gesammelte Werke* (Frankfort: Suhrkamp, 1967), II, 1234.

4. Georg Lukács, *Die Theorie des Romans* (Berlin: Neuwied, 1963), p. 35ff.

5. Jacques Derrida, "Le Retrait de la métaphore," in *Poésie*, No. 7 (1978), pp. 104–5; "The Retrait of Metaphor," *Enclitic* 2, No. 2 (Fall 1978), p. 7.

6. Ibid., p. 105; Eng., p. 7.

7. Franz Kafka, *Sämtliche Erzählungen*, ed. Paul Raabe (Frankfort: Fischer, 1970), p. 228.

8. Cf. Philippe Lacoue-Labarthe and Jean-Luc Nancy, *L'Absolu littéraire, Théorie de la littérature du romantisme allemand* (Paris: Seuil, 1978).

9. For a more thorough discussion of this question, see M. Frank, *Das Problem 'Zeit' in der deutschen Romantik* (Munich: Winkler, 1972).

10. Cf., for example, Schelling, *Sämtliche Werke* (Stuttgart, 1856–61), I, 5, p. 736: "In addition I only note that the most consummate union of all art forms—the joining of poetry and music through song, of poetry and painting through dance—once synthesized itself, is the most perfectly composed of theatrical spectacles."

11. *Kritische Ausgabe der Werke von Friedrich Schlegel*, ed. Ernst Behler (Munich: Schöningh, 1958–), II, 204, No. 238. (Henceforth abbreviated as Fr. Schlegel, *KA*.)

12. Novalis, *Schriften*, ed. Paul Kluckhohn and Richard Samuel, 2nd ed. (Stuttgart: Kohlhammer, 1960–), II, 110, No. 11, pp. 20–24.

13. I use Derrida's semiologically neutral term "mark," rather than "symbol," in order to avoid association with a particular linguistic theory.

14. *"sens tuteur"*; *"signifié* principal *du text"*: Jacques Derrida, *Positions* (Paris: Minuit, 1972), p. 61; English in: *Diacritics* 2, No. 4 (Winter 1972), p. 37.

15. Fr. Schlegel, *KA*, XVII, 128, No. 76.

16. Novalis, *Schriften*, III, 664, No. 603; II, 610, No. 402.

17. Ibid., II, 201, No. 284.

18. Ibid., III, 256, No. 87.

19. Fr. Schlegel, *KA*, II, 200, No. 220.

20. Derrida, *Positions*, pp. 61–62, 82 (passim); Eng. pp. 37, 43.

21. E. D. Hirsch, *Validity in Interpretation* (New Haven: Yale University Press, 1967).

22. Derrida, "Positions," p. 61; Eng. p. 37.

23. Ibid., p. 62; Eng. p. 37. Cf. p. 82; Eng. p. 43: "There is such a general text wherever (i.e., everywhere) this discourse and its order (essence, meaning, truth, intent, consciousness, ideality, etc.) are exceeded (*débordés*), i.e., wherever their occurrence is reset in the position of a mark within a chain, and it is the structurally necessary illusion of that discourse to want and to believe that it governs that chain. This general text, to be sure, is not limited, as one might have initially understood, to written marks on a page. Its writing lacks, moreover, any external boundary, except for a certain

Manfred Frank

re-mark. Writing on a page, and then "literature" are particular types of this re-mark. They must be examined in their specificity and at a new cost, if you wish, in the specificity of their 'history,' and in their articulation with the other historical regions of the general text."

24. Sartre, *L'Idiot de la famille* (Paris: Gallimard, 1971), II, p. 1984.

25. See also J. Derrida, "La Mythologie blanche," in *Marges de la philosophie* (Paris: Minuit, 1972), particularly pp. 274ff.; Eng. in *New Literary History* 6, No. 1 (Autumn 1974), pp. 5–74. See also M. Frank, "Die Aufhebung der Anschauung im Spiel der Metaphor," in *MLN* 93, No. 5 (December 1978), pp. 819–38.

26. J. G. Fichte, *Wissenschaftslehre 1798 (nova methodo)*, in *Nachgelassene Schriften*, ed. Hans Jacob (Berlin, 1937), II, p. 368.

27. J. Derrida, *La Dissémination* (Paris: Seuil, 1972), p. 378; *Dissemination*, trans. Barbara Johnson (Chicago: University of Chicago Press, 1981[?]), p. 378.

28. Ibid., p. 350; Eng. p. 350.

29 Novalis, *Schriften*, II, 127, No. 32, p. 20.

30. Fr. Schlegel, *KA*, XII, pp. 94–95, 77–78.

31. Beckett, *Endgame: A Play in One Act* (New York: Grove Press, 1958), p. 73.

32. Derrida, *La Dissémination*, p. 317. (Derrida plays upon Mallarmé's *Un coup de dés* [in *Œuvres complètes* (Paris: Pléiade, 1945), p. 475].)

33. Ibid., pp. 282ff.

34. Ibid., p. 309 *Œuvres complètes*, p. 310).

35. Jacques Lacan, *Ecrits* (Paris: Seuil, 1966), p. 505; Eng. in *Ecrits: A Selection*, trans. Alan Sheridan (New York: Norton, 1977), p. 155. ("What this structure of the signifying chain discloses is the possibility I have, precisely in so far as I have this language in common with other subjects, that is to say, in so far as it exists as a language, to use it in order to signify *something quite other* than what it says.")

36. Ibid., p. 502; Eng. p. 154.

37. Fr. Schlegel, *KA*, II, p. 348.

38. Ibid., XII, 211.

39. Ibid., 210. (See M. Frank, *Das Problem 'Zeit,'* p. 28ff. for a detailed discussion of this concept of allegory.)

40. Ibid., XIX, 25, No. 227.

41. ". . . that the Romantic is not so much a genre as an element, more or less predominant, of poetry which can never be fully absent. I think it must be clear to you: that I claim all poetry should be Romantic and why I make this demand and avoid and reject the novel, in so far as it wishes to be a particular genre." (Schlegel, *KA*, II, 335.)

42. Ibid., XII, 28.

43. Ibid., XVIII, 82, No. 634.

44. Ibid., XVIII, 418, No. 1168.

45. Novalis, *Schriften*, II, 362, No. 21; Schlegel, *KA*, X, 311.

46. Novalis, *Schriften*, II, 201, No. 612.

47. Ibid., II, 273, No. 568.

48. Ibid., III, 471, No. 112.

49. Ibid., II, 664.

50. Ibid., III, 571, No. 107.

51. Ibid., III, 429–30, No. 820.

52. Ibid., II, 281, No. 626.

53. Ibid., III, 378, No. 622.

54. Ibid., III, 558, No. 16.

55. Ibid., III, 664, No. 603.

56. Ibid., II, 610, No. 401.

57. Ibid., III, 283, No. 245.

58. Ibid., III, 257, No. 92.

59. Schlegel, "Deduction des Rhythmus," in: *KA*, XI, 220.

60. Ibid.

61. Ibid., 221.

62. Ibid., 220.

63. Ludwig Tieck, *Werke*, 4 vols., ed. Marianne Thalmann (Munich: Winkler, 1963), I, pp. 870–71.

64. Tieck, *Werke*, I, p. 928. Florestan earlier questions the necessity of ending: "And why must everything have an end, . . . and especially in . . . poetry! Does one begin to play only in order to stop?" (p. 862)

65. A. W. Schlegel, *Kritische Schriften und Briefe* II, ed. Edgar Lohner (Stuttgart: Kohlhammer, 1963), p. 209.

66. Ibid., p. 207.

67. Ibid., p. 209.

68. L. Tieck, *Das Buch über Shakespeare*, ed. Henry Lüdeke (Halle: Niemeyer, 1920), pp. 117–18.

69. Ibid., p. 117.

70. L. Tieck, *Kritische Schriften* (Leipzig, 1848), I, p. 65.

71. Ibid., p. 56.

72. T. W. Adorno, *Philosophie der neuen Musik* (Frankfurt: Europäische Verlagsanstalt, 1958), p. 57; *Philosophy of Modern Music*, trans. Anne G. Mitchell and Wesley V. Blomster (New York: Seabury, 1973), p. 58.

73. Ibid.

74. Ibid., p. 57; Eng. p. 56.

75. Novalis, *Schriften*, III, 261, No. 113.

76. Ibid.

77. Wagner, *GSD*, VII, p. 130.

78. "Zu Wagners Begriff der unendlichen Melodie," in *Das Drama Richard Wagners als musikalisches Kunstwerk*, ed. Carl Dahlhaus (Regensburg: Bosse, 1970), pp. 81–103.

79. Ibid., pp. 93, 99, 103.

80. Wagner, *GSD*, IX, p. 211.

81. Ibid., p. 309.

82. Ibid.

83. Ibid., X, p. 171.

84. Ibid., p. 185; Cf. IV, pp. 202, 322.

85. Ibid., III, p. 83.

86. Ibid., pp. 86–87.

87. This self-imposed discipline of the melody occasioned one of the principal objections of the contemporary Wagner-criticism: "No repetition, not even of a single syllable, in the entire opera; uninterrupted lively, rapid, fiery, stormy progression of the drama." (From a discussion of *Lohengrin* by F. von Biedenfeld in *Europa: Chronik der gebildeten Welt*, 19 Oct. 1850). Cf. Fr. D. in the Augsburg *Allgemeine Zeitung*, 4 Sept. 1850: "This proceeds without pause until the curtain falls: no recitative, no *andante*, no *cabaletta*,

and no duet . . . ; nowhere a rest-point, movement everywhere, haste and chase, a wild energy." [Rpt. in *Situationsgeschichte der Musikkritik* . . ., ed. Helmut Kirchmeyer (Regensburg: Bosse, 1968), 3, IV, cols. 735 and 695.

88. Wagner, *GSD*, IV, p. 327.

89. Ibid., p. 328.

90. Carl Dahlhaus, *Richard Wagners Musikdramen* (Hildesheim: Friedrich, 1971), p. 104.

91. Wagner, *GSD*, VI, pp. 201f. "Since he from thee was severed/our sire no more/sent us to warfare;/undirected/rode we, an awe-stricken host . . ." *Dusk of the Gods*, trans. H. and F. Corder (New York: F. Rullman, n.d.), p. 15.

92. Wagner, *GSD*, X, pp. 360f. "Cruel one!-Ha!-/Felt e'er thy nature/ For one fellow creature,/Then feel now my desolation! . . ." *Parsifal*, trans. H. and F. Corder (London: Schott, n.d.), p. 43.

93. Dahlhaus, pp. 104–5, 151–52.

94. *The Poems of Gerard Manley Hopkins*, ed. W. H. Gardner and N. H. Mackenzie, 4th ed. (London: Oxford University Press, 1967), p. 49.

95. Schelling, *Sämtliche Werke*, I, 5, pp. 635, 637.

96. Hopkins, *Poems*, p. 46.

97. Hopkins himself gives two examples: "Hóme to his móther's hoúse *private* retúrned," and "*Bút to vánquish* by wísdom héllish wíves." (*Paradise Regained* IV, 639, and I, 175.)

98. Hopkins, *Poems*, p. 46.

99. Ibid., p. 47.

100. "As strict," Hopkins writes, "as the other rhythm." (*Letters*, II, p. 39.) [Tr. Note: The author uses a bi-lingual edition of Hopkins' correspondences. As this edition is generally unavailable in this country, I refer the reader to two volumes edited by Claude Colleer Abbott: *The Letters of Gerard Manley Hopkins to Robert Bridges* and *The Correspondence of Gerard Manley Hopkins and Richard Watson Dixon* (London: Oxford Press, rev. 1955), here abbreviated as Letters, I and II, respectively.]

101. Tr. Note: Hopkins says that the lines are "rove over." (*Poems*, p. 48.)

102. *Poems*, p. 48.

103. Cf. *Letters*, II, v; I, xxxix; II, xii.

104. *Letters*, I, xxxvii, p. 45.

105. *Letters*, II, v, p. 22.

106. Ibid.

107. As one might in the case of Arno Holz.

108. L. Tieck, *Das Buch über Shakespeare*, p. 117.

109. Wagner, *GSD*, IV, p. 322.

110. Ibid., IV, p. 202.

111. Thomas Mann, *Doktor Faustus* (Frankfort: Fischer, 1965), pp. 254–55; *Doctor Faustus*, trans. H. T. Lowe-Porter (New York: Knopf, 1948), p. 191.

112. Hopkins, *Letters*, II, ii, p. 8.

113. Hopkins, *Poems*, p. 105.

114. Tr. Note: In the fourth edition of *Poems*, "rutpeel" is printed as one word. In their notes to the poems, the editors comment, "[W.H.G.]—L. 6: construction obscure: *rutpeel* may be a compound word, MS. uncertain. [R.B.] Comparing yestertempest's, shadowtackle, footfretted and matchwood,

we are compelled to take rutpeel as a compound also" (p. 294). And in his "Forward on the Revised Text," MacKenzie comments, 'rut peel' is "now accepted as being inscaped into one word" (lxiv).

115. Sartre, *L'Idiot de la famille*, III, p. 222.

116. Sartre, *Critique de la raison dialectique* (Paris: Gallimard, 1960), p. 462 (passim).

117. Fr. Schlegel, *KA*, II, 200, No. 220.

118. Ibid., XVIII, 123, No. 76.

FIVE

THE MIXTURE OF GENRES, THE MIXTURE OF STYLES, AND FIGURAL INTERPRETATION: *SYLVIE*, BY GERARD DE NERVAL

Rodolphe Gasché

CHEMISTRY, or rather chemism, simultaneously the art of separating and mixing, became the scientific model for burgeoning Romanticism, that of Iena. It provided the model for its double project: to work out, or rather finish, a theory of literary genres; and, to conceive of their intermixing in a work where universality would proceed from its organic individuality.[1] Claiming that the two Schlegel brothers shared this task may be somewhat arbitrary. Roughly speaking, however, A. W. Schlegel did conclude a movement initiated in the sixteenth and seventeenth centuries; as an historian and literary critic he was less interested in analysing and dissecting works of art than in developing a theory of the mixing of their elements. This task consisted in erroneously founding, as G. Genette has shown, a three-genre theory based upon the poetics of Plato and Aristotle.[2] According to this plan, F. Schlegel would then be at the origin of the idea of a fusion of genres into what Jean-Luc Nancy and Philippe Lacoue-Labarthe have called the Genre or the *Absolu littéraire*.[3] My attention here is to analyse a particular case of such a mixing. But in so doing, my goal is not to show that such a fusion could again be separated into its inassimilable elements. Such a maneuver would be pointless, for the precise reason that genres have already been predetermined in the perspective of their subsequent sublation. I am interested rather in trying to determine the *particular figure* such a mixing assumes. For the uniqueness of mixing, as well as its inevitable facticity, seems to transport the work to the very edge of its individuality.

The text I will examine is Nerval's *Sylvie*. The whole of *Les Filles du feu* would of course have to be considered in order to treat the problem of genre mixing;[4] it would not suffice to deal only with this one novella whose author, by the way, was rather familiar with the German Romantics.[5] One would also have to consider the dedication *To Alexandre Dumas*; there the motif of the *unwritable* book should not only guide the reading of the ensemble, but the (Romantic) topos of the *work's absence (absence d'oeuvre)* should as well preside over any analysis of Nervalian madness, as I will try to envisage it later.[6] The novel serves as the paradigm for the mixture of genres, while the novella is at most one of its elements. If it is true that "mixture" must not be confused with a simple association of elements each conserving its unalterable property, but instead, according to its strict meaning within the field of chemistry, must lead to the production of a new chemical body with unique properties, then the novella becomes more interesting. In a letter to George Sand, Nerval will say that it is "a short novel which is not quite a tale";[7] it can thus be seen simultaneously as a part of the ensemble of *Les Filles du feu* and as a representative part of this ensemble. Even if it is difficult to consider *Sylvie* as an organic whole, it can still be analysed as the outcome of a mixing of genres by looking at a good number of distinctions which are intimately intermixed within it.

Sylvie, indeed, proves to be a mixture of old and new, of real and representation, of autobiography and fiction, of Christianity and paganism, of folk poetry and philosophy, of lyricism and drama, etc. As I have said, such a mixture is always unique and tends to inhibit the mediation between singular and universal. In trying to analyse such a mixture now, I would hope to pinpoint that which hinders this mixture from being a true synthesis (*relève*) of each of the elements combined in this chemical mixture. Beyond this, such an analysis should also invalidate not only the reassuring image of a Nerval asserting his Valois roots,[8] but also that other image, hardly more complex, of a Nerval preserving in *Sylvie* the balance between the simple charms of real life and the fascination exerted by the dream. This balance is not upset by what some call Nerval's madness. What does upset this balance (and here madness does have a goodly share) is rather on the order of the supplement, without which the image of such a world, of such a wholeness, could not be born.

The double determination of burgeoning Romanticism as I exemplified it through the two Schlegel brothers is considerably complicated by the fact that the individual and organic unity aimed for by genre mixing is always thought of as being in excess with relation to literature, as its beyond. Now the construction of such a work is seen as something like the complex return of an essential Classicity.[9] It is a complex

Rodolphe Gasché

return, for if it is true that the novel as a mixed poem finds its partner in the Greek *epos*, the Romantic return nevertheless cannot be confused with a return to a natural past situation. Indeed, even by rigorously separating the genres (separating the philosophic from the poetic), such a natural situation could not possibly return.[10] For Romanticism the continuous history of art is fulfilled and completed. But this completion was to issue forth into a totally different art, into an art which would itself necessarily recognize its essence; this is what Hegel expected from philosophical reflection.[11] Yet, even so, this completion is never concluded and will continue to give rise to works of art as a result of that completed art. Thus two similar movements occur. On the one hand, Hegel detected a return to symbolism in art by determining, in the *Aesthetics*, the transitory form characterizing the end of Romanticism as a *"Vereinigung in dem Gegenstande."*[12] The ancient Persians and Arabs excelled in the production of this form. On the other hand, the mixture of genres, *before* poetic dissolution has completed its task, can only be conceived as a return to the original sources and archetypes (*Urbilder*) of the "first ensemble of Greek poetic art."[13] Before achieving the individual, organic and unique work which would be beyond all used past forms and figures, in truth impossible, Romanticism could neither avoid being a (regressive) return to what it conceived as poetry of nature, to a state of undifferentiated expression before any separation into genres has occurred, and ultimately to an original language where images and figures would reign supreme. A. W. Schlegel called this the "original figural quality of languages."[14] In other words, the search for the Romantic work beyond all division (and of which the novel [as *Mischgedicht*] is the model) is inseparable from its thematic project, from the uniqueness of a former figure.

But this is not yet everything. Even though the novel is created in the image of the former epic genre, it also has a privileged relationship to another genre, or rather, mode of enunciation, namely mimetic drama. As we shall see, this privileged place granted to this particular genre by the novel (because mixed), as well as by the Romantic work in its becoming, will curiously affect the expected dissolution. Hegel then sees the end of Romantic art in terms of prose and subjective virtuosity. He stresses the fact that the modern artist, because he has completely lost the immediate relation of natural interiority to given forms and figures, is necessarily the creator of mixtures which he directs as does the playwright his characters.[15] And in fact, Romanticism (F. Schlegel in particular) considered drama as the true foundation of the novel.[16] Thus, for the Romantics, only ancient drama serves as the ultimate model for the "complete work of art." But then why is there this return to a mode of mimetic representation so severely criticized by Plato in the *Republic*? In a certain way, it is the very absence of lyricism in the Romanticism of Iena which signals the answer to this query. In fact, the criterion for this total work of art resides essentially in the relationship that such a work has with itself. Now the construction of such a self-engendering work which contains its own theory can be imagined only in terms of a self-staging or self-production [*automise-en-scène*]. The relationship the Romantic work entertains with itself, its self-reflexivity (F. Schlegel's *Gespräche über die Poesie* are a beautiful example of this), is not created from a diegetic mode, but on the contrary according to a mode of mediation: the mimetic mode. It seems to me that this is the reason for Romanticism's privileging the particular genre of drama in the construction of a mixed work.

I

I will thus be concerned with two things in my reading of *Sylvie*: first, with the particular figure that the mixing of genres and styles provides in Nerval, and second, with the work of staging which must assure the text's relationship with itself. Let me begin by mentioning that, in order to work out their project for a work going beyond all generic differences, the Romantics did not rely solely on the ideal contained in the *poetry of nature*, but also on its decadent repetition manifested, for example, by the Alexandrian poets: a period of dissolution and effervescence. Thus, characterizing the "strange" period (both renovating and decadent) surrounding the tale of *Sylvie*, Nerval writes:[17]

It was an age in which activity, hesitation, and indolence were mixed up, together with dazzling Utopias, philosophies, and religious aspirations, vague enthusiams, mild ideas of a Renaissance, weariness with past struggles; insecure optimisms—somewhat like the period of Peregrinus and Apullius. (50)

(c'était un mélange d'activité, d'hésitation et de paresse, d'utopies brillantes, d'aspirations philosophiques ou religieuses, d'enthousiasmes vagues, mêlés de certains instincts de renaissance; d'ennui des discordes passées, d'espoirs incertains, quelque chose comme l'époque de Pérégrinus et d'Apulée.) (242)

And as one might expect after such a description, the action in *Sylvie* starts where the narrator—whom I shall call Nerval simply for convenience sake—during an outing at the theater, evokes his love for a star named Aurélia. If the space of *Sylvie* opens with this theatrical outing, it is because the narrative unfolds in a theatrical space. I will clarify the different scenes and the scenic levels of this space. In fact, already with the second chapter, "Adrienne," it is discovered that this love for an actress and the repeated frequentation of a theater are the function of a memory, of a forgotten scene from childhood. The fact that this memory is "half-dreamed," (53) "represented" (53) in a state of "half-sleep," (53) only increases its *tableau*-like quality. Here is the memory itself: a large square of green in the courtyard of a castle where

Adrienne, "the grandchild of one of the descendants of a family related to the ancient kings of France," (54) in a voice imitating the "quavering tones of ancestors," (54) sings an old ballad to her listeners, believing themselves "in paradise," (54) while the light from the rising moon was falling on her alone, "isolated . . . (from) our attentive circle." (54) The description has all the attributes of a theatrical stage (*scène*). When Nerval finally places a crown of "glistening leaves" on Adrienne's head, and then compares her to Dante's Beatrice, this early scene increasingly appears as the image of a literary scenario, of which it is the representation.

Articulating a double memory—on the one hand of Genre and of generics, and on the other, of the irruption of the difference in genres—the invocation of a celebration where social and temporal differences are abolished ("for this one day of festival she had been allowed to mix in our games" [54] and "the young voices . . . imitate . . . the quavering tones of ancestors," [54]), no doubt has a sense of reconciliation of differences in view. But, at the same time, this scene represents the origin of differences, and primarily, that of sexual difference. Indeed, when Adrienne and Nerval exchange a kiss, "an inexplicable confusion" takes hold of him. With this difference also emerges the "*double image*" between the ideal woman, the nun, and the real woman, Sylvie, between "Death—or the Dead Woman," as Nerval will say in *Artémis*, and life, but also between social classes, places (city and country) and times (past and present).

Through this dual determination as a scene of reconciliation and of opening to all differences, this scene functions as the matrix for the play on the same and the other, on identity and difference, on the innumerable doubles which haunt this narrative.

Additional features of this original scene, or rather those relating to the textual matrix, can be gleaned from the other chapters of *Sylvie* concerning Adrienne. The ruins of the Abbey of Châalis, which, as Nerval tells us in *Angélique*, are situated above graves,[18] and where, he says in Sylvie, "you (still) breathe a perfume of the Renaissance" (66) as well as "an air of pagan allegory," (66) set the background in chapter VII for the "countryside's solemnity." Having traversed the woods on "unfrequented roads," (66) their pony flying "as if to some witches' Sabbath," Nerval and Sylvie's brother enter on St. Bartholomew's Eve into this "private festival" where "a sort of allegorical representation, in which some of the pupils of the neighboring convent are to participate," will take place. The play is thus performed during a celebration which is somewhat different from the Rousseauist and popular celebration common in Nerval. Our characters watch it in a no less allegorical setting. It is "a mystery play of ancient times" on the destruction of the world and spiritual rebirth. Now, the spirit armed with a flaming sword (the angel of death) who, after the destruction of the world rises up from the abyss to sing the glory of Christ, vanquisher of hell, is none other than Adrienne. Her family had devoted her to a religious life, and she now is reborn doubly transfigured through her costume and vocation. Thus, Adrienne, whose apparition is always dependent on the existence of a scene or stage, on a theatrical system, is transfigured, here among the ruins constructed above funerary monuments, into a pure spirit, an ideal woman. The original scene, therefore, is the place where one is put to death (burial in a convent, allegorical destruction of the world, etc.). The real character is put to death in order to allow her rebirth as an ideal. Before trying to answer the question of the relationship between this double operation of the scene and of the allegory, recall that Nerval, while retracing the details of this memory, wonders if they are actually real, or if he dreamed them. Necessarily, this scene thus takes on an ideal quality. And so does everything which comes from the matrix I have been trying to elucidate. In fact, everything that Nerval now uses to prove the truth of the event in question is but another memory of an allegorical nature:

Sylvie's brother was a little drunk that evening. For a while we stopped at the keeper's house where I was greatly struck to see a swan with spread wings displayed above the door, and inside some tall cupboards of carved walnut, a large clock in its case, and trophies of bows and arrows of honor . . . But it the apparition of Adrienne as real as these details, as real as the indisputable existence of the Abbey of Châalis? Yet I am certain it was the keeper's son who took us into the hall where the play took place. (67)

(Le frère de Sylvie était up peu gris ce soir-là. Nous nous étions arrêtés quelques instants dans la maison du garde, où, ce qui m'a frappé beaucoup, il y avait un cygne éployé sur la porte, puis, au dedans, de hautes armoires en noyer sculpté, une grande horloge dans sa gaine, et des trophées d'arcs et de flèches d'honneur . . . Mais l'apparition d'Adrienne est-elle aussi vraie que ces détails et que l'existence incontestable de l'abbaye de Châalis? Pourtant c'est bien le fils du garde qui nous avait introduit dans la salle où avait lieu la repésentation.) (257–58)

Although this setting (anticipating the allegory) combined with the image of the flying swan tends to throw a cloud of doubt over the real existence of Adrienne, the spiritual meaning of the allegory is no less exact. "Perhaps this memory is an obsession!" (68) Nerval explains, indicating that Adrienne may very well have been absent from the scene. But this absence guarantees all the better the spiritual meaning of the allegory. For this mechanism of putting to death in order to be reborn as idea clearly demonstrates that the spiritual meaning of the allegory is a function of the ruin of the original. In order to better illustrate this aspect of the scene, I would like to analyse the beginning of chapter V entitled "The Village."

During the festival, one evening after bringing Sylvie back to her village, Nerval wanders off into the forest where the scene becomes a sort of prehistoric landscape badly illuminated by the moon which hides the clouds from time to time. Nerval falls into a slumber in this landscape of "Druidical rocks" "which still hold the memory of the sons of Armen whom the Romans put to death." He is in the near vicinity of the convent of Saint-S . . . where he believes Adrienne to be, (60) and has a dream which was eliminated from the final version of the tale. Where there is now just a simple dash, one formerly read the following:

Two beloved figures were battling in my mind: the one seemed to come down from the stars, the other to rise from the earth. The latter was saying, "I am simple and fresh as the flower from the fields," the other, "I am noble and pure like the immortal beauties conceived in the bosom of God."

(Deux figures aimées se combattaient dans mon esprit: l'une semblait descendre des étoiles et l'autre monter de la terre. La dernière disait; Je suis simple et fraîche comme les fleurs des champs; l'autre: Je suis noble et pure comme les beautés immortelles conçues dans le sein de Dieu.)[19]

Finally, when he awakens, this landscape which retained him during the night by triggering a distant past (Nerval, from the sublime height represented by the Druidical boulders, is unable to distinguish the pond where he had met Sylvie. the previous night), fully reveals its allegorical nature:

When I woke up, I gradually recognized the points near the spot where I had lost my way in the night. To my left, I saw the long line of the walls of the convent of Saint-S . . . , the Gens d'Armes hills, with the shattered ruins of the old Carolingian palace. Near it, above the tops of the trees, the tall ruins of the Abbey of Thiers outlined against the horizon its broken walls pierced with trefoils and ogives. Further on, the manorhouse of Pontarmé, still surrounded by its moat, began to reflect the first light of day, while to the south the tall keep of La Tournelle and the four towers of Bertrand-Fosse rose up on the first slopes of Montméliant. (60)

(En me réveillant, je reconnus peu à peu les points voisins du lieu où je m'étais égaré dans la nuit. A ma gauche, je vis se dessiner la longue ligne des murs du convent de Saint-S . . . , puis de l'autre côté de la vallée la butte aux Gens-d'Armes, avec les ruines ébréchées de l'antique résidence carlovingienne. Près de là, au-dessus des toffes de bois, les hautes masures de l'abbaye de Thiers découpaient sur l'horizon leurs pans de muraille percés de trèfles et d'ogives. Au delà, le manoir gothique de Pontarmé, entouré d'eau comme autrefois, refléta bientôt les premiers feux du jour, tandis qu'on voyait se dresser au midi le haut donjon de la Tournelle et les quatre tours de Bertrand-Foss sur les premiers coteaux de Montméliant.) (251)

The convent of Saint-S . . . which dominates this semiimaginary geography, and which Nerval believed for an instant to be "the one where Adrienne was," (60) is situated in a mnemonic landscape whose traces bear witness to an irremediably lost past. The convent where Nerval presumes Adrienne to be, because of the nearby megalithic tombs, is a crypt for the ideal which does not lack the cadaver of the ideal. This is what we learn in the last lines of the narrative from Sylvie:

Poor Adrienne! She died in the convent of Saint-S . . . about 1832. (85)

(Pauvre Adrienne! elle est morte au couvent de Saint-S . . . , vers 1832.) (273)

Let me thus clarify the nature of this scenic mechanism. It doesn't only demand the death of the original in order to prepare its resurrection as an ideal; the ideal itself is perceived as irretrievable. It belongs incontestably to the past. This means at least two things: the scenic matrix does not only assure the repeatability of the ideal through the death of the original, but is also constitutive of the allegory through the ruin of this same ideal. Now, this *double death*, being the condition of possibility of the allegorical meaning, cannot exist without a *third death* which destroys the allegorical meaning itself. This is confirmed in chapter VI, entitled "Othys."

This chapter relating the early morning visit by Sylvie and Nerval to her great-aunt is a veritable return to sources. Sylvie and Nerval, first of all, follow the Thève, "narrowing as it nears its source." (62) Secondly, the aunt's home itself becomes, through the fire which Sylvie carries with her, the place for a reconciliation of elements.[20] She thus declares her love for the little Parisian here. This return to the origin is at first a search for models, in this case models of lace. Sylvie: "Oh, yes, Aunt . . . if you have any old pieces, I could use them as patterns." (63) (Ah! oui, la tante! . . . Dites donc, si vous en avez des morceaux de l'ancienne, cela me fera des modèles.) (254)

Quickly going up the stairs which lead to the aunt's bedroom, Sylvie and Nerval enter into a veritable sanctuary of memories from days past:

In an oval gilt frame, hung at the head of the rustic bed, the portrait of a young man of the good old times smiled . . . his young bride, who could be seen from another medallion, attractive and mischievous-looking, lissom in her open corset laced with ribbons . . . (64)

(Le portrait d'un jeune homme du bon vieux temps souriait . . . dans un ovale au cadre doré, suspendu à la tête du lit rustique . . . sa jeune épouse, qu'on voyait dans un autre médaillon, attrayante, maligne, élancée dans son corsage ouvert à échelle de rubans . . .) (254)

In this sanctuary the two lovers find the earlier model for first love in the form of a *double image*. Now with this discovery the idyllic reconciliation and return to origins start to take on a fantastic (*funambulesque*) quality. Indeed, this love to which the aunt has remained faithful makes her seem like "the Funambules fairies who put wrinkled masks over their own charming faces, which they uncover at the end of the piece when the Temple of Love appears with its whirling sun shining with magic fires." (64) Modeling themselves after this first love, Sylvie and

Nerval themselves will not be able to escape the logic of representation, nor the loss of origin it implies. The transformation of the original model into a lowly street-play, certainly not lacking in charm, begins as soon as Sylvie and Nerval begin slipping on the wedding clothes of the aunt and her defunct husband. In the image of this couple from the past, in the image of the *double image*, they are transformed into the image of eternal youth which the old aunt's wrinkled mask hides. Doubles then appear in this *tableau vivant*, Sylvie being the same as the other, as the aunt, and, of course, conversely. The two lovers thus seem to challenge old age, death and the aunt's evocation of passing time. Now this synthesis of past and present, which, as theatrical synthesis, allows for the play of the same and the other, requires the death of the original in the double way I have shown. But it does so in an even more dramatic way than I have been able to demonstrate until now. When Nerval compares the production (through repetition) of the original model to a pictorial model, a painting by Greuze, the earlier model is consequently radically affected. Similarly, when their meal is transformed into a simulated wedding feast (Sylvie and Nerval become "bride and bridegroom for a whole summer morning" [66]) through the repetition of the naive wedding song of yesteryear, this scene is not the simple actualization of the aunt's memories. Instead, these memories mediating the love between Sylvie and Nerval are eclipsed, as if by the shadow of death, when the nuptial song, flowery and loving, is compared to the "Song of Songs" from Ecclesiastes. But isn't it the enormous bouquet of digitalis offered by Sylvie to her aunt which all the more eerily shrouds this scene, in that it announces the approaching death of the aunt? Although no repetition of an original model is possible in such a death, this tragic side of the tale does not hinder the repetition from taking on a carnavalesque appearance. On the contrary, when we learn of the aunt's death in chapter X, Nerval discovers what has happened to the wedding clothes of the old aunt:

"Ah! Dear Aunty," says Sylvie, "she lent me the dress for the dance at Dammartin carnival two years ago. Poor Aunt, the next year she died!"

She sighed and wept so that I could not ask her how she happened to go to a fancy-dress ball . . . (75)

("Ah! la bonne tante, dit Sylvie, elle m'avait prêté sa robe pour aller danser au carnaval à Dammartin, il y a de cela deux ans. L'année d'après, elle est morte, la pauvre tante!"

Elle soupirait et pleurait, si bien que je ne pus lui demander par quelle circonstance elle était allée à un bal masqué . . .) (264)

So the scene of a return to the origins, a return and repetition which are not accomplished without the death of that to which one returns, through the grotesque nature which they cannot avoid assuming, also represents the ruin of the eventual meaning of such an operation.

The matrix I have tried to construct out of this memory concerning Adrienne is thus a scenic mechanism. This process of allowing allegorical meaning, and I would add, meaning itself, simultaneously invalidates it because it transforms its operation into a sort of theatrical farce, one not devoid of charm, be it tragic or not, but farce nonetheless. The mechanism in question is thus to be understood as insuring its own exposition (*mise-en-scène*), or rather its own mockery, a reflexive operation by which the *output* of the matrix is disappropriated, incomplete and unaccomplished. This machine, as we have seen, not only engenders difference, but also organizes the whole play between the same and the other which haunts our narrative. Let me now go on to the analysis of these effects.

II

It is in a semidream state that Nerval finds "the memory of Adrienne, a flower of the night efflorescent in the moon's glimmer, flesh-colored and fair phantom gliding over the green grasses half-bathed in white vapors." (55) It resembles a "pencil drawing blurred by time that had been converted into a picture, like those old sketches of the masters you admire in some museum and then you find, somewhere else, the dazzling original." (55) It can be seen to represent the bud, as Nerval says, of this love for a woman of the theater which overcame him every evening during the performance. Thus, the image-bud, the figure which cannot be born without the death of the original, engenders a new original which comes after, and which is derivative of the former image. Being no more than a blurred drawing or sketch in relation to a stunning original to come, the image of Adrienne engenders the original of Aurélia. For her, Nerval appears every evening "in the proscenium boxes in the role of an ardent wooer." (49) The apparition of this theatrical star illuminates the empty space of the stage and gives life to a performance in a theater where Nerval himself, in the role of the suitor, lines up with the actors. "In her I felt myself alive, and she seemed to live for me alone." (49) Now, Aurélia, her natural beauty and the life she incarnates are but a function of the stage lights and of the artificial light of the chandelier. With all of its properties, the stage serves as a "magic mirror" which beautifies and idealizes what it reflects. But the memory of Adrienne reveals to Nerval that Aurélia is but a derived original of the image-bud, and that she is thus, as he was able to say of himself, but "a living tomb." The ideal of Aurélia is not only its own tomb; to the image of Adrienne it is also the crypt of this latter, as dead. This inspires Nerval with the following thought:

To love a nun in the form of an actress! . . . but what if they were one and the same!— (55)

Aimer une religieuse sous la forme d'une actrice! . . . et si c'était la même!—
(247)

Indeed, if the ideal is *per se* exchangeable (contrary to the real
woman), the substitution of an actress for a nun would imply that
the difference between the same and the other is without difference.
Because of the repetition without difference, the actress could well be
the same as the nun. But didn't we see that the function of the matrix
was to make possible the repetition of the same by the simultaneous
production of the differential other? If the other is the same, where
then is the difference? Before picking up on this question a bit later,
let me continue the analysis of this original which is the substitute for
an "empty image," (69) for an early image which Nerval pursues.

In chapter XIII Nerval returns to Paris and runs to the theater to
succumb, once again, to the charms of his actress. He abruptly leaves
Paris for Germany to "try and get (his) feelings into order." For this,
he undertakes "to put into poetic action the love of the painter Colonna
for the fair Laura, whom her parents made a nun, and whom he loved
until death." (81) This scenario is to put the theatrical ideal into a
play to be performed in "the purgatorial space" theater represents for
Nerval. Aurélia accepts the starring role in this play. At this moment
Nerval lets it be known that he was the stranger who sent her the
adulatory letters. The test fails, for Adrienne isn't the same as the nun,
and she does not recognize Nerval as being the little Parisian of before.
When another chance comes he makes another effort to clarify his love
for Aurélia, and once again in juxtaposing several scenes, Nerval suffers defeat one more time. When Nerval convinces the company he is
accompanying as "gentleman poet" to give a performance in Senlis and
Dammartin, Nerval tries yet once again to verify that the actress and
the nun are one and the same (and, I might add, to reassure himself
that he is also one and the same).

I had planned to take Aurélia to the château near Orry to the same square of
green where for the first time I saw Adrienne. —She showed no emotion. (82)

(J'avais projeté de conduire Aurélie au château, près d'Orry, sur la même
place verte où pour la première fois j'avais vu Adrienne. Nulle émotion ne
parut en elle.) (271)

Since Aurélia didn't seem to recognize the area, Nerval reveals his plan
to her, and the actress clearly admits that she is not the same person.

You expect me to say, "The actress is the same person as the nun; you are
simply looking for drama, that's all, and the end eludes you." (83)

(Vous attendez que je vous dise: "La comédienne est la même qua la
religieuse; vous cherchez un drame, voilà tout, et le dénoûement vous
échappe.)" (271)

That evening Nerval notices that Aurélia has a liking for the stage-manager. It is then that he must accept the fact that his love is for another, that she is not the same, just as the one that Aurélia loves is other than he. Thus, this scenario in the image of the memory of Adrienne, instead of engendering the same, only produces the other. Instead of insuring a repetition without difference, it creates difference. It gives birth to the other in the scenario of the same.

The day Aurélia performs at Dammartin, Nerval brings Sylvie to the performance. Sylvie has met Adrienne, and Nerval encourages her to tell him

if she did not think the actress like someone she knew.
"Whom do you mean?"
"Do you remember Adrienne?"
She burst out laughing and said, "What an idea!" Then, as if reproving herself, she sighed and added, "Poor Adrienne! She died in the convent of Saint-S . . . about 1832." (85)

(si elle ne trouvait pas que l'actrice ressemblait à une personne qu'elle avait connue déjà. "A qui donc?—Vous souvenez-vous d'Adrienne?"
Elle partit d'un grand éclat de rire en disant: "Quelle idée!" Puis, comme se le reprochant, elle reprit en soupirant: "Pauvre Adrienne! elle est morte au couvent de Saint-S . . . , vers 1832.") (273)

Thus the hope that another, here Sylvie, would recognize Aurélia as being the same fails and seems to put an end to any chance for a possible identity. Sylvie's burst of laughter implies that Aurélia cannot be the same person. With this failure, will the narrative then open up into what is called the recognition of the other and of the real? Far from that, because the very death of the model will keep the narrative within the framework of the specular of the same and the other, within the framework of a difference *of* the same.

III

Thus leaving this theater where he appeared every evening, Nerval does not get back to reality. On the contrary, he joins a circle of friends from whom he also departs, but first by way of a reading room. Mechanically leafing through a paper, he discovers that on that very day the *Fête du Bouquet provincial* was taking place in Senlis. This bit of news awakens in him the memory of a childhood scene: the performance of a provincial festival which is but the repetition "from age to age of a Druid festival that had survived the new monarchies and novel religions." (53) This final memory leads to the memory of Adrienne, which makes him realize that he loved a nun in the form of an actress. "But let us get back to reality," as Nerval says.

Rodolphe Gasché

Why have I for three years forgotten Sylvie, whom I loved so much? . . . (55)
She is waiting for me. Who would marry Sylvie? She is so poor! (56)

(Et Sylvie que j'aimais tant, pourquoi l'ai-je oubliée depuis trois ans . . .
Elle m'attend encore . . . Qui l'aurait épousée? elle est si pauvre!) (247)

Parenthesizing his love for Aurélia, who is but the derived original of
an earlier image and who is part of a series of substitutions, Nerval
turns toward the other one he had forgotten and who probably must
have remained the same. Not being the original in a chain of substitutions, Sylvie is to be unique and should not have changed. Yet, if she
remained the same, she remained identical with herself. Thus at the
outset this presumed identity equally opens into the logic of substitutions so that the question will not only concern whether she has been
able to stay the same, but also whether she ever was identical to herself.
Adrienne and the actress are a pair, but they are principally the same,
while Sylvie who is unique constitutes a pair when she differs from
herself.

What is she doing at this moment? Is she asleep? . . . No, she is not asleep;
today is the festival of the bow, the only celebration of the year when you
dance all night. —She's there . . .
      What time is it?
      I had no watch. (56)

(A cette heure, que fait-elle? Elle dort . . . Non, elle ne dort pas; c'est
aujourd'hui la fête de l'arc, la seule de l'année où l'on danse toute la nuit.
—Elle est à la fête . . .
      Quelle heure est-il?
      Je n'avais pas de montre.) (247)

Musing about Sylvie has stopped time. She has become a nocturnal figure
during a festival which could well be the same festival where he met
Adrienne. Now, the attribute *nocturnal* is typical of the latter. But
Sylvie's identity is problematized with "A Voyage to Cythèra" where
Nerval continues his narrative of memories about Sylvie.

Some years had gone by. The time when I had met Adrienne in front of the
château was already only a memory from childhood. I was at Loisy again,
at the time of the annual festival. (57)

(Quelques années s'étaient écoulées: l'époque où j'avais rencontré Adrienne
devant le château n'était plus déjà qu'un souvenir d'enfance. Je me retrouvai
à Loisy au moment de la fête patronale.) (248)

Skipping several years, Nerval comes to another festival which, if not
the same as the other, closely resembles it. It is this resemblance which
will lead to a progressive transformation of the different into the same.

The festival culminates in a meal given on a shady island in the middle of a pond. The island contains an oval-shaped temple built at the end of the eighteenth century, originally dedicated to Urania. This modern renovated ruin was to serve as the banqueting hall, as such conceived in the image of a painting, for "perhaps the crossing of the lake had been devised in order to recall Watteau's *Voyage à Cythère*." It is this resemblance which begins the blurring betwen the same and the other, between Sylvie and Adrienne.

Let me first recall that, in the coach which takes him to Loisy, Nerval, on Flanders road, remembers "a path lined with apple trees whose blossoms (he has) often seen burst in the night like stars of the earth." (57) These stars of earth correspond, in fact, to those which, occurring in the dream cut from chapter V, designated Sylvie. The celestial star was Adrienne. These two stars can be superimposed on the two Venuses, the Venus Urania and the Venus Pandemos which, as Poulet has shown, structure our narrative.[21] If there is a connection between Sylvie, the star of the earth, and Aphrodite Pandemos, what is she doing in a temple dedicated to Urania, to the celestial star, to Adrienne, and in addition placed in the atmosphere of a painting perhaps conceived from *Poliphilos' Dream* by Francesco Colonna and evoking the voyage to the Orient? Why would she be in this temple if not to be transformed into the other, and to be marked with celestial attributes?

All the boats reached land. The flower basket, ceremoniously carried, occupied the center of the table and everybody sat down, the most favored men next to the girls . . . That was why I found myself next to Sylvie . . .

A surprise had been arranged by those who had organized the festival. At the end of the meal we saw a wild swan which had been held captive under the flowers until then fly up from the depths of the huge basket. With its strong wings it lifted up a tangle of garlands and crowns of flowers, finally dispersing them on all sides. While the bird flew joyfully into the last gleams of the sun, we caught the flower-crowns at random and each man instantly decorated the brow of the girl beside him. I was lucky enough to get one of the finest and, smiling, Sylvie this time allowed me to kiss her more tenderly than before. I understood that I had erased the memory of another occasion. (59)

(Toutes les barques abordèrent en peu de temps. La corbeille portée en cérémonie occupa le centre de la table, et chacun prit place, les plus favorisés auprès des jeunes filles . . . Ce fut la cause qui fit que je me retrouvai près de Sylvie. . .

Une surprise avait été arrangée par les ordonnateurs de la fête. A la fin du repas, on vit s'envoler du fond de la vaste corbeille un cygne sauvage, jusque-là captif sous les fleurs, qui, de ses fortes ailes, soulevant le lacis de guirlandes et de couronnes, finit par les disperser de tous côtés. Pendant qu'il s'élançait joyeux vers les dernières lueurs du soleil, nous rattrapions au hasard les couronnes dont chacun parait aussitôt le front de sa voisine.

Rodolphe Gasché

J'eus le bonheur de saisir une des plus belles, et Sylvie, souriante, se laissa
embrasser cette fois plus tendrement que l'autre. Je compris que j'effaçais
ainsi le souvenir d'un autre temps.) (249–50)

Captive under the flowers of the earth up to that point, Sylvie, in this
temple consecrated to the celestial Venus, like the swan, bounds off
toward the last gleams of the setting sun. The crown on Sylvie's head
achieves her renaissance as a celestial star. Thus transformed into the
other, into Adrienne, she evidently appears completely different to
Nerval:

My admiration for her at this moment was undivided, she had become so
beautiful! She was no longer the little village girl I had scorned for someone
older and more schooled in the graces of society. Everything about her had
improved . . . her smile had something Athenian about it as it suddenly
illumined her irregular and placid features. I admired this countenance,
worthy of antique art in the midst of the irregular baby-faces of her companions. Her delicately tapering hands, her arms which had grown whiter as
they rounded, her lithe figure, all made her quite another creature from the
girl I had seen before. I could not resist telling her how different from herself
I found her. (59)

(Je l'admirai cette fois sans partage, elle était devenue si belle! Ce n'était
plus cette petite fille de village que j'avais dédaignée pour une plus grande
et plus faite aux grâces du monde. Tout en elle avait gagné . . . son sourire,
éclairant tout à coup des traits réguliers et placides, avait quelquechose
d'athénien. J'admirais cette physiognomie de l'art antique au milieu des
minois chiffonées de ses compagnes. Ses mains délicatement allongées, ses
bras qui avaient blanchi en s'arrondissant, sa taille dégagée, la faisaient tout
autre que je ne l'avais vue. Je ne pus m'empêcher de lui dire combien je la
trouvais différente d'elle-même . . .) (250)

Crowned as Adrienne had been before, reborn after having forgotten her
celestial features, the star of the earth, different from herself, starts to
resemble the celestial star. Transformed into an ancient ideal, and thus
belonging, like Adrienne, to ancient families, the indescribable Athenian
qualities which characterized her brings Sylvie even closer to that urban
quality which Aurélia represents; it completes the process which separated her socially from her companions. Thus, in order to be reborn
from forgetfulness, Sylvie will have to die one more time in order to
become another, different from herself. Different from herself she is
the same, the same as the other.

IV

But Sylvie is not only *not* herself, she differs as well from herself
in that she is *no longer* the same.

Nerval escapes this dreamlike world which had thrust him into
the world of memories representing this ancient mystery play at the

Abbey of Châalis. Upon reaching Loisy "on unfrequented roads," he again finds Sylvie at the ball, Sylvie whom he had not seen for years. Driving her back at the dawn of a gloomy day, he learns that she has changed, that she is *no longer* the same person. That, evidently, abruptly halts all repetition.

Do you remember the day we put on my aunt's wedding clothes? . . . The illustrations in the book (*La Nouvelle Héloïse*, R. G.) also showed lovers in old prints of yesteryear, so that for me you were Saint-Preux, and I saw myself in Julie. Ah! Why didn't you come back to me then? (69)

(Vous souvenez-vous du jour où nous avons revêtu les habits de noces de la tante? . . . Les gravures du livre présentaient aussi les amoureux sous de vieux estampes du temps passé, de sorte que pour moi vous étiez Saint-Preux, et je me retrouvais dans Julie. Ah, que n'êtes-vous revenue alors!) (259)

The image which Sylvie once had of herself as well as of her little Parisian no longer coincides with the present. In reproaching Sylvie for not realizing she is an ancient nymph, Nerval thus recognizes that she is no longer the same as his memory had retained her. If and only if she had resembled this other would she have remained the same. Now, the thing which kept Sylvie from coinciding with that other was precisely the "empty image" of this "fatal spectre" which misled Nerval. One side of the *double image* hinders the other from coinciding with itself. One part of this image always contaminates the process of identity with the other.

Here is the moment to discuss what Poulet (and others) have understood to be the "essential identity" of these two images, of the *double image*.[22] Nerval, in the last chapter of *Sylvie*, announces:

Ermononville! . . . You have lost your love stars which shone for me with a double light. Now blue, now rose-colored like the deceptive star of Aldebaran, it was Adrienne or Sylvie—two halves of a single love. One was the sublime ideal, the other the sweet reality. (83)

(Ermononville! . . . tu as perdu ta seule étoile, qui chatoyait pour moi d'un double éclat. Tout à tour bleue et rose comme l'astre trompeur d'Aldébaran, c'était Adrienne ou Sylvie,—c'étaient les deux moitiés d'un seul amour. L'une était l'idéal sublime, l'autre la douce réalité.) (272)

One would of course be tempted to apply Freud's development concerning love life to this double image of one love.[23] But how could this simulacrum of antiquity, this place of doubling and repetition which for Nerval is Valois—"land where the ancient Idylls still flower,—translated once again from Gessner!"—how could it still be under the sign of one star's resistance to splitting? Or rather, how could this *double image*, in this place of repetition, ever have been *one*? All the more so since this double image is not symmetrical? One image, that of Adrienne, always prevails over the other. One image of this *double image* is in fact eccentric with respect to the structure of doubling representative of the two halves of the same love. The image of Adrienne, as we have seen, is at the origin of *the* difference, and consequently, of the *double image* itself. It is this image which sets off the entire play on the same and the other, on identity and its loss which we just saw. In other words, the scenic mechanism tied only to Adrienne's name is in excess with relationship to the specular totality of the same and the other which it engenders and which at the same time makes it impossible.

Let us return again to Nerval's attempts to get Sylvie to accept the image he has of her:

"Save me!" I concluded, "I am coming back to you for ever."
She looked at me tenderly . . .
At that moment our conversation was interrupted by violent shouts of laughter. (70)

("Sauvez-moi!" ajoutai-je, "je reviens à vous pour toujours."
Elle tourna vers moi ses regards attendris . . .
En ce moment, notre entretien fut interrompu par de violents éclats de rire.) (259)

If this attempt fails (and notice that Nerval will not have the same change again), it is because of the violent laughter of Sylvie's brother (is it the Sylvain of chapter XIII, i.e. Sylvie's other?). It is he who brings the gallant to the ball, this latter being none other, we learn later, than Nerval's foster brother, his double, in short, the other. The other (but which other, then?) interrupts, through the violence of a laugh, any assimilation of Sylvie to her own image, which is that of the other. Just as Sylvie will interrupt through her outburst of laughter any possible identity between Adrienne and Aurélia, between the other and *herself*, this outburst closes all repetition, all return. This has multiple consequences. For them, let us read chapter XI entitled "Return."

The preceding chapter, "Big Curly," had already insisted on the fact that Sylvie was no longer the same. Her room has changed, she has become a glove maker, etc. The chapter "Return" continues this problematic by showing that Sylvie no longer reads Rousseau (she reads Walter Scott now), and does not read the landscape as a function of the past and of her childhood. Thus, the landscape is no longer the same. Upon reaching the ruins of Châalis, Nerval leads Sylvie into the room of the château where he had heard Adrienne sing:

"Oh, do let me hear you!" I said to her, "Let your dear voice echo beneath these roofs and drive away the spirit that torments me, whether it be from heaven or from hell!"
She repeated the words and the song after me . . .
"It's very sad," she said. (76)

("Oh! que je vous entende!" lui dis-je; "que votre voix chérie résonne sous ces voûtes et en chasse l'esprit qui me tourmente, fût-il divin ou bien fatal!—

Elle répéta les paroles et le chant après moi . . . —C'est bien triste!" me dit-elle. . . .") (265)

Without echo, this repetition reveals that the return to the place of the fantasm is but the very impossibility of return. In fact, the ruins, as memory traces of the landscape, have stopped signifying, and Nerval meets only empty signs, ruins of signs, or what I have called the ruin of allegory. The crisis in question dates at least from the visit to the uncle's house at Montagny. It begins with the chapter entitled "Ermononville."

Everything seemed to be in the same state as of old; only, I had to go to the farmer's house to get the key of the front door. (70)

(Tout semblait dans le même état qu'autrefois; seulement il fallut aller chez le fermier pour avoir la clef de la porte.) (260)

Once he has finished the visit to the house, a house whose interior now only points to a past without power over the present, Nerval feels the need "to see Sylvie again, the only living and still youthful face that linked me to the district." (71) Sylvie, however, since she is no longer the same, is not able to give a supplemental meaning to these ruins of the past.

This impossibility of giving the past meaning, of making it signify, will set off a crisis of recognition.[24] The crisis becomes unavoidable with the erasure of nature's signs:

For a moment I was nearly lost, for the sign-posts marking the different roads in various places had lost their lettering. (71)

(Un instant je risquai de me perdre, car les poteaux dont les palettes annoncent diverses routes n'offrent plus, par endroits, que des caractères effacés.) (261)

In broad daylight, this once familiar countryside becomes unrecognizable. Returning, because of the disappearance of the marks and characters of writing, to this former unsocial nature, Nerval runs the risk of losing himself in this landscape. What is upsetting here is that the loss of the possibility of repeating an identical trace leads not only to the ruin of any possible meaning, but even to the ruin of any possible recognition.

Finally, leaving the "Desert" to my left, I arrived at the dancing-ring, . . . All the memories of philosophical antiquity, revived by the former owner of the estate, crowded back on me at the sight of this picturesque realization of *Anacharsis* and *Emile*.

When I saw the water of the lake glittering . . . I . . . recognized . . . the "Temple of Philosophy" which its originator had not been fortunate enough to finish . . . This unfinished building is already no more than a ruin, with ivy gracefully festooning it, and the brambles invading its broken steps. As a child I had seen there those festivals at which girls dressed in

white came to receive prizes for study and good conduct . . . Fortunately
the privet of Virgil still flourishes, as if to support the master's words inscribed above the door: *Rerum cognoscere causas!* . . . Here are the island
poplars and the tomb of Rousseau, empty of his ashes. Oh wise man! You gave
us the milk of the strong and we were too weak to profit from it. We have
forgotten your lessons, which our fathers knew, and we have lost the meaning of your words, the last echo of the ancient wisdom. But do not let us
despair and, as you did in your last moment, let us turn our eyes to the
sun. (71–72)

(Enfin, laissant le *Désert* à gauche, j'arrivai au rond-point de la danse, . . .
Tous les souvenirs de l'antiquité philosophique, ressuscités par l'ancien pos-
sesseur du domaine, me revenaient en foule devant cette réalisation pit-
toresque de l'*Anacharsis* et de l'*Emile*.

Lorsque je vis briller les eaux du lac . . . je reconnus . . . le *Temple de la
philosophie,* que son fondateur n'a pas eu le bonheur de terminer. . . . Cet
édifice inachevé n'est déjà plus qu'une ruine, le lierre le festonne avec grâce,
la ronce envahit les marches disjointes. Là, tout enfant, j'ai vu des fêtes ou
les jeunes filles vêtues de blanc venaient recevoir des prix d'étude et de
sagesse . . . Heureusement le troème de Virgile fleurit encore, comme pour
appuyer la parole du maître inscrite au-dessus de la porte: *Rerum cognoscere
causas!* . . .

Voici les peupliers de l'île, et la tombe de Rousseau, vide de ses cendres.
O sage! tu nous avais donné le lait des forts et nous étions trop faibles pour
qu'il pût nous profiter. Nous avons oublié les leçons que savaient nos pères,
et nous avons perdu le sens de ta parole, dernier écho des sagesses antiques.
Pourtant ne désespérons pas, et, comme tu fis à ton suprême instant, tournons
nos yeux vers le soleil.) (261–62)

Before showing that this glance at the sun, instead of insuring
truth, unleashes madness, I would first note that these ruins of ruins
once (allegorically) signified wisdom. But now, all that they signify is
the ruin of philosophy, ruined thought and the loss of thought. Of
course this loss is that of its allegorical signification, but also that of all
thought. This is what Nerval perceives, what he painfully undergoes. He
realizes that the erasure of difference coincides with the collapse of the
same, and not with its return. The interruption of the repetition of the
same brought about through the disappearance of differential marks
causes the mnemonic landscape, of allegorical signification, to return to
"a savage unsocial state," indeed, even to in-difference, to an undifferentiated state. Thus, a tomb without ashes is left, just as the convent of
Saint-S . . . no longer contained the living Adrienne: an empty sign.
However, the collapse of distinctions, and consequently a collapse of
the same, of recognition and of consciousness, *is* madness.

Madness *in* this particular text is in fact reliant on this apparently
abyssal play between the same and the other, the abortion of which we
have been able to witness. This play, what seems to be the very condition
of all identity, and consequently all consciousness as recognition, causes
an emptying of the sign, a halt of return and repetition, the contrary of

all thought. But the play between the same and the other, its almost abyssal specularity, is *already* madness. Nerval writes:

To love a nun in the form of an actress! . . . but what if they were one and the same!—It was enough to drive you mad! That fascination is fatal in which the unknown leads you on like a will-o-the-wisp hovering over the reeds in still water . . . (55)

(Aimer une religieuse sous la forme d'une actrice! . . . et si c'était la même! —Il y a de quoi devenir fou! C'est un entraînement fatal où l'inconnu vous attire comme le feu follet fuyant sur les joncs d'une eau morte . . .) (247)

In this way the identical image reflected by all women, the image which allows for the identification of the same from the different and which underlies all cognizance of the other as recognition (of the same), already brings on madness. It brings it on all the more so because this cognizance of the other through the same always turns into its specular contrary: the appearance of nonidentity, absence of recognition and cognition. Thus, the *double image*, and all its possible implication as "essential identity," turn into a total absence of identity. In fact, the celestial star and the star of the earth (even idealized) gradually turn into a water star. In the chapter "The Ball of Loisy," where we learn that Sylvie is no longer the same, we read:

I offered to take her home. It was now broad daylight but the sky was overcast. The Thève murmured on our left, leaving pools of still water at each winding in its course, and here white and yellow water lilies bloomed and the frail embroidery of the water flowers spread out like daisies. (68)

(Je lui offris de l'accompagner chez elle. Il faisait grand jour, mais le temps était sombre. La Thève bruissait à notre gauche, laissant à ses coudes des remous d'eau stagnante où s'épanouissaient les nénuphars jaunes et blancs, où éclatait comme des pâquerettes la frêle broderie des étoiles d'eau.) (258–59)

Sparkling like a will-o-the-wisp on still water, the water star has affected Nerval, even if it hasn't yet fatally intoxicated him:

The fields were covered with stooks and hayricks whose odor went to my head without inebriation, as had at other times the fresh scent of the woods and thorn thickets. (69)

(Les plaines étaient couvertes de javelles et de meules de foin, dont l'odeur me portait à la tête sans m'enivrer, comme faisait autrefois la fraîche senteur des bois et des halliers d'épines fleuries.) (259)

But the pull of the water flowers can no longer be doubted with the chapter "Ermononville," where, as we saw, the unhinging of the faculty of thought through the disappearance of identical signs occurs.

I saw the château again, the peaceful waters surrounding it, the waterfall murmuring among the rocks, and that raised walk connecting the two parts of the village marked with four dove-coats at its corners, and the lawn that stretches out beyond like a savannah overlooked by shady slopes; Gabrielle's tower is reflected from afar in the waters of an artificial lake starry with ephemeral flowers; the water foams, the insects hum . . . You must shun the treacherous air it exhales and gain the dusty rocks of the "Desert" and then the moors where the purple broom relieves the green of the ferns. (72–73)

(J'ai revu le château, leseaux paisibles qui le bordent, la cascade qui gémit dans les roches, et cette chaussées réunissant les deux parties du village, dont quatre colombiers marquent les angles, la pelouse qui s'étend au-delà comme une savane, dominée par des coteaux ombreux; la tour de Gabrielle se reflète de loin sur les eaux d'un lac factice étoilé de fleurs éphémères! l'écume bouillonne, l'insecte bruit . . . Il faut échapper à l'air perfide qui s'exhale en gagnant les grès poudreux du désert et les landes où la bruyère rose relève le vert des fougères.) (262)

The abolition of Gabrielle's tower,[25] its reflection and fall into the calm waters of the lake, convert the celestial star (to which Nerval's soul aspired) into an ephemeral water star which, like a will-o-the-wisp, runs along the surface of the water to lead the solitary stroller astray. Just as in the following chapter where, later visiting the now remodeled room that belonged to Sylvie, Nerval is "anxious to leave the room, for it contained nothing of the past," (73) he tries to escape from the treacherous air, from the will-o-the-wisp (*feu follet*), from madness (*folie*).

In "Last Leaves" Nerval notes down that "the ponds, dug at such great expense, are expanses of stagnant water disdained by the swan." (84) This remark follows the evocation of sadness with the memory of the "fugitive traces of a time when the natural was affected." (83) Madness is thus not only the erasure of writing, it is also the mutation of the swan (*cygne*) into an empty sign (*signe*), into roving signs, just like the will-o-the-wisp upon the stagnant water of a countryside where Adrienne has died in her convent, where Rousseau's tomb has been emptied of its ashes, and where Sylvie is missing from her rightful place because she is no longer the same.

How solitary it all is and how sad! Sylvie's enchanting gaze, her wild running, her happy cries, once gave such charm to the places I have just been through. (73)

(Que tout cela est solitaire et triste! Le regard enchanté de Sylvie, ses courses folles, ses cris joyeux, donnaient autrefois tant de charme aux lieux que je viens de parcourir! . . .) (262)

Sylvie, the daughter of fire (*fille du feu*), once a lively young girl (*fille follette*), is henceforth a will-o-the-wisp (*feu follet*). The madness (*folie*) here is double. There is the madness of the origin, the good madness, the good wildness, on the one hand, and on the other, there is the loss of the origin, the will-o-the-wisp, savagery, the violence of an undifferentiated nature. There is the good madness of full signs and mastered difference of the same, and empty vagabond signs which subvert repetition. Don't these empty and hollow signs represent the finalization of the idealizing movement which characterizes good madness? And doesn't the privilege of repetition without difference fall on them? The empty signs which appear in *Sylvie* as a result of the loss of the only star which sparkled with a double shine, like the deceitful star of Aldebaran, are in fact *the* condition of possibility of good madness, of the madness of identity. Only an empty sign is a discontinuous unity capable of being repeated identically. *Sylvie*, consequently, can be read as a tale about the cyclical logic whereby the sign becoming arbitrary is the condition of possibility of symbolic and allegorical signification; or also as a tale about the erasure of natural writing as artificial writing, and the natural violence of the established sign. But that must not concern us here. Of utmost importance, however, is the perfect symmetry and specular relationship between the logic of the same and its collapse.

Of course I have not exhausted all the reflexive categories. Such a categorization is theoretically possible, the specularity being infinite, and not abyssal. But neither the categories of the relationships between the same and the other, nor of the madness of plenitude and of that of absence, allow one to postulate rigorously the specularity of the text of *Sylvie*. Remember, however, that this tale is constructed formally so that its chapters echo each other, sometimes like a circle.[26] Thematically, on the other hand, one has simply to recall the reflection of the tower of Gabrielle in the lake, the magic mirror on the stage, the double shining of the star, etc., but especially the calculated circularity of "A Voyage to Cythèra." Perhaps imagined to echo Watteau's painting, the crossing of the lake, through its reflection in the water, again doubles the model. "This graceful *theoria*, a revival from the days of antiquity, was reflected in the calm waters of the pool separating it from the banks of the island . . ." (58) ("Cette gracieuse *théorie* renouvelée des jours antiques se reflétait dans les eaux calmes de l'étang qui la séparait du bord de l'île . . ."). (249) This infinite specularity, this ensemble of reflexive determinations, that is what I have called the madness *of* the text. "Last Leaves" does not escape from this madness. Instead of interrupting the reflexive logic of the preceding thirteen chapters, it *reflects* exactly as last leaf the pages facing it. But what is this last chapter about? Nerval describes the loss of illusions, the teachings of experience and sad homecomings. Now, this chapter also reports the activity of writing, and represents the place where the text reflects its own production. The "Last Leaves" begin this way:

Such are the delusions which charm and beguile us in the morning of life. I have tried to set them down without too much order, but many hearts will understand mine. (83)

(Telles sont les chimères qui charment et égarent au matin de la vie. J'ai essayé de les fixer sans beaucoup d'ordre, mais bien des coeurs me comprendront.) (271)

For this double madness, for the loss of natural writing through the erasure of identical marks, Nerval here substitutes the signs of a writing which will be capable of mastery. Reflexive, controlling writing which will master itself adds to and completes the mirror-like structure of the text. In other words, the madness *of* writing comes to complete the madness *of* the text. It is its truth.

Illusions fall, like the husks of a fruit, one after another, and what is left is experience. It has a bitter taste, but there is something tonic in its sharpness. (83)

(Les illusions tombent l'une après l'autre, comme les écorces d'un fruit, et le fruit, c'est l'expérience. Sa saveur est amère; elle a pourtant quelque chose d'âcre qui fortifie . . .) (271)

V

Such is this text's unity. It is a specular totality which is held together by the whole of its reflexive determinations. Such a textual totality, where the reflection is continually brought to a higher power and multiplies in an infinite series of mirrors (to quote from fragment 116 of the *Athenaeum*[27]), is the product of a chemical mixture of genres and styles, of the passage from literature to Literature, to literality, to the textual, etc. If one must trace the history of the mixture of genres back to the Greek Cynics and to the Roman *satura*,[28] I would suggest nonetheless another origin here, the mixture of prose and of tragedy in the *Scriptures*. Religious history, and consequently secular, clearly impeded the formation of literary genres from its inception. In fact, everything in the *Scriptures* which can still be separated into genres first belongs to a global order.[29] In accordance with the Auerbachian interpretation, the radical mixing of styles and of genres (Auerbach calls it the "levels of style")[30] that nineteenth century realism brought about is not only the completion and fulfillment of Romanticism, but even more the fulfillment of the figural representation of the Middle Ages, where the mixture of genres and styles had already culminated in a tragic realism. Although Auerbach uses in *Mimesis* and in his article "Figura" the notion of *figura* solely for analysing the representation of reality in late antiquity and during the Middle Ages, his analysis of realism in the nineteenth century does not in the least narrow the scope of figural interpretation. On the contrary, it increases its effectiveness to a maximum. One would simply have to compare the two types of analysis to prove it. It is true for Auerbach that figural interpretation is the characteristic mark of aging cultures. Thus its distinguishing feature is something extremely old through which these cultures return to their origin.[31] I would emphasize however the following point, the most important for our problematic: the difference between *figura* and both symbol and allegory. The *figura* is a function of both a representation and a vertical and religious construction of the world (*religiös vertikalen Aufbaus*).[32] It differs from the symbol and from allegory because these animate a purely spiritual, ahistorical interpretation.[33] The *figura*, on the contrary, is always necessarily historical in the following way:

Figural prophecy implies the interpretation of one worldly event through another; the first signifies the second, the second fulfills the first. Both remain historical events; yet both, looked at in this way, have something provisional and incomplete about them; they point to one another and both point to something in the future, something still to come, which will be the actual, real, and definitive event. This is true not only of Old Testament prefiguration, which points forward to the incarnation and the proclamation of the gospel, but also of these latter events, for they too are not the ultimate fulfillment, but themselves a promise of the end of time and the true kingdom of God.[34]

But what is this coming event, on which the fullness of meaning of those intra-historical events depends. Auerbach defines it in the following passage with relation to the *figura*:

Thus the figures are not only tentative; they are also the tentative form of something eternal and timeless; they point not only to the concrete future, but also to something that always has been and always will be; they point to something which is in need of interpretation, which will indeed be fulfilled in the concrete future, but which is at all times present, fulfilled in God's providence, which knows no difference of time. This eternal thing is already figured in them and thus they are both tentative fragmentary reality, and veiled eternal reality.[35]

The following question should thus concern us here: how does the *figura* provide unity for the mixture of genres and styles? Without touching on the delicate problem of its relationship to the Hegelian *Gestalt* as the living incarnation of the concept in a history, the *figura* confers unity to the mixture of genres in being their transgression toward that which founds them beyond their separation. What founds them as their common essence is a figure whose *figura* takes place until the immutable and always already prefigured Eternal is accomplished at the end of history. Without being the unity to come, but based upon it, and replacing it, the unity that the *figura* confers on the mixture of genres and styles thus necessarily remains disproportionate to itself. Now, the Romanticism of Iena had already conceived chemical mixing (which Novalis has affirmed destroyed all figures)[36] as producing the religious. It is true that it was to be the result of the mixing of philosophy and poetry. But for the Romantics, for Schelling in particular, the exemplary historical figure of such a mixture is, as for Auerbach, the *Divine Comedy* of Dante. The difference between the Romantic *menstrum universale* is however a function of the double notion of religion which characterized Romanticism itself. On the one hand, there is the religion of F. Schlegel and of Schelling, on the other the Christianity of Novalis. Now, this double conception of the religious, its two Romantic sides, is also found in Nerval.

In fact, the specular reflection constitutive of *Sylvie*'s unity, a specularity which the Romantics aimed for through the mixing of genres, is related to the religious such as Schelling intended it, i.e., to art thought of as the absolute representation of truth. And, as Lacoue-Labarthe and Nancy have shown, it is "the becoming-artist of the work or absolute self-production itself,"[37] the question of the subject of the work as Subject of the work, of the work-subject, that speculative metaphysics aims for on the level of art and of form, and not on the level of the concept as in Hegel. This question of the work-subject is, in fact, *the* religious question. (The madness *of* writing in *Sylvie*, seen autobiographically, must then be viewed in the perspective of the creation of such a self-reflexive and self-engendering work.[38] The Nervalian practice of self-plagiarism must also be understood in this sense.[39]) The specular unity of *Sylvie*, an apparently faultless unity, sustaining itself, seems then to exclude any question of figurality. But is it really so, for doesn't it also go hand in hand precisely with what has been named the "syncretism" of Nerval? "Nerval," writes Jean Richer, is he "who refuses to choose, who wants to reconcile contraries: mysticism and sensualism, paganism and Christianity."[40] This syncretism is very close to the other side of Romanticism's religious concept. Although what has been called the theomaniacal delirium of Nerval and which, as the texts show (*Aurélia* in particular), is rather a spiritual alchemy or an aspiration to become pure spirit through the reconciliation or reintegration (to use Martines de Pasqualy's term) of all religions, this religious syncretism is not without relation to the specular unity produced from genre mixing. The mixing of religions is theoretically tied to the mixing of genres. That is what fragment 327 of the *Athenaeum* proves:

Wanting to reunite into one all genres of religions is a very natural and almost inevitable desire. Its realization, however, is palpably called the mixture of poetic genres.

(Es ist ein sehr natürlicher, ja fast unvermeidlicher Wunsch, alle Gattungen der Religion in sich vereinigen zu wollen. In der Ausführung ists damit aber ungefähr, wie mit der Vermischung der Dichtarten.)[41]

Now this reconciliation of religions within Nerval's syncretism, a mixture parallel to the mixture of genres and of styles, if it doesn't necessarily represent a return to Christian faith as Richer seems to suggest,[42] it is nonetheless brought about under the auspices of Christianity, despite all avowed paganism. Thus the mixture in question will not escape from figural unity. Only the *figura* can allow for some sort of mixture of religions. Doesn't Nerval write in *Diorama*: "Indicating the ruins of a world being born is a poetic idea" ("C'est une idée poétique que d'avoir indiqué les ruines d'un monde naissant")?[43] Nerval's use of figural representation, of the *figura*, is thus allegorical, but allegorical in the sense that it ruins that which it promises. So being, the figural unity would coincide with the specular unity, and thus with the totality that the madness *of* the text confers upon it. But doesn't he also use it in the sense that Auerbach intends it, that is, a unity imposed upon the mixture from the outside? Nerval's religious experience, in fact, coincides with a spiritual madness, but it is also the madness of *religion*. This is certainly more obvious for *Aurélia* (especially the ending) than for *Sylvie*. But if such is the case, the figure then opens out into religious delirium and can, as figure, be founded on the promise of a unity yet to come and not yet realized. The real unity will remain incomplete.

How do we then deal with these two, or even three, religions: the madness *of* the text, the madness *of* religion and the madness of *religion*; or again, the question of the relationship between the specular, religious and figural unity? In formulating the two problems which were to guide my reading of *Sylvie*, I first raised the question of the particular figure that the mixture of genres and styles in Nerval takes. The unity of *Sylvie* which relies on the madness *of* the text as well as on the madness *of* religion and which takes the form of a specular and religious unity is not independent, it seems to me, of the figural unity and the religious madness on which this letter is based. Now, that would mean that the specular unity would be wanting, would hold to a unity always incomplete with relation to itself. It would be wanting, and would also hold to, an experience as particular as the madness of *religion*. To say it again in another way: an experience and a particular figure must come to the aid of a specular and religious unity of the text that against all appearance is found lacking.

That brings me to reformulate the second question I raised in reference to *Sylvie*, namely, where is the scenic- or stage-work in this relationship of the text with itself? First, it should be noted that for Romanticism, the *menstrum universale*, the producer of the religious, is clearly poetry. This role of mediator (or *relève*) which poetry assumes is not free of problems. It is not, as Paul de Man suggests in "The Rhetoric of Temporality," that the artwork-becoming-subject is problematized under the figure of secular allegory or even that of irony.[44] On the contrary, as the case of *Sylvie* has clearly shown, instead of subverting the work's organic totality, allegory's (or irony's) negative function contributes to this end essentially in that this organic quality relies on an infinite specularity, that is *unendlich* and not *endlos*. If the reflexive totality encounters mishaps, if the mixture of genres, and consequently of religions, creates problems, the reason is due rather to what Antonio, in *Gespräch über die Poesie*, calls *diction*, namely, the "center of every letter"; in other words, it is due to what, concerning the specific mode of composition of a genre, is of the order of writing.[45] Romanticism, as has been seen in Nerval's *Sylvie*, masters writing by inscribing it into the reflexive weaving of its text. Thus, it is not a question of the writing I mentioned earlier: the madness *of* writing. That which, on the other hand, will not allow itself to be inscribed without remainder in the play of mirrors of the specular and religious text, that which always exists as supplementary with relation to that textual totality, and that which always overflows into what it cannot take into account is precisely that very thing which organizes the multiple self-relationships of the text. What is always in excess in the mixture of genres and of styles regarding the self-engendering and autonomy of the work is the theatrical. In fact, the specular mirage can only take place under the *direction* of writing. But simultaneously, this same scenic-work never stops disappropriating the self-mirroring of the text. Just as the theatrical space, Nerval's purgatory, already upsets the symmetrical and specular play of the same and of the other, so also the theatrical space opened up by writing is the always excessive discontinuous space upon which the representation of a continuous universe becomes possible. But, as such, this space fatally interrupts any direct relationship between spaces and times. Nerval writes: "Today there is no direct road to Ermononville. Sometimes I go there by way of Creil and Senlis, sometimes by Dammartin." (84) ("Pour se rendre à Ermononville, on ne trouve plus aujourd'hui de route directe. Quelquefois j'y vais par Creil et Senlis, d'autres fois par Dammartin.") (272)

Let me try to bring this paper to a close, a paper which no doubt has raised more questions than it has answered, by recalling Nerval's remarks during the visit to the home of the uncle who had passed away. He notices "two Flemish paintings said to be the work of an ancient painter, an ancestor of ours." But that is not all:

On the table was a stuffed dog which I had known alive as the old friend of my wanderings through the woods, the last King Charles (*carlin*) perhaps, because it belonged to that lost breed . . .

"Let's go and see the parrot," I said . . . The parrot asked for food as it had done in its happiest days . . . (71–72)

(Sur la table, [je perçus] un chien empaillé que j'avais connu vivant, ancien compagnon de mes courses dans les bois, le dernier carlin peut-être, car il appartenait à cette race perdue . . .

"Allons voir le perroquet," dis-je au fermier. Le perroquet demandait à déjeuner comme en ses plus beaux jours . . .") (260–61)

Thus, at the beginning, a painter, a tableaux-maker, a scene-maker, perhaps even a thaumaturgist. But also a race of actors, the *carlin* named from the Italian actor Carlo Bertinazzi. What is left is the foolish, senseless and sterile repetition of a word stretching towards the past. All, within the *mise en scène* of the text.

Translated by Robert Vollrath

NOTES

1. Peter Kapitza, *Die frühromantische Theorie der Mischung* (Munich: W. Fink, 1968).
2. Gérard Genette, "Genres, types, modes," in *Poétique*, 32.
3. Jean-Luc Nancy and Philippe Lacoue-Labarthe, *L'Absolu littéraire* (Paris: Seuil, 1978).
4. The ensemble of the epistolary novel *Angélique, Sylvie*, about which I will speak, *Chansons et légendes du Valois*, folklore and philological essay combined, the novella *Octavie*, the poetical and philosophical history of religion entitled *Isis* and the play *Corilla*.
5. Cf. Albert Béguin, *L'Ame romantique et le rêve* (Paris: Corti, 1946).
6. Recall that Michel Foucault, in his preface to the first edition of *Folie et déraison: Histoire de la folie à l'âge classique* (Paris: Plon, 1961), defined madness in general as the *absence of work (absence d'oeuvre)*. See consequently *De Foucault à Nerval:* Aurélia *ou "le livre infaisable"* as well as the very beautiful text "La répétition: Folie du lyrisme" by Shoshona Felman in her book *La Folie at la chose littéraire* (Paris: Seuil, 1978).
7. Letter of 6 November 1853, quoted in Sarah Kofman, *Nerval, le charme de la répétition* (Lausanne: L'Age d'homme, 1979), p. 11.
8. Raymond Jean, *Nerval par lui-même* (Paris: Seuil, 1964), p. 8.
9. Jean-Luc Nancy and Philippe Lacoue-Labarthe, p. 390.
10. Kapitza, pp. 115–16.
11. G. W. F. Hegel, *Vorlesungen über die Aesthetik*, vol. I, *Werke in Zwanzig Bänden* (Frankfort: Suhrkamp, 1970), pp. 25–26.
12. *Ibid.*, vol. II, pp. 240ff.
13. Friedrich Schlegel, *Gespräch über die Poesie*, in *Schriften zur Literatur* (Munich: dtv, 1972), p. 287.
14. August Wilhelm Schlegel, *Leçons sur l'art et la littérature*, in *L'Absolu littéraire*, pp. 364–65.
15. Hegel, vol. II, p. 235.
16. Friedrich Schlegel, *L'Absolu littéraire*, p. 318.
17. All French quotes from Nerval are from the *Oeuvres* (Bibliothèque de la Pléiade, 1966), Tome I. The English quotes are taken from *Selected Writings of Gérard de Nerval*, translated with a critical introduction and notes by Geoffrey Wagner (London: Peter Owen, 1958). The page numbers following the English quotations refer to this edition. I have modified a certain number of them for the present paper.—trans.
18. *Oeuvres*, p. 223.
19. *Ibid.*, p. 1268.
20. "Upon the arrival of her niece, the house was ablaze." ("*Sa nièce arrivant, c'était la feu dans la maison.*") The house itself was constructed

Rodolphe Gasché

"of unequal blocks of sandstone covered with vines of hops and of Virginia creeper." (". . . *en pierre de grès inégales que revêtaient des treillages de houblon et de vigne vierge.*") (253) Let me recall, as Jean-Pierre Richard does, that sandstone is a mixture of petrified mud, a mixture of earth and humidity. (Jean-Pierre Richard, *Poésie et profondeur* [Paris: Seuil, 1955], pp. 51ff.)

21. "Sylvie ou la pensée de Nerval," in *Trois essais de mythologie romantique* (Paris: Corti, 1966), p. 29.

22. *Ibid.*, p. 44.

23. S. Freud, *Beiträge zur Psychologie des Liebeslebens*, in *Ges. Werke*, Bd. XVIII (London: Imago, 1940–52).

24. Chapter XII, "Father Dodu," is especially significant here, for it shows us that not only is the tomb of Rousseau empty, but even his memory is deformed. The only thing which remains of Rousseau in this countryside is his double, father Dodu, who ends up transforming Rousseau into Socrates.

25. Cf. Poulet for "the abolished tower" [*la tour abolie*], p. 48.

26. Cf. S. Kofman, pp. 40–41.

27. Friedrich Schlegel, *Athenäums-Fragmente*, in *Schriften zur Literatur*, pp. 37–38.

28. Philippe Lacoue-Labarthe/Jean-Luc Nancy, "Le Dialogue des genres," in *Poétique*, 21.

29. Erich Auerbach, *Mimesis. The Representation of Reality in Western Literature*, trans. by W. R. Trask (Princeton: Princeton University, 1971), p. 20.

30. "Höhenlagen des Stils," *Ibid.*, p. 554.

31. Erich Auerbach, "Figura," in Auerbach, *Scenes from the Drama of European Literature* (Gloucester, Mass: Peter Smith, 1973), p. 57: "Thus figural interpretation is a product of late cultures, far more indirect, complex, and charged with history than the symbol or myth. Indeed, seen from this point of view, it has something vastly old about it: a great culture had to reach its culmination and indeed to show signs of old age, before an interpretative tradition could produce something on the order of figural prophecy."

32. *Mimesis*, p. 20.

33. "Figura," p. 55.

34. *Ibid.*, p. 80.

35. *Ibid.*, p. 81.

36. "Das chemische Prinzip ist dem figurierenden Prinzip zuwider—es zerstört die Figuren." Quoted from Kapitza, p. 101.

37. *L'Absolu littéraire*, pp. 203–4.

38. Cf. for example Albert Béguin who writes that Nerval's works are "those with the most intimate ties to the existence of their author," and that the works become, "because Nerval wants it, the very place where their destiny is decided." (p. 358).

39. Cf. J. P. Richard, p. 75.

40. Jean Richer, *Gérard de Nerval et les doctrines ésotériques.* (Neuchatel: Griffon d'or, 1947), p. xvii.

41. *Athenäums-Fragmente*, p. 62.

42. Richer, pp. 173–74.

43. Quoted in Richer, p. 69.

44. Paul de Man, in *Interpretation, Theory and Practice* (Baltimore: The Johns Hopkins University, 1969).

45. *Gespräch über die Poesie*, p. 329.

SIX
THE POLITICS OF PROSE AND THE ART
OF AWAKENING: WALTER BENJAMIN'S VERSION
OF A GERMAN ROMANTIC MOTIF
Irving Wohlfarth

For Marcus Bullock

Is health inherently—prose?
Friedrich Schlegel

BENJAMIN'S RECENTLY published notes to his *Theses on the Philosophy of History* contain two seminal fragments which associate the Messianic age with the idea of prose:

The idea of prose coincides with the Messianic idea of universal history (Lesskov).

The Messianic world is the world of all-sided and integral actuality. Only in it is there universal history. But not in writing, rather as festive performance. This feast is cleansed of all ceremony. It knows no festive songs. Its language is liberated prose which has burst the fetters of writing. (The idea of prose coincides with the Messianic idea of universal history. Cf. in *The Storyteller* the modes of literary prose [*Kunstprosa*] as the spectrum of the historical ones).[1]

Messianism in general—and Benjamin's is no exception—is governed by a triadic scheme: Origin, Fall, and Redemption.[2] The distinctive feature of the above quotations is the introduction of prose as the medium in which the Messianic scheme is enacted. In *The Storyteller*, to which the above quotations refer, Benjamin had written:

For if the record kept by memory—historiography—constitutes the creative indifference (*schöpferische Indifferenz*) of the various epic forms (as great prose is the creative indifference of the various metrical forms), its oldest form, the epic, encompasses in undifferentiated form (*kraft einer Art von Indifferenz*) the story and the novel. (*I*, p. 97)

It is out of such "creative indifference" that the triadic scheme emerges, and it is to it that it returns. Three such interrelated points of origin and finality are here singled out—historiography as the indifference of epic forms, the epic as that of its own family tree, great prose as that of the various metrical forms. The relation of historiography to the epic forms—that is, of indifference to difference—is described as that of "white light," pure, colorless, and all-inclusive, "to the colors of the spectrum" (*I*, p. 95).

Already here historiographical, historical, and esthetic categories are peculiarly interchangeable. But Benjamin is far from being the first to extend *prose* and the *epic* far beyond any narrowly literary meaning. Consider, for example, the implicit equation of history with prose in the following passage from Friedrich Schlegel:

History is, so to speak, formless, the highest, most universal and natural form of the human mind, for which it requires no other preparation. We are receptive to poetry only in a state of heightened emotion, of enthusiasm; philosophy is itself an artificial condition which has to be brought about by exertion. History is the most universally intelligible, natural, objective form of knowledge.[3]

Such interchangeability of esthetic and extra-esthetic categories— notably between literary terms and historical periods—belongs, generally speaking, to the heritage of German Idealist esthetics. Thence it entered a certain Marxist esthetics via Lukács's *Theory of the Novel*. In Hegel's *Asthetik*, for example, "prose" and "contemporary prosaic conditions" refer both to the literary medium and the extra-literary structure of the modern bourgeois phase of world history; its symmetrical counter-part, "the general epic condition of the world," has the same double connotation; and the double genitive of Lukács's "age of the epic" like-wise makes each meaning the other's frame of reference. Benjamin's equation of prose with a Messianic version of "universal history" invests the third stage of the triad with an analogous double structure, thereby reawakening the latent Messianism of German Idealist esthetics. In this context, the "poetics of prose" (Todorov) is also its politics.

A close parallel to such a Messianic politics of prose is to be found in the celebrated letter in which Flaubert dreams of a "book about nothing":

Je crois que l'avenir de l'Art est dans ces voies. Je le vois, à mesure qu'il grandit, s'éthérisant tant qu'il peut. . . . La forme en devenant habile, s'atténue, elle quitte toute liturgie, toute règle, toute mesure; elle abandonne l'épique pour le roman, le vers pour la prose; elle ne se connaît plus d'ortho-doxie et est libre comme chaque volonté qui la produit. Cet affranchissement de la matérialité se retrouve en tout et les gouvernements l'ont suivi, depuis les despotismes orientaux jusqu'aux socialismes futurs.

C'est pour cela qu'il n'y a ni beaux ni vilains sujets et qu'on pourrait presque établir comme axiome, en se posant au point de vue l'Art pur, qu'il n'y en a aucun, le style étant à lui tout seul une manière absolue de voir les choses.[4]

For this disconcerting conjunction of Hegelian idealism with a socialist perspective Benjamin will substitute a Messianic materialism, but, more disconcerting yet, this hardly affects the rigor of the parallel. In each case an implacable critic of "progress" finds in a more or less idealist perspective on the world-historical evolution of esthetic forms the model for the progress, actual or desired, of world history itself.[5] "L'idéal n'est fécond," writes Flaubert, "que lorsqu'on y fait *tout* rentrer. C'est un travail d'amour et non d'exclusion" (p. 164). The substitution of a positive for a negative conception of progress, a loving for an exclusive version of sublimation, involves a revised model of demythologization. It is synonymous neither with the "disenchantment of the world" nor with an enlightenment philosophy of history. If it is "progress in the consciousness of freedom," it nevertheless takes unorthodox, non-Hegelian forms, for it terminates not in a philosophy of the state but in the celebration of its withering away. The absolute style which dissolves all subject matter thereby dissolves style itself as the imposition of an alien order. The effacement of formal restraints is equated with the abolition of hierarchical standards. From the absolute Flaubertian standpoint of style no discriminations can be made between beautiful and ugly, just as, according to Benjamin, the chronicler—who occupies the similarly absolute vantage point of the Last Judgment—makes no distinction between major and minor events (*I*, p. 254). All pre-existing canons, all pre-scriptions, indeed—in Benjamin's version—the written word itself are to be superseded. Language then sloughs off its fixed liturgical forms, and formulates its newfound freedom in informal, performative modes that are no longer constrained by the bound rhythms, formulas, songs, and rituals of the world-historical past. Language thus aspires to the Messianic condition of prose. According to certain "anarchistic" versions of Jewish Messianism, the redeemed world will be a place of "free fulfilment" liberated from the taboos that were made necessary by the Fall.[6] Benjamin calls such freedom prose, and finds its rhythms prefigured in surrealism:

wherever action itself is and puts forth the image, tears it back and devours it (*aus sich herausstellt und ist, in sich hineinreißt und frißt*) where proximity looks itself in the eye, the sought-for space of images opens up, the world of all-sided and integral actuality. (*R*, pp. 191–92)

There is thus nothing less "prosaic" than Benjamin's conception of prose. In the dedication to *Le Spleen de Paris* Baudelaire evoked *le mira-*

cle d'une prose poétique musicale sans rythme et sans rime. At moments
Messianic prose is even more "poetic" than that. *Aus sich herausstellt
und ist, in sich hineinreißt und frißt (GS, 2, 1, p.* 309) marks a dithy-
rambic return to rhyme and meter. The free verse of Messianic prose
also communicates with the "hymnic" "rhythm of Messianic nature,"
which Benjamin's own prose enacts as follows:

und der Rhythmus dieses ewig vergehenden, in seiner Totalität vergehenden,
in seiner räumlichen, aber auch zeitlichen Totalität vergehenden Weltlichen,
der Rhythmus der messianischen Natur ist Glück. (*GS*, 2, 1, p. 204)

Free rhythm in celebration of freedom from rhythm—such is the paradoxical medium of "profane illumination."

The basis of all subsequent esthetics was, according to Benjamin's
dissertation, *The Concept of Criticism* (Kunstkritik) *in German Romanticism*, laid by the German Romantic esthetics of Friedrich Schlegel
and Novalis. That inaugural study, which culminates in an interpretation of their conception of prose, also lays some of the groundwork for
his own esthetics. Since, as Benjamin shows, their idea of prose is co-
terminous with their theory of criticism, it is first necessary to recapitulate his analytical exposition of that theory in order to situate prose as
the *Aufhebung* of all genres. The early Romantic conception of the
absolute is, he shows, that of a self-reflexive medium of systematically,
continuously unfolding forms whose "point of indifference" (*GS*, 1, 1,
p. 39) and progressive development are chiefly identified with (the
"idea" of) art. Art is a coherent continuum of forms which immanently
tend toward self-reflexion, that is, toward self-dissolution in higher,
more reflexive forms that better approximate to the idea of art, with
which the absolute work of art will finally coincide. In this process,
Romantic art—notably the novel (*Roman*)—and criticism mark a
qualitatively new stage, and prose is their characteristic medium. All
objects being, according to Romantic epistemology, self-reflexive *subjects*, criticism is nothing other than the self-reflexion of its "object."
It is thus immanent both to the total movement of art and to the individual work, which it "unfolds," "completes," "universalizes," "systema-
tizes," "classifies," "dissolves," and "romanticizes"—that is, relates to
its own (at once immanent and transcendent) idea. Therein criticism
is related to the objective dimension of Romantic irony. Novalis relates
it in turn to translation—an *aperçu* which Benjamin interprets, in con-
formity with his own subsequent (and itself profoundly Romantic)
theology of translation, as the "medial," serial rendering of one language
into another, higher one (p. 70). There as here the continuum tends
toward the final unity of a "realm of fulfillment" (*Erfüllungsbereich*)—
the multiplicity of languages toward a single language ("the language
into which every text . . . is to be translated" [*GS*, 1, 3, p. 1239]), and all

of literature toward a " 'single book' " (*GS*, 1, 1, p. 90). Just as the work of art tends toward the idea of art, so that idea is itself a single work invisibly in the making, the reconciliation of all its forms: such is the "mystical thesis" (p. 91) of the early Romantics. Benjamin thus expounds a very different version of Romantic self-reflexion than Paul de Man, who in his essay "The Rhetoric of Temporality" presents Romantic irony as a dizzy, endless regress which undermines the finality of any assertion, let alone a "mystical thesis."

In the celebrated 116th *Athenäumsfragment*, to which Benjamin's dissertation repeatedly refers, Schlegel calls this ideal unity "universal poetry" (*Universalpoesie*)—a medium of seemingly universal mediation which also links, among others, the terms of our initial quotation, prose and "universal history" (*Universalgeschichte*):

Romantic poetry is a progressive universal poetry. Its vocation is not merely to unite all the separate genres of poetry and to bring poetry into relation with philosophy and rhetoric. It wants, and should want (*will und soll auch*) to mix and fuse poetry and prose, genius and criticism, artful and natural poetry (*Kuntspoesie und Naturpoesie*), to make poetry alive and sociable, life and society poetic, to poeticize wit. . . . Only it can, like the epic, become a mirror of the whole surrounding world, an image of the age. . . . It is capable of the highest, most all-sided development (*allseitigste Bildung*). . . .[7]

The mingling of poetry and prose in the final *Gesamtkunstwerk* is not, on Benjamin's selective interpretation, the amalgamation of two genres among many, still less, despite the term *Universalpoesie*, the absorption of prose into poetry. "The idea of poetry is prose" (pp. 100–101). Whatever its philological merits, this thesis is invested with undeniable "theoretical affect":

In this apparently paradoxical but in reality very profound conception the Romantics find ᷆ completely new ground for aesthetics. . . . Prose is the definitive characterization of the idea of art, and the real meaning of the theory of the novel. . . . The conception of the idea of poetry as prose is decisive for the whole Romantic philosophy of art. . . . it was fertile in historical consequences. (pp. 100–103)

Defined as the idea of poetry, prose represents both a higher stage of aesthetic self-reflexion and the basis of the previous stages. As the originary and final point of indifference, it is at once the *undoing* of hallowed forms ("ceremony," "liturgy") *and* their "canonic" *ground*:

It is the creative ground of all poetic forms. In it they àre mediated and dissolved as in their canonic creative ground. In prose all bound rhythms merge into a new prosaic unity, which Novalis calls the "Romantic rhythm." (p. 102)

Novalis also describes the process of self-limitation and self-extension whereby poetry transforms itself into prose in terms of correspondingly "more colorless and transparent expression" and of "all-roundness" (*Allfähigkeit*) "in all directions" (*nach allen Seiten*) (p. 101). As such it coincides with his description of philosophy as "a mystical . . . penetrating idea which ceaselessly drives us in all directions" (p. 47). This motif, Schlegel's *allseitigste Bildung*, will be echoed in Benjamin's characterization of the world of Messianic prose as "all-sided" (*allseitig*) and integral actuality." Novalis's notion of "more colorless and transparent" expressions has to do with the implicitly optical model of a *Reflexionsmedium*, which the early Romantics occasionally represent as light (p. 104). All thoughts, writes Schlegel, are "merely refracted color-images" (*gebrochene Farbbilder*) of a hidden inner light (p. 37). It is in this context that Benjamin's metaphor of white light (as the creative indifference of the colors into which it is "broken" down) has its place. His dissertation concludes with an original variation of this metaphor. The relation of criticism to the literary work is visualized as

the production of a blinding (*Blendung*) in the work. This blinding, sober light extinguishes the multiplicity of works. It is the idea. (p. 119)

The idea of art is to the individual work as white light to a color of the spectrum. It comprehends it—in every sense—as the universal medium of which it already partakes. Hegel claimed that Schlegel's effacement of differences resulted in a night in which all cats were grey. Will, then, the blinding effect whereby multiplicity is extinguished produce a light in which all colors are white? Benjamin stresses that Schlegel was at pains to accentuate the highly definite, even individual, nature of the absolute idea (pp. 88–90). It is universal but not abstract. Hence, indeed, its equation with prose. Prose is, it seems, both the sober light of the new day[8] (compared with which all that went before is as a "broken" spectrum of scattered colors) and, as its *Reflexionsmedium*, the sustaining medium of the old. Flashes of blinding critical illumination, of wit and mysticism, would thus represent anticipatory moments at which the white light of the past and/or future both dissolves and makes visible the present. The "Romantic" poetry envisaged by Schlegel can mingle "poetry and prose, genius and criticism" only because prose is at once the ulterior, but immanent, unfolding of the poetic work and its originary ground, its already existing "kernel":

The rationale of criticism . . . consists in its prosaic nature. Criticism is the preparation (*Darstellung*) of the prosaic kernel in every work. Preparation is to be understood here in a chemical sense as the production of a substance by a particular process to which others are subjected. . . . Criticism grasps the prosaic element in both senses—literally, in its own non-metrical language (*ungebundene Rede*), and figuratively in the form of its object, the eternally sober nucleus (*Bestand*) of the work. (p. 109)

"Knowledge is self-knowledge" (pp. 53–61): in the act of criticism—the exposition of the work's core—prose "automatically" comes into its own.[9] It "encounters itself"—like the "righteous man" in the epic figure of the storyteller (*I*, p. 109).

Such a theory of prose plainly rests on idealist premises. The "idea" that is both core and telos, synthesis *a priori* and *a posteriori*, has the same circular structure as Hegel's *Geist*. Both enact a process of developing self-recognition in the medium of prose. But Benjamin's idea of prose is indebted to Romantic rather than Hegelian precedent. These differ inasmuch as the Romantics see prose as inherent to poetry and aspire to their ultimate union, whereas the Hegelian periodization of history has a divided, contradictory world of—"prosaic"—prose (in which poetry can survive only as a protected enclosure) succeed a harmonious epic world of poetry, the two opposites finally and all along being implicitly reconciled in the medium of *philosophical* prose. Here as elsewhere the differences represent variations within a triadic structure. Since the first and third stages must always mark points of creative indifference, the *Geist* must have been latently prosaic throughout its gestation, the better to perform, in its final, explicitly prosaic form, the *Aufhebung* of its poetic past. But there is prose and prose. However prosaic its core, Romantic *Universalpoesie* incorporates philosophical prose as only one of its elements. And it in turn differs markedly from surrealist prose, the closest of the three to Benjamin's conception of Messianic prose. For if *Universalpoesie* exceeds art—which, like philosophy, is merely one element of its progressive synthesis—it nevertheless constitutes the unbroken expansion of a primarily literary category, a steady continuum of integral forms; even where the "limbs" of its "organic" totality are without order, the organizing center holds. "Only the mingling of the limbs," writes Novalis,

is lawless; their order and relation to the whole is still the same. Within it all its impulses spread in all directions. Here too the limbs move about a single whole that is eternally at rest. (p. 101)

Much the same applies to Hegel's "Bacchantic ecstasy in which no limb is not drunk"—an ecstasy which is immediately qualified as "transparent and simple calm."[10] The self-intoxication of the Hegelian system causes no disorderliness in its seried ranks. All this is in decisive contrast to surrealist prose, in which "no limb remains unrent" (*R*, p. 192), and to its Messianic counterpart, which bursts the fetters of the written word. Such materialist prose is the collective medium of self-division,[11] not of self-penetration (p. 38) or auto-affection (p. 63). For the later Benjamin, "continuum" becomes a primarily negative category—already *The Origin of German Baroque Drama* replaces the unitary *Reflexionsmedium* with a discontinuous plurality of ideas (cf. *GS*, 1, 3, pp. 889, 938)—and the romantic faith in a sustaining center persists only in muted form. Surrealist fragmentation is that much more centrifugal than the Romantic fragment; the surrealist version of "unbound speech" (p. 109) is far more literal, anarchic and wrenching than the Romantic intermingling of "bound rhythms" (p. 102).

But such major differences do not obviate the clear parallel established by the category of prose between Schlegel's *Universalpoesie* and Benjamin's *Universalgeschichte*. The relation of universal history to the "multiplicity of histories" (*GS*, 1, 3, p. 1238) is that of a universal language to the "multiplicity of languages," and of critical prose to the "multiplicity of works." Hence the equation between "the idea of prose" and the "Messianic idea of universal history." To put the parallel another way, the relation of the redeemed world to its prehistory would be that of criticism to the work of art. The Messianic world is in this sense the "criticism" of its past. It not merely "cites" it (*I*, pp. 254, 261); it comprehends it, completing and fulfilling it, like criticism a text and realized happiness a wish (*I*, p. 179). The promiscuity of genres postulated by Schlegel, like happiness according to Benjamin's *Theologico-Political Fragment*, is both a vocation and a wish: *Sie will und soll auch*. Just as criticism responds to the immanent tendency, the inner wish, of the literary work, so the past carries with it a "temporal index" (*I*, p. 254) which signals its secret need and wish for redemption.

Does, then, Benjamin's definition of the Messianic world represent the transposition of an esthetic to a historical model, the superimposition of the "idea" of art on the "idea" of the Messianic world? No, because this interchangeability is already built into Hegelian and Romantic esthetics alike.[12] The formal structure of the *Geist* and the *Reflexionsmedium* allows for such substitutions of content. "What metaphysical quality one might wish to ascribe to this point of reflexive indifference is an open matter" (*GS*, 1, 1, p. 39). At one moment Schlegel equates it, in Fichte's wake, with the ego (*Ich*), at others with *Bildung*, harmony, genius, irony, religion, organization, history, and art (p. 44). Benjamin's dissertation singles out the esthetic medium as the most fruitful of these identifications, but also accords a special place to history[13]—thereby pointing to a correlation between historical and esthetic categories dear to both the Romantics and himself. While confining himself to the Romantic theory of criticism, Benjamin specifically characterizes its larger perspective as that of "Romantic Messianism" (pp. 12–13). Hence its parallels with his own position. The unfolding Messianic idea would, given its self-universalizing movement, necessarily comprehend history *and* art, and each in their totality, as so many prismatic moments—or else as the privileged, comprehensive medium of the other. Esthetic categories thus tend to exceed esthetics. And if history is thereby estheticized, esthetics is by the same token historicized, if only according to a circular idealist model. Schlegel's idea of *Universalpoesie* is not merely a literary or even an interdisciplinary utopia. It calls for the socialization of poetry and the literarization of life, though in still quite "superstructural" terms when compared with

Benjamin's Marxist version of that postulate in *The Author As Producer* (*R*, pp. 225, 231).

The profoundest insight contained in early Romantic esthetics is, Benjamin maintains, Hölderlin's "notion of the soberness of art":

This notion is the essentially new basis of the Romantic philosophy of art. It marks it as perhaps the greatest epoch in the Western philosophy of art, and continues to exercise an unforeseeable impact. (*GS*, 1, 1, p. 103)

Benjamin's own conception of Messianic prose will retrospectively confirm this prediction inasmuch as the twin epithets *prosaic* and *sober*—"prosaic is . . . a metaphorical designation for sober" (p. 103)—will prove to be among the most far-reaching for his own subsequent writings. Hölderlin's term is "holy-sober," *heilignüchtern* (p. 104). "Soberness is allowed, called for," writes Benjamin in *Two Poems by Hölderlin*, "because it is inherently holy, beyond all elevated sublimity (*Erhebung im Erhabnen*)" (*GS*, 2, 1, p. 125). It is with the same apparently paradoxical conjunction of seeming opposites that Benjamin will identify the idea of Messianic prose as a feast cleansed of festive songs. Far from being dissolved by "sober" rationality, the "holy" coincides with it; far from ruining the feast, the critical activity of stripping it of ceremony exposes its prosaic kernel by liberating it from the particular metrical constraints of festive song. The white light of Messianic prose is at once mystical and sober.[14] The celebrated term Benjamin coins for it in the essay on surrealism—"profane illumination" (*R*, p. 190)—is a variation of the same oxymoron. And just as Schlegel's Messianism is, according to the dissertation, at its most authentic when it is uncontaminated by religiosity, so too it is *against* religion that Benjamin vindicates something in the order of mystical illumination:

It is a cardinal error to believe that, of "Surrealist experiences," we know only the religious ecstasies or the ecstasies of drugs . . . the true, creative overcoming of religious illumination certainly does not lie in narcotics. It resides in a *profane illumination*, a materialistic, anthropological inspiration, to which hashish, opium or whatever else can give an introductory lesson. (*R*, p. 179)

Surrealist illumination is, Benjamin notes, occasionally clouded by spiritism, as Romantic mysticism had been by religiosity. But at its strongest such intoxication is *heilignüchtern*. "The dialectics of intoxication," he observes in connection with Erich Auerbach's account of courtly love and André Breton's *Nadja*, "are indeed curious":

Is not perhaps all ecstasy in one world humiliating sobriety in that complementary to it? What is it that courtly love (*Minne*) seeks—and it, not love, binds Breton to the telepathic girl—if not to make chastity, too, a transport? Into a world that borders not only on tombs of the Sacred Heart or altars to the Virgin, but also on the morning before a battle or after a victory. (*R*, p. 181)

Irving Wohlfarth

Courtly love, which is usually taken to be the historical source of modern Romantic love, is here decisively distinguished from bourgeois/Romantic versions of erotic satisfaction. Two dialectics of intoxication—that is, two versions of the intimate, non-contradictory relation between intoxication and soberness—would seem to be implicitly contrasted. On the one hand, the postcoital sadness, the morning after, which retrospectively unmasks the illusory and destructible nature of a momentary euphoria—Bataille's *fête servile*, a weak interdependence of two states on the model of, say, a manic-depressive cycle, *spleen et idéal*, etc.; this would perhaps explain why drugs can serve as no more than a preliminary initiation to profane illumination. On the other hand, a *strong* dialectic of intoxication. Its inviolable chastity puts shameless consummation to shame. It does not culminate in the moment (of climax) but takes place before (a battle) or after (a victory). Not that it is pre- or anticlimactic. Not being generated by the intoxication of sexual climax, it knows no sobering disenchantment. Nor is this a matter of pietist sublimation, spiritual elevation, *Erhebung im Erhabenen*. An intimate relation obtains between *Minnesang* and the *un*bound Messianic eros whose literal prose *breaks* the forms of festive song. Its arena is not the religious interiority of the "sacred heart" but the wide-open city; its future lies not in churches but in communism:

Transparency is the sign of the coming age—transparency not merely of rooms but—if we are to believe the Russians, who are planning to abolish Sundays in favor of movable holidays—even of weeks. (*GS*, 3, p. 197)

Movable holidays (*bewegliche Feierschichten*) scratch movable feasts (*bewegliche Feiertage*) from the calendar. But such rationalization does not remove illumination, it democratizes it. "Soberness" is not the aftermath but the medium of intoxication.

The conventionally "prosaic" relation of prose to poetry is here reversed by a logic which harks back to the German Romantic equation of the idea of poetry with prose, and of mysticism with criticism. Reflexion is, on that theory, "the opposite of ecstasy," and is represented as sunlight (*Besonnenheit*) (*GS*, 1, 1, p. 104): it is almost as if such Apollonian composure were the "creative ground" of the Dionysian. Conventional notions about Romanticism to the contrary, the model for a certain canonic form of Romantic love proves to be the Romantic theory of prose. Far from representing an exterior, destructive antithesis to poetry, critical insight likewise discloses poetry's prosaic essence.[15] Criticism, pseudo-Romantics often declare, is a cruel dissection of the living work of art. But the German Romantics' theory of prose distances itself from the standard definition of the "Romantic" (p. 107); and so does surrealism, properly understood:

Benjamin's German Romantic Motif

The aesthetic of the painter, the poet, *en état de surprise*, . . . is enmeshed in a number of pernicious romantic prejudices. Any serious exploration of occult, surrealistic, phantasmagoric gifts and phenomena presupposes a dialectical intertwinement to which a romantic turn of mind is impervious. For histrionic or fanatical stress on the mysterious side of the mysterious takes us no further; we penetrate the mystery only to the degree that we recognize it in the everyday world, by virtue of a dialectical optic that perceives the everyday as impenetrable, the impenetrable as everyday. (*R*, pp. 189–90)

What the "Romantic" cannot grasp is that—unlike so-called "realism" and "Romanticism"—the everyday and the mysterious, poetry and prose, are not mutually exclusive opposites. To that extent "Romantic" and "realist" agree: both oppose the real to the surreal. The impressive examples of "profane illumination" that Benjamin proceeds to enumerate are so many reversals of such "Romantic" common sense:

The most passionate investigation of telepathic phenomena, for example, will not teach us half as much about reading (which is an eminently telepathic process), as the profane illumination of reading about telepathic phenomena. And the most passionate investigation of the hashish trance will not teach us half as much about thinking (which is eminently narcotic) as the profane illumination of thinking about the hashish trance. Reading, thinking, waiting, strolling are no lesser forms of illumination than eating opium, dreaming, ecstasy. And more profane ones. (*R*, p. 190)[16]

The profaner, the better. The hidden kernel would be destined to exteriorize itself, to be translated into the public arena of Messianic prose. *Profane* illumination would be the—always already profane—"idea" of *all* illumination. It is, Scholem has insisted, "still illumination and nothing else"[17] but, as Benjamin insisted before him, it represents the "true, creative overcoming of religious illumination." Conversely, if it is the sober light of day that casts more light on esoteric, occult phenomena than *vice versa*, this is because such enlightenment is itself an exoteric form of illumination. There is, clearly, demythologization and demythologization. Benjamin associates *his* version of *die Entzauberung der Welt* with Judaism, fairy tales and story telling, not with, say, "clear and distinct ideas," the "reality-principle," the "iron cage," etc. The process which converts poetry into prose cannot harm it because prose is its "eternal nucleus," its inviolable, indecomposable kernel. It is because profanation does not dispel illumination but rather displaces and transforms it[18] that Benjamin can assent to it so unreservedly. The very radicality of its profanation seems at times to function for the later Benjamin as the surest sign of such palingenesis.[19] His transvaluation of the "decay of aura"[20] is thus an act of faith—faith that what is lost in depth is gained in breadth (*R*, p. 225), faith in the potency of self-dissemination.[21] There would be something self-consumingly mystical at the heart of Benjaminian demystification.

It is difficult to tell whether the logic that governs such thinking partakes of a "restricted" or a "general" economy.[22] Benjamin's materialism undeniably rests on idealist premises inasmuch as it varies motifs from German Romantic esthetics. Idealisms can always afford to immerse themselves in the world because they are always sure of recuperating themselves in the process. But the resulting affinities with materialism are not always necessarily elective. It might seem that only the early Benjamin was substantially indebted to Romantic esthetics; and that, in true Romantic fashion, his dissertation provided a metacritical commentary on aspects of his intellectual youth. But inasmuch as "soberness" is the very basis of the *Reflexionsmedium*, the revolutionary destruction of aura affirmed by the later Benjamin may well conceal *some* "idealist" continuity within "materialist" discontinuity: not merely aura, but even its seemingly *anti*-Romantic negation is already built into Benjamin's Romantic "idea of prose." In his middle writings that *hermetic* idea can perhaps be said to find its consummation in the no longer reflexive medium of the revolutionary *public*. The self-organizing Brechtian film-audience postulated in *The Work of Art in the Age of Mechanical Reproduction*, a critical mass where quantity transforms itself into quality, was for a time the object of Benjamin's chaste expectancy ("the morning before a battle"), its own prosaic, aura-destroying Messiah, for whom it was thus no longer necessary to wait. And Tretiakov's Russia—the scene of a "mighty recasting of literary forms, a melting down" of existing antinomies that obliged Westerners "to rethink our conceptions of literary forms or genres" (*R*, p. 224), "a metal from which an unknown substance is . . . to be extracted" (*R*, p. 106)—seemed to be the place where Schlegel's alchemical program of "mixing" and "fusing" the genres had become the object of a "world-historical experiment" (*R*, p. 111), which actually made poetry "alive and sociable" and "life and society poetic." In making it his first major task to re-elaborate a theory of criticism which gravitates towards the idea of prose, was, then, Benjamin programming his own future development? Does the relation of his "materialist" to his "idealist" phase resemble that of prose to poetry—according to a pre-Marxist model, whereby the later illuminates the earlier (so far, so good: Marx's celebrated "anatomy" lesson makes the same point) because it is already *contained within* it? And if the break with the esoteric—or, at least its exoteric destination—is thus anticipated, doesn't such teleology "organically" articulate even the most violent rupture? Deceptively steeped in materiality though it may be, is, then, Messianic prose an irreducibly idealist category, a comprehensive *Aufhebung* of all genres which, like all *Aufhebung, contains* within itself the possibilities that exceed it?[23] Or is it the name for a heterogeneous materialist force-field where a medium—as a graphologist, receptive hypnotic subject, etc., Benjamin was a medium in the best Romantic tradition—began to re-fuse the relations between "materialism" and "idealism." But can a post-Romantic *medium* think through a *break*? But isn't the notion of a break itself too easy and hense illusory—in Benjamin's terminology, too phantasmagorical—a way out? Benjamin once likened himself to a blotter steeped in holy writ—a blotter which, if it had its way would *blot out* all the theology it had soaked up (*GS*, 1, 3, p. 1235). His, though, was no copy, pale or otherwise, of German Romantic theology. Unlike Albert Béguin, Benjamin will not want to relive the Romantic dream—the dream of a synthesis of waking and dreaming[24]—but, unlike the deconstructors, who "solicit" it, he continues, in "citing" it, to visualize the awakening as its prosaic telos.[25]

NOTES

1. *Gesammelte Schriften* (hereafter *GS*), ed. R. Tiedemann and H. Schweppenhäuser (Frankfort: Suhrkamp, 1971–), 1, 3, p. 1235. For references in the text, abbreviations, followed immediately by the appropriate page numbers, will be used: *I* for *Illuminations*, ed. H. Arendt (New York: Harcourt Brace, 1968); *R* for *Reflections*, ed. P. Demetz (New York: Harcourt Brace, 1978). Translations are, where necessary, emended.

2. Cf. my "On the Messianic Structure of Walter Benjamin's Last Reflections," in *Glyph* 3 (1978), pp. 148–212.

3. Friedrich Schlegel, *Kritische Ausgabe*, ed. E. Behler (Munich: Schöningh, 1964), vol. 13, p. 24.

4. Flaubert, *Préface à la Vie d'Ecrivain*, ed. G. Bollème (Paris: Seuil, 1963), p. 62. Flaubert's conception of prose combines a metaphysical terminology of "Forms" and "Ideas" with a contrary nominalist emphasis on the liberation of prose from codified rhetoric (pp. 285–86) or Poetics (p. 168)— a symptom, this, of the problem of reconciling the universal with the particular—and gravitates toward a "Platonic" conception of the Beautiful as the "splendor of the True" (p. 188), a "Pythagorean" equation between truth and number (p. 271). If it harks back to the classical rhetoric of *le style nombreux*, it also looks forward to the unprecedented: "un style . . . que quelqu'un fera à quelque jour, . . . et qui serait rythmé comme le vers, précis comme le langage des sciences, et avec des ondulations. . . . La prose est née d'hier; voilà ce qu'il faut se dire. Le vers est la forme par excellence des littératures anciennes. Toutes les combinaisons prosodiques ont été faites; mais celles de la prose, tant s'en faut" (p. 71). "Nous avons trop de choses et pas assez de formes" (p. 111). "Je tourne à une espèce de mysticisme esthétique . . . , et je voudrais qu'il fût plus fort. . . . Mais, la base théologique manquant, où sera maintenant le point d'appui de cet enthousiasme qui s'ignore? . . . Alors la prose (la prose surtout, forme plus jeune) pourra jouer" (p. 86). *Otherwise* a *different* prose will result: "Les pions feront la loi. L'humanité ne fera plus de barbarismes dans son thème insipide; mais

quel foutu style, quelle absence de tournure, de rythme, et d'élan!" (p. 51).
It is, of course, with *this prosaic* prose that Flaubert generally associates
socialism. The letter of the *livre sur rien* is a notable exception. Despite obvious differences, Flaubert's and Benjamin's conceptions of prose share certain
features in common. Esthetic categories are also political ones. Prose enacts
an interplay of prosody and prose, the "once again" and the "unprecedented"
(*I*, p. 204). In Benjamin's case, a self-liquidating theology, which is destined,
precisely, to find its unruly *Aufhebung* in prose, releases the "force" that
Flaubert is afraid his post-theological "mysticism" lacks.

5. Benjamin distinguishes in his dissertation between the realized particularity of the Messianic *Erfüllungsprozess* and the modern misconception
of progress as a *Werdeprozess*, an empty movement towards an indefinite ideal
(*GS*, 1, 1, pp. 12–13, footnote 3, and pp. 91–93).

6. Cf. Gershom Scholem, *The Messianic Idea in Judaism* (New York:
Schocken, 1971), pp. 20–24.

7. *Kritische Ausgabe*, 2, 1, pp. 182–83.

8. "In every true work of art there is a place at which . . . for the first
time something truly new makes itself felt with the soberness of early morning (*mit der Nüchternheit der Frühe*)" (cit. Rolf Tiedemann, *Studien zur
Philosophie Walter Benjamins* [Frankfurt: Suhrkamp, 1965], pp. 103–4).

9. Cf. Schlegel on prose as the completion of its object's self-knowledge:
"(We actually only know that which knows itself). Consequences thereof:
What cannot be understood exists in an imperfect state.—It is gradually to
be made intelligible. . . . knowledge is prose—indifference" (*Kr. A.*, 3, p. 302).
Benjamin himself cites in this context Novalis's dictum "Perceivability is
attentiveness" (*GS*, 1, 1, p. 55), which later recurs, significantly, in connection with his theory of "aura" (*I*, p. 188). The *correspondances* evoked in
"auratic" experience—and all full-bodied experience is auratic for Benjamin—
presuppose something in the order of a *Reflexionsmedium* in which there
are no things, only subjects attending to themselves, and thereby communi-
cating with kindred spirits. Even if the attentiveness Novalis had in mind
refers to the observed subject's attention to its observer, that attention is—
so Benjamin argues in the dissertation—itself only a symptom for its capacity to see itself (*GS*, 1, 1, pp. 55–56). All "objects" are self-perceiving
subjects which "radiate" (p. 57) this auratic self-knowledge. Such "magical
observation" (p. 60), which Brecht accurately described as "mysticism
coupled with an anti-mystical stance" (prose, its telos, being a "sober" form
of the "mystical"), is also the basis of the early Romantic/Benjaminian
theory of criticism. Benjamin's notion that the salvation of the past, criticism and salvation in one, rests on a "secret rendez-vous" (*Verabredung*)
(*I*, p. 254) between past and present generations echoes Novalis's characterization of the relation between classical antiquity and modern criticism. Far
from representing a classical perfection that lives on, self-sufficiently, in
the perfect tense, antiquity is "made" by the moderns like a "beloved by her
friend's prearranged [*verabredet*] sign in the night, like the spark through
contact with the conductors" (*GS*, 1, 1, p. 116). Experience, beauty, in-
voluntary memory, aura and criticism, all interrelated, are all a matter of
elective affinities. "The past carries with it a temporal index by which it is
referred to redemption" (*I*, p. 254). Benjamin originally wrote "secret"
index. The secrecy of the rendez-vous, the hieroglyphic nature of the signals
(Schlegel speaks of the "secret affiliations" [*Ordensverbindungen*] between
words [*GS*, 1, 1, p. 49], Benjamin of their "aura" [*I*, p. 200]), and the powers

of "divination" (*GS*, 1, 1, p. 89) required to decipher them are so many Romantic motifs. Novalis's rendez-vous takes place "in the night."

10. *Phänomenologie des Geistes* (Hamburg: Meiner, 1952), p. 39.

11. Cf. *R*, p. 192. "All-sided and integral actuality" coincides with the festive disruption of bodily integrity. But the Messianic perspective cannot but project a recuperative redemption, *a restitutio in integrum* (*R*, p. 313), "Sober" may be a "metaphor" for "prose," but prose in turn embodies the ideal of the literal, the telos of all translation, the *parousia* of the proper. "Proximity looks itself in the eye." Surrealist anarchy promises future order: thus even integral *actuality defers* to the future.

12. Cf., on *Stilgeschichte* as a model for actual historiography, H. R. Jauss, "Geschichte der Kunst und Historie," in *Literaturgeschichte als Provokation* (Frankfort: Suhrkamp, 1970), pp. 222–26. Cf. also Philippe Lacoue-Labarthe and Jean-Luc Nancy, in *L'Absolu littéraire* (Paris: Seuil, 1978), p. 54: "L'eïdetique peut toujours s'infléchir en esthétique. Une telle eïdesthetique . . . est de fait ce qui trace, dans le paysage de l'idéalisme en général, l'horizon propre du romantisme."

13. "And there is no denying that in a different context one of the other determinations—e.g. history rather than art—could quite conceivably be inserted as the absolute . . ." (*GS*, 1, 1, p. 44). (On the other hand, certain "displacements," "superimpositions" and "confusions" between the various absolutes—e.g. between art and religion—merely serve, Benjamin argues, [pp. 44, 73–74], to cloud the issues; prematurely synthesized, the components of *Universalpoesie* amount to what Benjamin will later call "esperanto" [*GS*, 1, 3, p. 1235]). The exposition of a work's "prosaic kernel" will, indeed, coincide in Benjamin's own later writings with that of its "temporal core" (*Zeitkern*, Tiedemann, p. 130), its inner historicity. The inner essence is in each case inaccessible to the outer senses. The kernel is as "tasteless" as prose is "colorless." "The nourishing fruit of what has been historically understood contains time within it as the precious (fruitful) but, to be sure, tasteless (sober) seed (kernel)" (*GS*, 1, 3, p. 1250). Metaphors of seeds and kernels find their most systematic exposition in *The Task of the Translator*, according to which translation aids the germination or historical "unfolding" of the original towards true language, its "holy growth"; it is the ripening of the "concealed seed" of "pure language," the "exposition" of its "inviolable" kernel (*I*, pp. 71–76). Such partial "exposition" (*Darstellung*) is also the "germ of its production" (*Herstellung*). Exposition of the kernel, production of the seed—the two metaphors together define the double temporality of a process which both uncovers the originary kernel and brings the seed to fruition. Both meanings are telescoped in the dissertation: the Romantics are said to have understood *Darstellung* in a chemical sense—that is, as *Herstellung* (*GS*, 1, 1, p. 109). When the seed has come to full fruition and the kernel is fully exposed, time itself will presumably be capable of being fully tasted. This is to conceive time as a *Reflexionsmedium*. Why, then, isn't Benjamin's "historical materialism"—the emphasis on the *Zeitkern*—merely the "unfolding" of his earlier Romantic idealism? Cf. footnote 20.

14. Benjamin variously represents this light as the totality of the visible spectrum or as its ultraviolet extreme. The latter too is invisible to the naked eye, but prosaically, scientifically, so: "The historical materialist who investigates the structure of history performs his version of spectrum analysis. Just as the physicist ascertains the existence of ultraviolet in the solar system, so *he* ascertains that of a messianic force in history. Whoever wants to

know what a 'redeemed humanity' would look like . . . poses questions to which there is no answer. He might as well enquire after the color of ultra-violet rays" (*GS*, 1, 3, p. 1232). The image of invisible rays combines the Jewish–Marxist taboo on graven images with the motif of a Messianic light that already illuminates profane history. As the invisible source of visibility, they make possible the "invisible work" of mystical unification toward which the Romantic idea of art immanently tends (*GS*, 1, 1, p. 91). But whereas the earlier Benjamin valorizes the blinding, "sober light" that extinguishes the spectrum (*GS*, 1, 1, p. 119), the materialist's reference to the color of ultraviolet rays reduces it to absurdity. The grid, however, remains the same. The origins of Benjamin's "materialist" theory of historiography can be traced to (his account of) the German Romantic theory of criticism. Or, more or less synonymously, to his early theology of language and translation. The text of history is comparable to the language of nature that is there com-pared to a "secret password" (*R*, p. 331) relayed from one sentry to the next. The materialist redeemer of the past, be he historian or critic, would be a higher sentry who transmits, a translator who renders, it into a language closer to the universal language of Messianic redemption. Its prose "is un-derstood by all men like the language of the birds by Sunday's children" (*GS*, 1, 3, p. 1239).

15. Cf. Benjamin's account of Romantic irony: "Criticism wholly sacri-fices the work for the sake of all-encompassing unity. By contrast, the pro-cedure which, while preserving the work, is nonetheless able to bring out the full extent of its connectedness to the idea of art is . . . irony. Not merely does it not destroy the work, it renders it well-nigh indestructible. . . . The kernel of the work remains indestructible because it is not founded on ecstasy—which can be decomposed—but on an inviolable, sober, prosaic form" (*GS*, 1, 1, pp. 86, 106). The core of the work is indestructible because it is not founded on ecstasy; and a certain ecstasy is indecomposable be-cause it is founded on soberness. Instead of destroying Romantic love, Ro-mantic irony—another medium of Messianic light like wit, mysticism and criticism—could thus be considered its basis. If, then, irony points in the same direction as prose, it would follow that prose has an ironic relation to poetry. Such is the thrust of Nietzsche's fragment "Prosa und Poesie" in *Die fröhliche Wissenschaft* (*Werke*, ed. K. Schlechta [Munich: Hanser, 1960], 2, p. 99).

16. Thus, waiting for the Messiah is a far more authentic—because demythologized—form of illumination than hearkening to soothsayers (*I*, p. 264).

17. In *Zur Aktualität Walter Benjamins*, ed. S. Unseld (Frankfort: Suhrkamp, 1972), p. 127. Cf. Also J. Habermas's contrasting discussion, p. 201 passim.

18. Consider, for example, *On the Mimetic Faculty*, for a scheme which combines the preservation, transformation, decay and liquidation of the occult (*R*, pp. 333–36).

19. "I speak here of an identity," writes the younger Benjamin," which emerges only from the paradoxical reversal [*Umschlagen*] (in whatever direc-tion) of one into the other" (*Briefe*, ed. G. Scholem and T. W. Adorno [Frank-fort: Suhrkamp, 1966], p. 425). He is referring to the relation of politics to religion. Such logic recalls Novalis's definition of philosophy as a "mystical . . . penetrating idea which irresistibly drives us in all directions" (*GS*, 1, 1, p. 47). "To penetrate into the depths," Benjamin once told Brecht, "is my way

of travelling to the antipodes." (*Understanding Brecht* [London: NLB, 1973], p. 110).

20. Benjamin defines aura as "the unique appearance of a distance, *however near it may be*" (*I*, p. 222, emphasis added). It is destroyed by "the desire of contemporary masses to bring things 'closer' spatially and humanly." As Benjamin's definition suggests, proximity *can* be built into its structure. But in the case of art, mechanical reproduction affects a "most sensitive kernel" (p. 221). So much for the idealist model of an inviolable prosaic kernel: history is not an unbroken continuum. Thus the materialist Benjamin also breaks with the idealism to which he continues to remain indebted. Hence such paradoxes as the post-auratic aura of Messianic prose "where proximity looks itself in the face." It is doubtful whether they are describable in terms either of organic development or an epistemological break.

21. Cf., on such faith in the productivity of mystico-dialectical reversal, *The Work of Art in the Age of Mechanical Reproduction*: "The mass is a matrix from which all traditional attitudes to works of art today emerge newly born. Quantity has turned (*umgeschlagen*) into quality" (*I*, p. 239. Cf., on *Umschlagen*, note 19 above). Cf. also *The Author as Producer*: "it is in the theater of the unbridled debasement of the word—the newspaper—that its salvation is being prepared" (*R*, p. 225). There are, clearly, no *guarantees* that the prose of profane illumination will succeed in leavening an all-too-prosaic world.

22. Cf. Jacques Derrida, "De l'économie restreinte à l'économie générale," in *L'Ecriture et la Différence* (Paris: Seuil, 1967), pp. 369–407.

23. To emerge from the sleep of Hegelian reason—a sleep over which the logic of *Aufhebung* vigilantly and cunningly presides—it is first necessary, Derrida argues, to spend the night with it. But since the ensuing *dawn*— "Ce matin-là et non un autre" (p. 370) bears a deceptive resemblance to the *dusk* when, according to Hegel, philosophy ("the owl of Minerva") awakens, *redoubled* alertness is called for. It is the same "vigilance" that *L'Absolu littéraire* would have us bring to our *German Romantic* sleep.

24. Cf. Béguin's quotations from Steffens, Schelling, Novalis, Schubert, etc. (*L'Ame Romantique et les Rêves* [Paris: Corti, 1946], pp. 82, 86, 111, 208, 210). "On ne peut que romantiquement parler du romantisme," he claims (xiii). Such a declaration of empathy is, in Benjamin's terms, a case of *mythical* fascination and, in de Man's, an unwitting version of Romantic *irony*!

25. "The realization of dream elements upon awakening is the textbook example of dialectical thinking. For this reason dialectical thinking is the organ of historical awakening. Each epoch not only dreams the next, but also, in dreaming, strives toward the moment of awakening. It bears its end in itself and unfolds—as Hegel already saw—with cunning" (*R*, p. 162). Does, then, even the central Benjaminian notion of "presence of mind," subjected to *still soberer* deconstructionist analysis, seem firmly trapped in Hegelian/Romantic phantasms? But such was the materialist Benjamin's own objection to *L'Ame Romantique et le Rêve*. While endorsing Albert Béguin's contention that "disinterested" research is self-betrayal, he argued that Béguin's all-too-immediate self-identification with Romantic dream-theories was no substitute for a—no less "intensive"—investigation of the historical "constellation" in which they arose. "He fails to reckon with the possibility that the true, synthetic kernel of the object could send out a

Irving Wohlfarth

light in which the Romantic dream theories fall apart" (*GS*, 3, p. 560). Even here Benjamin's categories—constellation, kernel, irradiation—characteristically betray Romantic affinities. They thus corrode themselves. A difficult state of affairs, but it is precisely deconstructionist analyses which have taught us to consider such practicable contradictions as strategically indispensable to the complex program they share in common with Benjamin—namely, waking up.

SEVEN

THE THEORY OF ACCIDENTS
Denis Kambouchner

This text is dedicated to Philippe Lacoue-Labarthe
and Jean-Luc Nancy

LET US INTRODUCE, in close association with the question of genre, that of generality. Let us then raise the question: *how is generality in literary theory possible?*—or even more simply, if we persist in recognizing generality as the fundamental condition of theoretical discourse: *how is a theory of literature possible?* Supposing at least that literary theory would accept a question of this sort. Supposing that a question of this sort is even acceptable—an assumption which is not altogether certain.

This question, with its Kantian tone, may appear at first provocative, or, worse, impertinent, meaning that the provocation would be of no benefit and would only reveal the somewhat ridiculous ambitiousness of a legislative investigation. To whomever would like to examine the possibility of approaching literature within a theoretical framework— once this possibility has been legitimized—the immediate response would be that literary theory *exists*, and that the many studies recently having constituted its configuration and having furnished its program have generally shown themselves to be concerned with methodological questions and attentive to their own operations, so that the general prejudicial question of the conditions of possibility must be rejected as anachronistic, if not as hyperbolic and speculative. Literary theory, in its reality and its positivity, has no need of a transcendental foundation, whose procedures and reasoning, acting on an object such as a text, are moreover barely imaginable; it has need only of principles and concepts that it alone can elaborate—this elaboration, forever in progress, being after all the surest gauge of its reality.

The following must be established immediately: in opening up this question, we are neither contesting the existence of literary theory, nor binding works of literary theory to a strictly philosophical jurisdiction. It should be recognized simply that this term "literary theory" can be taken in two ways and can be understood on two distinct levels. In its broader and more diluted sense this term, or title, would denote the totality of texts, theoretical in nature, devoted to literature, without discriminating as to their object, orientation or validity. In its second stricter and stronger sense, it would designate only the general constitution of a coherent, unified theory. We would say then—and in no way paradoxically—that all works which remain within the scope of literary theory in its second meaning (of *telos* or achieved configuration) belong to literary theory in its first meaning (of a generic and institutional title). This having been said, it should be recognized that the present reality of the former does not mean that the latter is not still to be realized. In addition: if any endeavor is regularly defined by a self-assigned *telos* and if this *telos* is as much a problem as an object, then the possibility of literary theory in the stricter sense is not an issue irrelevant to works of literary theory in the larger sense: rather it is—more or less openly—their essential concern and constant preoccupation. To raise the question is, then, neither arbitrary nor arrogant.

There are, however, two points in these broad arguments which might lend themselves to certain objections. It can first be asked if it is not an undue simplification to maintain that a work's self-proposed *telos* is the sole criterion of its status. This work can certainly be defined equally well by its style, its processes, or the order of its objects—or even by its lexical choices and its mode of discursiveness. As for generality, it is then scarcely feasible that any work could call itself theoretical if this generality were not already present therein, either as the object or as the modality of its *énoncés*. It becomes difficult, therefore, to postulate a strict distinction between the two positions of theory (the actual and the teleological positions) and to consider generality as still potential and problematic when this generality is, in one way or another, already to be found in a certain number of studies that might readily be cited. Next (and this is the second point), it can be asked if the theoretical *telos* in fact has, at least for "modernity," the systematizing and synthesizing properties conferred on it here. It is obviously easy to contrast abstractly the notion of a general theory with the reality of individual and parcellary works; it is easy to oppose the achieved generality, sure and definitive, of the former in opposition to the provisional generality, uncertain and incessantly menaced, characteristic of the latter. But this opposition probably loses its pertinence whenever the ideal of the achieved theory is abandoned or decried as illusory and inaccessible, whenever theoretical works give up their pretensions to system and recognize in this precarious generality their one true element—thereby trying simply and modestly to diminish its precariousness.

These objections, which are not negligible and which at this time make no concessions to the ordinary ease of a positivist pragmatism—these objections cannot be immediately put aside. At least the following must be conceded, that the generality which is our object or our concern here cannot in fact be accorded a simple position, and that the traditional position of science or of theory *qua* science or theory of the general now requires more than one criticism and more than one readjustment. However much this position remains (or has become) in itself problematic—and the whole task here is to examine its fate—it seems just as adventurous, and debatable, to accord an absolute significance and unlimited value to the signs by which many recent studies have signaled their divergence from any classical theoretical position. Certainly the express representation of an orderly, exhaustive theory, guaranteed *a priori* as to its generality, has recently suffered an eclipse in literary studies as it has elsewhere. It is unlikely, though, that the comprehensive understanding of the *"fait littéraire"* (literary reality) in its specific composition, its status, and its correlates, is a goal that has been generally abandoned. So that the question remains intact and insistent: how do we know under precisely which conditions this understanding is possible—in other words, how can something like "the literary text in general" (or "literature in general") be established, structured as a theoretical object? That we could find in the corpus of works devoted to literature declarations which bear on the text in general, that there could be in the works which compose this corpus a dimension or areas of generality, these facts in themselves do not put an end to the question. First because here it is not a matter of opening or closing the possibility of this generality (as if it were to appear in the future or as if, to the contrary, it could never exist), but rather a matter of knowing which status belongs to it in its area of insistence or declaration. Secondly, there is an appreciable and persistent difference between the lacunary character, episodic or discrete, of generality currently attained and the organic character, strict and regular, of the projected generality—between the positions to which the "text in general" gives rise and its constitution as object.

What is at issue here, then, is, in one word, the *constitution* of the literary text, or the constitution of literature. Moreover, this word *constitution* should be interpreted in its strongest sense, according to

Denis Kambouchner

which the theoretical constitution of an object at once involves certain features ordinarily associated only with juridico-political constitutions. There is nothing arbitrary in that. In general, the labor of theory can be demonstrably foreign to all normative objectives, disavow all juridical categories and procedures, sidestep any dogmatic positions, and deny itself any position of authority in regard to its objects. But insofar as it sets up for itself an object (however this "object" might be defined), the labor of theory cannot deny that it seeks to give this object its proper place or function, its definition, and its value within a general range (of objects, but also of categories) which itself must possess or acquire a stable configuration. Hence the chief or controlling imperative will always have been to structure, to divide or to break down into certain categories the realm of acts or of objects that today we call *literature* (but which elsewhere have been called *mythos, Dichtung,* etc., names which emphasize other divisions and implications) so that this realm will not remain irregular, unstable, or disquieting in respect to the general configuration of knoweldge, and in respect to the definition of other cultural and societal phenomena. Nothing there that goes beyond the current meaning of the term *constitution*—according to which any object is "constituted" when a stable structure and meaning in it can be perceived. But accepting this imperative is only one step away from domesticating (programmatically at least) the "literary reality" (the *mythos,* the *Dichtung,* etc.), from assigning to it the status of heteronomy, fixing its position within an order of representations which would acquire its laws elsewhere and which could, as such, fashion the element or object of legislation. These operations are inevitable, and this step is always taken, to the extent that in no hypothesis can this reality attain absolute autonomy nor impose by itself its modalities of comprehension. To this extent, the theoretical operation cannot be absolutely exclusive of a juridical dimension. Between one constitution and another (or between one aspect of the constitution and another), there is more than just homonymy and coincidence.

This association can remain, almost always, in the background. But we have only to refer, for example, to Book II of Plato's *Republic* (or *Constitution*) to find, if not its basic foundation, at least its exemplary actualization. *Prôton dè hèmin epistateon tois mythopoiois*— "we must first of all supervise the fable-makers" (examine their work, direct them): this program, or slogan, is articulated just after the (not yet legislative) provision listing the City-State's basic components. And the primary task, from the Platonic point of view, seems not to be the handing down of laws and regulations which would compose the *Politeia* (the system of laws, the constitution, the political organization), but rather the examination and specification of the use, terms and form of these *mythoi* (myths, fictions, fables) told to children—the essential object of the prescription being the reference to gods and heroes (the manner in which the *mythoi* represent them). The first task is, we would say, to guarantee the political constitution, in its indispensable stability, by the regulation or establishment of a symbolic constitution whose primary element is the *mythos*. The same necessity can be observed in certain works by Rousseau, for example in *The Letter to D'Alembert*, where the theater appears as the very thing which threatens community and political contractuality: "We think that in going to the theater we are coming together, and yet it is just there that each of us withdraws; it is there that we are going to forget our friends, our neighbors, our family to become absorbed in fictions, to lament the misfortunes of the dead, or to laugh at the expense of the living." ("L'on croit s'assembler au spectacle, et c'est là que chacun s'isole; c'est là qu'on va oublier ses amis, ses voisins, ses proches, pour s'intéresser à des fables, pour pleurer les malheurs des morts, ou rire aux dépens des vivants.") In both instances, the *epistèmè* or that which takes its place—theoretical or philosophical comprehension of literature, theater or fable—remains whole under the necessity (and within the limits) of the *epistasis*, of supervision and regimentation.

Undoubtedly, it cannot be maintained that every theoretical treatment of literature (let the word be taken, if possible, in its strictly referential aspect, and as a summary of all the other names) is comprehensible within the same framework or admits of the same implications. The theoretical constitution of literature cannot be absolutely, nor even necessarily, its juridical, civic or normative constitution. A treatment may take diverse forms, according to its explicit orientation toward a juridico-political or an esthetic normativity, or toward a simply epistemic concern. But even supposing that it would always be possible to distinguish strictly among the three instances, they would still coincide in a way that would make the Platonic or Rousseauist position something other than an accident (exception or excess) in relation to the usual status of theory. On the one hand, if theory wants to *comprehend* the text or literature, in the absolute use of the term, namely to determine its constitutive elements, define its program and guarantee its place and function, the theoretical program thus established cannot exist without external correlates: the moment that it seems to be fulfilled is also that moment when the text (literature) seems to become controllable—seems therefore to sustain submission to a practical (or pragmatic) program, whose *telos* is no longer internal to the theory. This practical program, due to its nonspecific character (in as much as it does not concern a single text) is also necessarily prescriptive, normative—so that the horizon of normativity can never be absolutely abolished by a theoretical operation, even if it were "pure." On the other hand, and more radically, if in theory there is no

Denis Kambouchner

operation which is not a decision, it is never certain that the decision is imposed by "the thing itself" rather than imposed on it with some measure of arbitrariness or authority. It must be assumed that as the urgency to have any object comprehended, defined, and stabilized increases, so does the prescriptive value of the theoretical decision—and the resulting legality or regularity becomes in fact increasingly an imposed legality or regularity. Because the position of the urgency is subject to variations from one theoretical undertaking to another, the sphere of activity and the modes of prescription can shift; but no venture, no matter what its validity and precautions, can absolutely deny itself every prescriptive dimension. From both points of view— considering the position in which theory is established and the positions taken within theory—the pursuit of legality is also the testing of legislation. And juridical regulation may well differ widely from theoretical regularity: theory, nevertheless, seeks and instantly imposes its own jurisdiction.

The theoretical constitution, in this respect, is no more a simple act or simple decree than is the juridical constitution. It concerns, rather, the differential position of a complex and regular system of places, functions, values, and signs, in which and through references to which every act, every endeavor, every event should be defined, according to a distribution by *topos* or *casus*. By means of the constitution, reality is described and, at the same time, organized. In the constitution and in reference to it the *composite*, the *example* and the *case* assume their meanings: the *composite* as a concrete, individual organization of constitutive elements; the *example* as a concrete or "real" element which fills precisely any function or place; and the *case* as a structurally defined possibility or as an exceptional case, seen as atypical or abnormal but not as imprescriptible or indefinable. With the special clause here— assuring the difference between the theoretical and the juridical, and the possible prevalence of the first over the second—the elements recognized as constitutive should constitute not only the conditions governing the definition, the reconstitution and the judgment of the real, but also the real itself in all its aspects. The constitutive elements, in other words, are not only the means of defining the real, but also that by which the real takes its form. Therefore the constitution under its theoretical, even more than its juridical, status has the two inseparable values of *diagram* and *program*: diagram of the actual and program of the potential, so that, theoretically, nothing can remain resistant or irreducible to it.

Within this configuration—of which only a minimal outline has been set forth here—the question of generality and the opposing of the general (or generic) to the particular are immediately involved in such a way that, in fact, there is no constitution which is not constituted according to this opposition and, reciprocally, no occurrence of this opposition which is not grounded in a constitutional frame of reference. From one point of view, the constitution as act—insofar as it is elaborated, written down, and decreed in founding texts—implies a position of generality as a starting point for defining generally some general structures as well as categories, namely concepts and values. Were this position to be lacking, no specification could take place. And from another point of view, the constitution as a fundamental structure—assigned to the "things themselves" and pertinent thereto—can admit only of *general* (or generic) places, functions, values—again, categories as classes—in which individual elements and facts are placed and constituted. And inasmuch as the constitution results in planning or speculation, inasmuch as it is the object of calculation and theory, the essential problem of this calculating and theorizing is to assure that the particular is constantly compared to and constituted with regard to the general, that it is considered, known (*epistamenon*) and watched over (*epistatêmenon*) by it. In the realm of political constitutions, the *Social Contract*, for example, can be wholly understood through an accentuation of this problem—the particular (as individual or subject) being, in relation to the general (the State, the sovereign, the assembly, or the convention), capable of imminent deviation, infraction, resistance, or even (a more radical hypothesis) amnesia, forgetting, infraction, resistance, forgetfulness which then bear on its own condition. In the realm of theoretical constitutions, an infraction may be less obvious, a threat less immediate or less precise. But the risk is the same: that a particular object or fact would remain (at least partially) unassimilated, irreducible to the ordinary modalities of assignment, and that the theory would therefore be left (at least ultimately) limited, fragile, unstable.

What is at issue, then, in the constituting of the literary text? To constitute the text (or literature) theoretically means, on the one hand, to establish the general configuration within which *all* available texts (determined by a cursory delineation of the corpus) should be classified (in such a way that their similarities and dissimilarities are apparent) and on the other, to provide an enumeration, definition, and analysis of the text's constitutive elements (in such a way that nothing belonging to literary reality, or at least to the observable portion thereof, noticeably eludes the grasp of theoretical discourse). From both viewpoints, then, it is a matter of elaborating the *fundamental categories* of literature: those which alone can establish discourse on the mode of literature's development, on its function and place among cultural phenomena; those which any scholarly (cognitive) discourse on literature, whatever its specific object may be, must recognize, actualize, and confirm. These categories acquire and maintain their determination

Denis Kambouchner

and form independently of any individual text. And the generality here at issue is nothing other than the status pertaining to them—that which also belongs to any discourse dedicated strictly to explaining and constituting them. Since there would be no cognitive discourse on literature if such categories were not already available or constituable, this generality (or this constitution) is already a reality. But because, in its very reality, it requires extension, verification and guarantee, and because the existing consitution may always appear incomplete, the question of justification (*quid juris?*) persists; and since there has been no response to this question by the act of a general foundation, generality and constitution remain entirely unrealized with respect to their absolute values.

Two problems—for there are problems—surface immediately. The first concerns the circumscription and the unity of the literary corpus, which implies that all texts are recognized as possessing a certain number of characteristics in common. If the corpus is not unified, or at least classified, no criterion will guarantee that we can speak of one text as we do of another, or that what is said of the text in general can be applied to all texts: a theoretical constitution would be impossible. The second problem concerns the provenance and the mode of elaborating general categories or, essentially, the status of the example. If, in fact, these categories can only be fixed and elaborated through an investigation of particular texts, if whatever is tested or constructed within the element of particularity cannot then be abstracted from this particularity, if the example cannot be simply a sample, and if, briefly, the individuality of each text demands a different analytical mode, we will not have well-grounded generality but only precarious generalizations, and nothing will guarantee the general stability of the constitution. These problems stem directly from the status here accorded to the constitution; works of literary theory have generally abstained from questioning this status. But this does not imply that these problems are purely speculative and have never been treated *in concreto.* Quite the opposite: their persistence has been such that a fundamental schema of literary theory (one of the oldest and one of the most resistant, taking into account its diverse affectations) can be construed as replying directly to them. This is precisely the distinction among genres, which constitutes at least a provisional solution to the first problem, and which is an ever-present recourse for the second, as valuable as it is cumbersome, in that it encompasses all the pressing difficulties encountered here.

In the first case, the advantage of this distinction is clear enough: the genres having been hypothesized as highly distinctive, categorizing units (which does not imply that their definition would be absolutely rigorous, but only that their differentiation brings some sharp contrasts into play), texts are then distributed into the different genres, not only because of formal differences, not only because of a diversity of types and institutional uses, but also, correlatively, because they impose different sorts of handling—the distinction between them consequently coinciding with the opposition or arrangement of the fundamental categories of discourse concerning them. The literary corpus need not be fully delimited; theoretical generality, though, is guaranteed due to the instituting of genre as the general framework for comparing individual texts and as the elaborative framework of a rigorous conceptual apparatus. Not that the genre distinctions would be absolute and absolutely exclusive, as could be suggested by an unnecessarily direct or automatic reference to the Aristotelian meaning of the term. In his *Poetics*, Aristotle speaks not of the *genos* but of the *eidos*. The category of "literary genre," in its common as well as in its most advantageous usage, cannot have the value of absolute insuperability attached to the *genos* in Aristotelian logic and metaphysics. The overlapping of genre boundaries can be acknowledged by a generic constituting of literature, without appearing as a threatening distortion, if it is assigned, declared as such, and given the status of exception. Thus it is still possible to speak of differences among genres, of their occasional overlapping, or even of newly defined genres, without constitutional generality suffering as a result. It is not necessary, to speak succinctly, for the genre *qua* unity to have an absolute form and position; it is only necessary that genre exist, as a frame of reference and as a guarantee of generalization.

Like every other constitutional element, genre does not serve uniquely as a frame of reference: it exists too as *program*. And this is not only because it is and has been possible to determine a canon, a set of esthetic norms or a list of distinguishing signs. For each genre (as type of texts) there is a corresponding genre of interests, namely a specification which affects not only theoretical discourse (with its categories and secondary objects), but also the ordinary act of reading (in so far as it is predetermined by certain presumptions, anticipations, postulations, expectations) and the act of writing (to the extent that it depends upon a formal design). The position of genre is active, or insistent, within each order of operations. It intervenes in the writing act from the very moment of the text's conception, through which are defined, at least in their general modalities, the principal elements to be presented, the action or motives organizing them, the referential or differential ties situating the text within a broader context or tradition —so that every text is defined, projected, and in some way written within the limits of generic forms. It intervenes in reading too, to the extent that the initial interest of the reader is directed not to an as yet unknown text's achieved individuality, but toward a textual type or

Denis Kambouchner

ideal, toward a form or a program that this particular text should provide or actualize. Undoubtedly the idiom, and with it the singularity of the elements presented, appear very quickly: the reading cannot be sustained without this singularity. This fundamental condition remains: what we expect of our genre (the lyric poem, for example) is not what we expect from another (for example, the novel); genre's position predetermines the objects of interest and the degree of attention to literalness. Nor can an absolute exclusivity or prescription exist here: it is not impossible to read a novel as a poem. This operation—reading within the mixing or blurring of genres—should simply start with a particular decision, which does not in itself threaten the consistency of genre but which theoretically remains foreign to reading's normal operations.

From this programmatic nature of genre, and from its frequent and regular occurrence in the act of reading, just as in the act of writing (the former as the moment of recognizing and institutionalizing the text being more decisive here than the latter), the following proceeds directly if the constitution leaves something unassimilated, if something from the text is not comprised within it, this residue is theoretically inoffensive and discreet. The essential point, in other words, is as follows: that no hiatus exists between the theoretical constitution of genre and the particular experience of reading a text; that the generic categories are active even at a level which might seem to be the most empirical. *Genre carves out the text.* And this carving out is not a carving up or dividing up which affects equally constituted and homogeneous elements: it is precisely the act which institutes the text, by which the text acquires its physiognomy, its characteristics, its usage, its evaluative criteria. It says what the text is and how it should be received. The residue remains discreet or even inoffensive: some operations or elements not comprised within any generic division can surely be found in the achieved singularity of the text; but it is inconceivable that designating these operations or elements would precipitate a crumbling of the generic constitution, as long as the programs for reading and for theory support each other, reciprocally corroborating their present positions. These programs are not complete; the possibility of, or pretention to, a reading which would be sustained (or which would maintain the text) in the absence of any genre determinations, or of an act of writing which would encounter only literature in general, beyond all genre, can never entirely disappear from the realm of literary reality, nor from discourse concerning literature. But if the generic program could or should ever be disassembled, it would necessitate not only a change in the status of writing, not only a theoretical challenge: it would necessitate significant reform in the metabolic relationship between reading and theory.

It is precisely from this quarter—the metabolism of this relationship—that the constitution's second fundamental problem arises: the problem which bears on the general categories' provenance and mode of establishment, or on the status of the example. The issue, in its most formal aspect, can be presented thus: theoretical elaboration in literature necessarily deals with reading, as the most fundamental modality of relating to texts. If literary theory wants to be a complete theory, at least three conditions must be respected: first of all, that a reading should yield no appreciable residue (that not a single constitutive element of the text should remain illegible or unread); next, that what results from a reading of a particular text should be wholly assimilable to or determinable by general theory; finally, that reading, in its relationship with theory, should keep its experimental or confirmational function, the mode of elaborating theoretical categories being *a priori* exempt from any empirical limitation. If these three conditions cannot be respected, the fundamental adherence or correspondence of the general and particular will not be absolutely guaranteed—adherence or correspondence which alone can exclude on principle (namely, in any way not accidental, contingent, defective and reparable) the risk of the one infringing upon the other (with either theory remaining abstract, failing to encompass particularities, or reading, as a particular reading, being misguided or detached from any theoretical order). But this hypothesis cannot be rejected *a priori*, and it is advisable first to examine these conditions in their most problematic aspects.

Everything up to this point would be simple enough if we could see in the reading act—at least in a scholarly reading, to be distinguished from ordinary readings—a purely empirical or experimental moment without real subsistence or specific program. But a scholarly reading is not simply an operation, or even a set of operations: it is a discipline (in the institutional sense of the term), a genre of research which has its own specific *telos* and function within the general field of discourse on literature. As an institution of literary instruction, or medium of cultural celebration and integration of the "great texts," reading does not fall exactly within the bounds of theory. "Genre of research": this occurrence of the word *"genre"* is not fortuitous. In the relationship between theory and reading (or between *poetics* and *criticism*), the question of genre is implied twice: first, to the extent that theory should direct this generality's elaboration, in which or in reference to which a particularity, dealt with in the reading, takes its place; second, to the extent that, in the general field of "literary studies" or discourse concerning literature, reading and theory (criticism and poetics) can be presented as two distinct genres. There is nothing out of the ordinary about this division of one discipline or sphere into genres (distinct epistemic modalities or subdivisions): it can be said that this division, with respect to the claims of an epistomological generality, has the same relationship that the division of objects into genres has with the claims of a theoretical generality. This division, in particular, is absolutely necessary for the methical or methodological constituting of theory—the genre of discipline, questions or activity alone furnishing the strict boundaries and guarantee of unity to a method's position. The distinction made between research genres does not have an absolute position any more than does the distinction between object genres: a scholarly discourse may well mix genres together and thus, for example, cause reading and theory to coexist by means of a highly complex interlacing. Such discourse does not thereby become illegitimate, since each genre can be, in fact, recognized within it—which is to say that its forms and rules are respected as to *locus*. The problem there is this: how is the genre distinction between reading and theory compatible with the fundamental (hierarchical, architectonic) prevalence of the latter over the former? Can we permit a significant distinction if this distinction constantly threatens the reciprocal adherence between reading and theory?

First we must rule out two equally abstract and *a priori* untenable positions. The first would have theory follow or simply emanate from reading through synthesis or generalization: but the generality thus obtained could never be guaranteed, and the very constitution of the theoretical elements (which, hypothetically, should be constituted and active in the reading) would become almost incomprehensible. Inversely, according to the second position, readings would only follow an already constructed theory, applying it to the particularity of various texts: but in that case the principle of this construction would not be made any more intelligible. Rather an essential contemporaneity must be postulated between reading and theory—theory having the task of elaborating, discussing, systematizing the schemas and categories used in reading. Readings would be concerned with the structure of a given narrative, with the characters found in a specific novel, with the metaphors of a particular poem; theory should, generally, be devoted to questions such as: "what is a narrative structure?" "what is a character?" "what is a metaphor?" etc. Reading should analyze the positive singularity of texts by means of categories and schemas constituted and guaranteed by their objective validity, then used as neutral instruments; theory should constitute the positive generality of these schemas and categories with reference to examples (texts or text fragments considered to be *topoi*, sequences of a supposedly neutral reading). Theory and reading should, therefore, maintain a relationship of reciprocal instrumentality, the former providing its operations to and borrowing its examples from the latter. It would be of no importance that each is actually incomplete, that theory is possibly less advanced than reading: they should each ultimately come to rest in their own *telos* (the complete constitution of generality, the exhaustive comprehending of particularity), with theory being naturally predominant in its scope, stability, and interest.

This position of the relationship is seductive, and hardly seems controvertible. It is found often enough in texts dealing with literary theory; and if literary theory is possible, it certainly appears that it could not assume any other position with respect to reading. Not, nevertheless, that this position would be self-evident or that it should be accepted without precautions or examination. At the least it postulates this—that between reading and theory there is community, coincidence, or correspondence (at least partial, but potentially complete) of schemas and categories. Yet this is not absolutely certain. Assuredly, many of the words (or categories) which critical discourse (or reading) uses to describe a text's form or to reconstruct a signifying complexity are also found, as objects or concepts, in theoretical discourse. Assuredly, many of the schemas (that is to say, at least, the determining modes and figures) through which critical discourse defines and qualifies a text correspond to a concept of literature, of text, that theoretical discourse can and should determine or explain. But empirically verifying the existence of this correspondence, or community, does not yet establish its fundamental or general principle. There remains a question, which bears more essentially on the schemas than on the categories —first because each category contains a schematizing function (whereas not every schema is given a name), next because the recurrence of a word or the use of identical words can appear to indicate an identity of categories, whereas the coincidence of schemas cannot be thus represented and offers no immediate assurance. The question remains: do both critical discourse and theoretical discourse use or depend upon the same schematism? Or, if we admit that theoretical discourse *is* both discourse *par excellence* on schema and schematic discourse (elaborating its own schemas and those of *praxis*), is reading itself, as *praxis*, a schematizing activity, and can it be, as such, subject to regulation by theory? There is no more crucial question than this. All questions previously raised—concerning the provenance of general categories, the exhaustiveness of critical and theoretical treatments of texts, and, finally, the genre distinction between reading and theory —belong to this question, whose extent and meaning must still be clarified.

There are very few ways of passing from a text's particularity to a theoretical generality (of schematizing the former within the latter). Theory, as the constituting of generality, deals, in a text and consequently in a reading, only with that which either can be described in general terms and general forms, or can be translated into a system of significations (into a code) seen as determinative and admitting of an autonomous presentation. Theory is dealing, thus, either with structures and schemas which the text actualizes (in applying them to particular elements), or with constitutive (general) elements which the text assembles into a particular composition, or even with a general focus of meaning which would determine the whole or the essential part of the text—the text having no function other than to constitute one particular actualization, version or translation of it. In all the above instances, we are concerned with elements or factors whose consistency and determination are *a priori* independent of any particularity whatsoever, and which therefore determine the text rather than being determined therein. In this way, even when theoretical discourse in using a particular text seems to name or constitute something which will take on a general aspect, the work of theory in relation to the text is always *a priori* determining, in the Kantian sense of the word: it subsumes the particular under the general—the general being itself preconstituted, determinative, and strictly determinable within theory. The fact that reading itself would be schematizing and would use schemas elaborated within a theoretical framework should signify, consequently, that it is itself essentially determining and that, if the schematization here can consist only of describing and translating, reading is essentially descriptive and translative. It remains to be seen if this is indeed the case.

The following can be recognized without difficulty: reading (still a matter of scholarly or critical reading, it will later be seen why this is an absolutely imposed qualification) can indeed be integrally descriptive or translative, it can consist entirely of a schematizing activity (namely, determining the text only in relation to generality), when it considers brief and strictly limited text sequences. More generally, every reading, whatever its scope, avails itself of descriptive and translative schemas, through which a text's form is related to certain generic categories or signs, and its signifying complexity linked to certain fundamental orders of meaning. But when a reading does not permit itself a preliminary segmenting of the text, but rather agrees to confront the text in its general depth, density, and complexity, it should, in order to record this complexity or simply to take its bearings from it, effect at least two types of operations which belong neither to description nor to translation: they are *accentuation* (through which any text element deemed significant is noted, or reformulated, retranscribed, but without being linked to any generality whatsoever) and *liaison* (by which two or more elements are associated and determined with respect to one another through an affinity of meaning, the mode of determining here affecting only the particularity—the particular determining the particular). Neither accentuation nor liaison implies the usage or occurrence of constitutional schemas: the elements to which they are applied do not lend themselves, in their singularity, to any anticipation, and if it happens that the liaison is typical (corresponding to a type of relationship already elaborated), it usually constitutes a *pure relationship*, without determined form.

These two operations—accentuation and liaison—would remain inessential and nonthreatening to the schematizing (determining) character of reading, if they were only the necessary preliminaries to description and translation, if they could be integrally submitted to these two, or if they could be maintained within the limits of a strictly determinable program. It is not fortuitous that these conditions recall those which affected the general relationship between reading and theory: the problem's dimensions have shrunk, description and translation now representing that part of reading which *a priori* tolerates theorization. But two forceful arguments cause these conditions not to be respected, and they cause reading to remain at least partially, but perhaps fundamentally, insubordinate to the status of theoretical determination.

The first is that accentuation and liaison are both bound to an activity, or event, of singular status, which is the *observation*. Observation is not just one operation among others: it is the fundamental act of scholarly reading without which nothing can be said, represented or explained about a text. A reading of a text can be useful to the constituting of a general theory, and this theory can take possession of a text, only if all the observations occasioned by the text coincide with the rigorously established program of its theorization. The problem is that between observation and program, there is not an incompatibility, but rather a persistent inadequateness. Certainly any observation implies a certain capacity for attentiveness and a certain orientation of this attentiveness; this orientation is itself correlative to interests, questions or categories of reference which can attain their coherence in an established theory, and in this way the observation can be the object of a *discipline* (a declaration in the form of: "such and such must be noted" is not an aberrant statement). But, from another point of view, an observation occurs only if something absolutely singular and unforeseeable is discovered and makes itself obvious: an observation which would, however, correspond to the form of questions and reference categories could always fail to occur, while another could occur which no general prescription would have determined. The attentiveness brought to the text is never strictly programmable, and the observation is at least as much an unforeseeable event as it is a preformed operation: in it the latter is lost in the former. The liaison, therefore, and the accentuation, as forms of observation, cannot be anticipated, not only with respect to their object (textual particularity), but also with respect to their execution, so that they cannot respect or constitute any program, and so that, for reading, there is no principle of complete synthesis (neither in relation to the text, nor in relation to theory).

From another standpoint—and this is the second argument—the particularity exhibited by liaison and accentuation is not of such a nature that it could be subsumed, converted, or surpassed (*aufgehoben*) without residue within a descriptive or translative generality. It is not even essentially devoted to either description or translation, but much more to a development which should reach its conclusion (or *telos*) in a complete liaison (an integral reconstitution of particularity). It is an established fact that description and translation are necessary to point out formal relations within the text or to relate elements belonging to different orders of signification. The labors of general constitution and complete liaison cannot then be sustained in absolute externality. But just as certainly description and translation are, in relation to textual particularity, only partially active: description cannot affect the particularities of *meaning*, and translation, when it relates the particularities of meaning to the generality of a fundamental code (or of an original constituting of significations) does not suppress them as such in any instance. It is a general paradox: every translation is inherently incomplete (omitting certain determinations from what is translated); and the more the fundamental code (in which the *traductum* is inserted) is restricted, the more the particularity of the original remains, as such, incomprehensible. These particularities of meaning are not absolutely exclusive of any general dimension, nor do generality and particularity form two separate spheres or elements. But, as regards meaning, the generality to which the text is immediately related (that within which the text is elaborated, and which it elaborates) is not the generality of a fundamental code, structured and organic, but rather, punctual and discrete, the generality of referent, motif or theme. And because these elements—referent, motives, themes—are inherently innumerable, because they do not correspond to stable entities, because their conjunction is never simply combinative, their generality is not that which forms the object, element or quality of the theoretical constitution. And if it is not theoretically impossible to consider each text as a peculiar composition of general elements (in which case particularity can be *a priori* completely resolved within the schematic determining), in fact this generality is too unequal, diverse and diffuse to be synthesized or exhausted in any theory whatsoever.

Reading is thus bound to the text, to its particularity: in its fundamental acts, it deals with generality as such only incidentally, and even when it must recognize in the text elements of a general dimension, it is, nevertheless, not necessarily, nor very often, a matter of theoretically determinable generality. Even though in reading there is one part (description, translation) devoted to theory, reading in its entirety cannot be called schematizing or determining, nor can it be submitted, on account of its partial schematism, to a general theoretical program. Assuredly, according to the interests, questions and categories which contribute to defining its style, the importance of its determining part (that devoted to theory) can be subject to variation. But the more a reading insists on observing only that which can be inserted in a given theoretical framework or program, the more likely it is to overlook the particularity of the text—and the less it reads. Hence, with respect to the genre distinction between reading and theory, this special situation obtains: either these two activities constitute only a single genre (when reading is entirely schematizing—which can happen, if it can happen, only when it affects small text units—but in that case reading is only the empirical moment of theoretical activity); or the difference between the two is considerable and so complex that the schema of generic distinction (in so far as it implies a broad and strongly marked opposition) is in no way sufficient to describe it. And because the first hypothesis does not correspond to reading's usual status, but rather to a practice extremely limited in its scope as well as in its comprehension, there is no hope that theory (as the constituting of generality) and reading (as the exploration of particularity) will ever exist in a harmonious, architectonic interrelationship.

Up until now we have dealt only with scholarly reading—to wit, that which claims to know what reading is and intends to know what it reads. But the screw is tightened one more turn if it proves that this reading with its pretensions to knowledge does not comprehend, does not capture all the effects relating to the text and all the constitutive phenomena of literary reality. Yet another form of reading obviously exists, namely *ordinary reading*, which is not directed toward an epistemic *telos*—or at least not to the same one—with which scholarly reading maintains a remarkable relationship. On one hand, scholarly reading sets for itself the task of pointing out, in the body of the text, everything an ordinary reading usually fails to note—the discrete elements of which the text is composed and whose composition gives the text, at the same time, its unique physiognomy, its characteristics, and its efficacity. It makes a discipline of the observation in order to reconstitute a certain program: not the generic program of which the text would be the example, but the individual program which it elaborates or effects. And in so far as the text's program is also a program for reading (whose phases and effects the ordinary reading records, but without taking note of them), the scholarly reading in some way reconstitutes the progress and course of the ordinary reading, and brings out its truth. But, on the other hand, the reconstitution is in no way repetitive or mimetic; and if scholarly reading indeed claims to restore the truth of the ordinary reading, it also abolishes, misconstrues, or discards one of its essential dimensions. An ordinary reading does not have to know a text's program as such, and even less the generic program of which the text would be one instance; or, at least, if it does recognize something as a program, it is only to the extent that it discovers or comes across—incidentally, unforeseeably—elements which retroactively reveal the coherence of what is being read. Its first concern is not a program but accidents or events. This is precisely what scholarly reading does not comprehend (or can scarcely comprehend— less and less as it is increasingly devoted to an absolute position of programmaticity): for scholarly reading, everything is connected in advance—and the undefined power and resonance of accident or event dissolve in the program.

All that—this dissolution, this disappearance of the reading event —would be clearly without interest or consequences if it—the event— was a merely contingent phenomenon or secondary effect, not essentially related to the very nature of the text. The ordinary reading would be, therefore, event-centered and would encounter accidents and surprises (because of its discovery of the text, but also because of its own irregularities); but these surprises, accidents, or events would relate only to a defective approach, to an imperfect knowledge of the text's reality. For two reasons of primary importance, however, this is not a tenable position and, to the contrary, between the literary text and the dimension of event (or accident: the two words should be seen as synonyms, both referring to the Aristotelian *symbebêkos*), we must admit the strictest, most fundamental relation.

At issue here is, very simply and first of all, the text's *esthetic* dimension, which usually makes reading a pleasurable experience, or, more generally, the experience of an affect or series of affects. We shall easily recognize not only that the interest and dynamics of reading consist in large measure of the interest and dynamics of affects, but also that even in the act of writing the greatest importance is attached to the affect as such (to provoke or transmit) so that every program here (generic or particular) is a program of possible affects and that generally the act of writing, at least for literature, can be considered as a calculation of affects. The literary text is thus an affected text— bearing affects—we could say: affectual. And even if these affects cannot be absolutely determined (for it is in the affect's nature not to be absolutely determined), even if there are always unknowns, the determination of the affects provoked in reading is absolutely not contingent, and it in no way depends only on the subjectivity of the reader. Yet the relation between affect and event is one of direct implication. Certainly momentary, brusque, intense affects, attached to brief sequences or to precisely localized elements, must be distinguished from durable affects, more continuous, stable, discreet, linked to a text's style or general tone. Only the former have an obvious relationship with assignable events: events of reference (of narrative) or events of meaning (of discourse). But the latter cannot subsist in the absence of any event. Not only is it necessary that they be inaugurated, established, put into position by certain events (of meaning, at least); but they must also be continuously or at least regularly sustained and reactivated by infinitesimal, discreet, minor and homogeneous events. In any case, therefore, the affect occurs, or survives, because something occurs in the text; if the dimension of event disappears from scholarly reading, this reading then fails to comprehend not only the status of ordinary reading, but also the text itself, to the extent that it is elaborated to produce in this reading certain affects.

Secondly, it must be noted that the comprehension and value of what we have called the particularities of meaning will be necessarily different acccording to the reading's orientation toward program or toward event. It is certain that the text implies a generic or particular program, and that nothing within the text is determined outside of any programmaticity: it is from this that the scholarly reading takes its authority. But the notion, which scholarly reading insistently postulates, that every element, every particularity of the text could be *integrally* comprised in *one* (albeit extremely complex) program is indeed questionable. To the extent that a scholarly reading pursues the *telos* of a complete liaison and attempts to reconstitute the integral program of a text, it accords each element, each text sequence, an essentially functional signification; which is to say that each element, each sequence takes on its meaning and necessity in its relationship to other sequences or elements, that this meaning and necessity are thus in themselves absolutely determined, and that any other effects of meaning (supplementary, absolutely localized, without a strict association to the whole) are essentially contingent, arbitrary, fortuitous, nonpertinent. Polysemics, ambiguity, plurivocity, or over-determination can be carried to an extreme degree in writing without contradicting this postulate: they rather confirm the program's pertinence and the calculation's effectivity. And if, in having to consider too many elements and significations, a reading cannot reconstitute the whole program of the text, whatever it does manage to reconstitute is at least substantial, exemplary, essential, and absolutely pertinent. However, in three respects, this postulation proves to be insufficient or eminently reductive. First, we cannot, without undue haste, assume the unity of the program from the unity of the text; we cannot *a priori* exclude the possibility that a text responds to several programs, of diverse types, which would be neither rigorously articulated nor absolutely specified: attributing to each text element a determined functional or programmatic signification could not then pass uncontested. Next, writing's operations are never absolutely determined by a preestablished program (either generic or particular): not only are decisions made during the writing itself, of which neither the object nor the necessity was at first foreseeable, but also there exists an element of luck (or bad luck) as a result of which what is obtained is not exactly what was sought, due to which, consequently, there are also events of writing, and according to which a writer finds himself choosing a given element for motives which do not relate exclusively to its functional signification. In this regard, unless we believe in an absolute program which would proscribe all unknowns (but this is an empty or theological position), it remains impossible to reduce the meaning of a text element to its function within the same text, and to exhaust a text's signifying force through the complete interrelating of all its elements.

Finally and above all, a fundamental discordance exists between the idea of a complete determination of meaning and the affectual, event centered experience of reading. The affects produced in reading are surely linked to determined and assignable text elements. But the exact signification of these elements (in their relationship to affect), the very quality of the affect, and the definition of the event which the affect points out or constitutes—all this is, nonetheless, not assignable or determinable. And if it is possible, in fact, that typical elements or well-known text events (a certain kind of evocation, peripeteia, narrative or poetic procedure) provoke affects which are themselves equally characteristic (already tested, easily named), it is, nonetheless, the case that reading's most striking events, those in which literature seems to attain its greatest and most essential power, are invariably the most enigmatic. Not that these events owe nothing to a program, nor that they are not determined in a calculation. Simply that, beyond their functional signification, they imply something remarkable: they provoke, in the mind of the reader, a resonance as intense as it is difficult to express. In other words, the text becomes decisive and creates a powerful event just when its signification is proving to be essentially infinite (undefined, unlimited); and if no analysis of the calculations, no programmatic reconstitution can account for this event and the affect connected with it, this is not due to a contingent or conjectural insufficiency: it is because the resonance of this event is not comprised within any body of knowledge, and that it takes place, as Kant says, *in the absence of any concept (ohne Begriff)*. Since it is not simply an affinity between two or among several elements, but rather an infinite contamination by one element of the others, or a dissemination of one throughout the rest, the resonance, in fact, weakens the fundamental postulation—namely, the postulation of the complete determination (or determinability) of meaning—on which any constitution of knowledge or concept rests.

A single example—admitting that we will find thousands of others throughout the whole literary corpus, and especially in the works of such authors as Hölderlin or Kafka. In the brief text entitled *Lenz*, Büchner recreates, from information he has gathered, some of the first episodes of the poet's madness. To begin with, it is hardly a matter of indifference that this admirable text would be understood as reporting "real" events: in this way its resonance is at once heightened (why? how? this remains to be seen). In the beginning of the narrative, after a long meandering walk in the mountains, Lenz comes to the pastor Oberlin's house, where he will be offered shelter for a while.

Oberlin welcomed him, he took him for an artisan: "Welcome, although I do not know you. —I am a friend of Kaufmann, and I bring you his greetings. —What name, please? —Lenz. —Ah! well! Now hasn't it been in print? It seems to me I have read some dramatic works attributed to a certain gentleman of that name. —Yes, but please do not judge me by them."

"Yes, but please do not judge me by them" (*"Ja, aber belieben Sie, mich nicht darnach zu beurteilen"*): we suppose that these words will not have left the reader indifferent. Although they are strongly integrated into the economy of the narrative (into the program of what it records, and into its general style, or its specific *Darstellungsart*), their own punctual effect does not depend on any determined procedure of literary composition. That which precedes, as that which follows, certainly resounds with these words, partially determines their meaning, and accentuates their impact; this functional relationship, however, does not prevent these words from being detached from the text and taking on, in the reading experience, an absolutely singular intensity. "Yes, but please do not judge me by them." In other circumstances this could be simply a gesture of courtesy, the expression of an elegant reserve ("yes, I am a writer, but never mind, our dealings should be simple"). But everything that precedes these words, as well as everything that follows—the seriousness, the pain and passion of the walk in the mountains ("everything was so tight against him, so close to his body, so drenched"), just as later the reply to Kaufmann ("What does my father want? Can he give me more? Impossible! Let me have some peace!") expressly proscribes such an interpretation, and what remains in these simple words is one word—*Sprache*: event of meaning—of mourning or of infinite renunciation. How then can we understand their resonance?

A writer—according to the image we have of the writer, but also according to his own self-image—cannot say of his writings: "Please do not judge me by them," unless he says it out of some conventional sense of courtesy, to the extent that he can pretend to disavow this image. He cannot say it with real seriousness, and insofar as writer *is* a signatory and wants to monumentalize his name through his writings, these are exactly *the words he cannot pronounce*. Here the event is tied to this impossibility and to its exception; the singularity of the episode is not that of a particular case (comprised within a given generality), but that of a fundamental anomaly, of an *atopon*. Yet this condition—the fact that what occurs contravenes the normal or general constitution of representations—does not have a purely localized effect, minor and limited; this effect would possibly remain minor if the representations thus challenged were of less significance, but here, in any case, they (the name, identity, work, signature, judgment) are of such cardinal importance that the infraction or contravention itself becomes cardinal, and the *atopon* reverberates over every *topos*: hence the infinity of the resonance and the actual infinitizing of this motif or motion that we have named "mourning" or "renunciation." This is surely not easy to understand, and this dimension of signification or event will escape any reading (or theory) anxious to reduce the elements and acts of a text to their functional programmaticity. But there is more: "mourning" or "renunciation" (like, moreover, "name," "work," "identity," etc.) are terms which certainly qualify or determine (at least partially) what is at issue here, but invoking them does not alone suffice to explain what is happening, nor does it reintegrate the event into any constituted body of knowledge (or even if it claims to do so, there is inevitable reduction). And, for example, if mourning has lent itself to theorization (for example, through psychoanalysis), it is not at all certain that the mourning of the works, or of the name, or even the infinite mourning echoing throughout Lenz's words belongs to the realm of facts or objects whose definition can be supplied by this theory in its current state. If there is mourning here, this mourning is not only infinite in its objects, but also indefinite in its modality. *A fortiori* the interest of this mourning—the attention mobilized by these words and the esthetic dimension of this event—remains insistently enigmatic. Hence the question: what theory will encompass all this? How is a theory of this event possible?

Such is finally, for literary theory, the ultimate test: that of the event (or accident) of meaning (or reading), to the degree that it weakens or exceeds all programmaticity. Literary theory in the strong sense (as general constitution) would be possible if the schemas elaborated within it could wholly constitute the reading's program, and if the reading thus programmed could reconstitute, in a particular program, all or the essential particularities of a text. But these conditions have now been invalidated twice. First by the observation, as the fundamental act of scholarly reading, which even if it can be intended for the reconstitution of a program cannot be strictly bound to any single process of programming, nor can it strictly coincide with a determination of the particular by the general. Second and more especially by the event, which on one hand does not correspond to any theoretically constituted generality, and, on the other hand, reverberates or takes place well beyond the particular program which gives a text's elements their reciprocal functionality. Thus in so far as scholarly reading as well as theory (critical discourse as well as poetics) remains intrinsically attached to the value of program and theory (more precisely, to this general architectonic program which is the constitution), it is the event, with its signification and intensity, which forms their absolute limit. And if this event, as such, proves not to be contingent but constitutive of literary reality, theory and scholarly reading may well retain, analyze, or reconstitute certain aspects or dimensions of this reality—but they can neither comprehend it entirely nor secure this comprehension (albeit partial) by a general guarantee. Thus they fall short of their own *telos*.

Is this to say that the event as such must generally remain absolutely enigmatic, incomprehensible, ineffable, and that theory in general (every attempt at analysis, synthesis or schematization) must therefore be dedicated to an interminable misfortune (which it would by no means have provoked and from which it would have absolutely no recourse)? Certainly not. If the event remains essentially insubordinate to a specific theoretical order (albeit extremely powerful), or, more precisely, to theory *qua* programmatic constitution and to whatever corresponds to it in the empirical order of reading, it does not remain inaccessible to all discourse: rather this theoretical order (that of the constitution) will have been set up precisely *against* event—or to reduce its power. And all that for the strongest of motives. For any constituting (or even reconstituting) project, in so far as it tries to encompass a real program and, at the same time, set up a virtual program, in as much, then, as it is tied to an absolute position of programmaticity or of regularity, any constituting project postulates a fundamental stability for its objects. It could well be that these objects are not presently stable, and that the constitution has to establish a legality or regularity where only disorder seems to reign: however, stabilization must be possible, and disorder, no matter how large and durable it seems, must be only accidental, inessential with regard to the true nature of the objects it affects. And this "must be" is unconditioned, since the constitution itself is unconditionally necessary and anterior, in its primordial necessity, to every determined project. Yet the event as such is precisely a sign, effect or element of instability: its chance to exist is due to nothing other than a general instability, and is itself an act or factor of destabilization. It thus constitutes the very

Denis Kambouchner

thing the constitution wants to reduce, which it should make disappear in its regularity. But if the constitution's object cannot be hypotheticized in the absence of the event dimension, then event has the power to weaken radically any constitutional order. Such indeed seems to be the case of literary theory: in order to define a text's constitutive elements in their positions and forms it would have to bind, not only form, but also signification, to the status of absolute determination (or determinability). The principle of stability cannot be more directly expressed. But the event, with its indefiniteness and resonance, constantly weakens this status. If then the incomprehensiveness of event results above all from the principle of stability's absolute position, the question is still open as to which conditions make possible a discourse of event.

Let us be precise. In the general field of discourse on texts or on literature, the discourse concerning theoretical constituting has never exclusively prevailed, and we can find without difficulty discourses taking into account or taking over what we here call the "event" (or "accident") of meaning (or reading). Literary theory has ordinarily strayed from, underrated, minimized, misconstrued the ultimate interest of these discourses, classifying them under two equally pejorative headings: "critical subjectivism" and "metaphysics of literature." Not that these discourses would be, each one in its genre, uniform and possessing equal compass. Very much to the contrary: to the extent that these labels have been established with an *a priori* negative value, and only to preserve the positivity of a constituting theory, these "genres" are quite likely to bring together the least comparable of works. These discourses will simply have, each in its "genre," at least this much in common—that they have been interested either in the particular *efficacity* of a text, in the affects it provokes, in the events it presents or constitutes, or in literary efficacity in general, namely in this question: "how is literature possible?" or even: "what comprises literature's essential interest?" They will be thus placed either prior to or beyond programmaticity: hence—depending on the individual case, but sometimes collectively—their power and their weakness. Thus the problem becomes this: is it possible to reduce the exclusivity or incompatibility between these discourses and those of theoretical constitution? Is it possible to *hold together*, at least partially or punctually, the discourse of program and the discourse of event? Or again: as soon as the meaning-event is recognized as the essential dimension of literary texts, how do we deal with this event without sacrificing either to the undefined and deregulated particularization of a simply associative discourse (which would attempt, without much hope, to translate or reconstitute the event's resonance) or to the abstract generality of a purely speculative discourse (which would be restricted to affirming the resonance and the indeterminability of meaning)? How can the theoretical urgency of an active interrelationship between the general and the particular be maintained on event?

If the project defined in these questions is not absolutely unrealizable, the theoretical treatment of literary texts—which includes esstablishing a schematic generality, but also putting into practice a sort of reading which would be interested in its own events—should acquire the remarkable status of a *theory of accidents*. A highly paradoxical status, certainly, with regard to this Aristotelian assertion, resounding throughout the whole of Occidental metaphysics and even well beyond its perceptible frontiers: *"Peri tou kata sumbebêkos oudemia esti theôria"*—"Concerning that which is by accident there is no possible theory" (*Metaphysics* E 2, 1026 b 3). "Is by accident" that which is neither necessary (always there and always in the same state) nor frequent; in this sense, the Aristotelian assertion is, in fact, a direct statement of the principle of stability (hence, its fundamental value), and the possibility of formulating a theory of accidents obviously rests upon successfully challenging this principle. Not, however, upon simply rejecting it. Accident (or event) is just as inconceivable in an absolute instability as in an absolute stability; in order to possess meaning or resonance the accident must provoke or manifest an appreciable destabilization, and then affect or call into question supposedly stable elements. Theoretical discourse, therefore, is certainly not concerned to affirm an absolute instability (in which, moreover, it would itself lose meaning): it is rather concerned to grant a fundamental dimension to the accidental, namely to recognize in it a general necessity, to acknowledge the stability of the instability from which it proceeds, and to consider that every stable element's or configuration's position contains an essential instability.

In this regard, the theory of accidents in literary texts should be elaborated at two distinct levels. On one hand, as the theory of accident (or event) of meaning in general, it should conceive of the literary text as the organization (constitution, composition, program) of a stable assemblage of representations (or symbolic elements) whose stability is not otherwise assured and, at the same time, as the perturbation (accident or set of accidents, destabilization) arising within the configuration (supposed to be stable and constituted elsewhere) of the elements it affects. This theory should consequently investigate the form and general stability of symbolic formation, the symbolic dimension of accident (or event), and the interest given to accident (or event) as such. The determination of the literary, as an arena of events or as the distinctive character of certain forms of accidents can no longer be effected except on the basis of such an investigation. On the other hand, this theory, as the theory of accidents linked to a particular text, should certainly attempt to reconstitute the text's individual program (and understand the text as a programmatic constitution), but not in postulating its complete autonomy and stability: if this program can be reconstituted, it is *in reference* to the general, common, or even extratextual state of the elements that it brings into play. Thus it will also be a matter of appreciating *as events* the occurrence of these elements or the destiny the text assigns them, of analyzing the *mode of event* peculiar to this text, and of determining, through the form and organization of these events, through the value of the elements on which they bear, the amplitude of its resonance. This does not imply that the indefiniteness of meaning would be reduced, nor that the text's resonance would be thus exhausted. Apart from the fact that this indefiniteness can never be absolute, it is less a determined hermeneutic obstacle than a general condition of representations or symbolic elements; it does not prohibit determining activity, but only makes it interminable. It is thus not reduced—it has only retreated, and the resonance persists beyond its qualification.

Here we must, however, insist: if the theory of accidents is possible (if literary theory is possible as a theory of accidents), this possibility is bound not simply to a new position for the "text"-object and its elements, but also to a mutation within the status of theory itself. To the degree that the principle of stability loses its absolute position, theory can no longer claim to constitute an absolutely stable generality, complete and sure, nor can it *a priori* avoid all factors or dimensions of instability. And if generality is no longer absolutely constituted, or at the very least constitutable, and can no longer, consequently, constitute particularity, theory cannot resume its opposing of the two registers (general-particular) in the absolute form previously allowed. Moreover, the difference between the two levels of theoretical activity proposed here is not that which separates general theory (or poetics) from particular readings (criticism), establishing the architectonic prevalence of theory. It is not only that the first of these levels (theory of accident [or event] of meaning in general) far exceeds the limits into which literary theory had been inserted. It is also, and above all, that the second (theory of accidents tied to a particular text) is neither less theoretical nor less general than the first: it is the theory (that is to say only the *attempt at constituting*) of a generality of another order— that implied by the text's reference and resonance, that which was inaccessible to a general constitution. And the generality of both, not being (and not being able to be) absolute and formally guaranteed, can be defined by precisely this—that *the theories resound*, echoing each upon the other, upon the text, and upon an indefinite number of texts: the generality assumed by a declaration of discourse is only a function of the resonance it acquires. But there is more: the link between the theory of accidents and the text can thus no longer be simply the classical relation of theory to its objects. The text itself is a theory of accidents, a general theory. Of a different order, to be sure. Certainly, at least, between the two neither prevalence nor subjugation can obtain—but only the more or less resounding encounter of diverse symbolic constructions incessantly seeking their improper cohesion.

Translated by Evelyn Perry

EIGHT

LA LOI DU GENRE/THE LAW OF GENRE
Jacques Derrida

NE PAS MELER les genres.

Je ne mêlerai pas les genres.

Je répète: ne pas mêler les genres. Je ne le ferai pas.

Supposez maintenant que je laisse ces énoncés résonner tout seuls.

Supposez: je les abandonne à leur sort, je libère leurs virtualités aléatoires et les livre à votre écoute, à ce qu'il leur reste et que vous lui donnez de mouvement pour engendrer, sans que je me tienne derrière eux pour en répondre, des effets de toute espèce.

J'ai seulement dit, puis répété: ne pas mêler les genres, je ne les mêlerai pas.

Tant que je laisse à cela—à ce que d'autres appelleraient des actes de langage—une forme encore aussi peu déterminée en le contexte ouvert où je viens de les donner à entendre depuis "ma" langue, vous hésitez sans doute entre plusieurs interprétations. Elles sont en très grand nombre, je pourrais le démontrer. Elles forment une série ouverte et par essence imprévisible. Mais vos hésitations oscillent *pour le moins*, entre deux types d'écoute, deux modes d'interprétation ou, si vous préférez laisser à tous ces mots plus de chances, deux genres d'hypothèses. Lesquelles?

Dans un cas, il peut s'agir de discours fragmentaire dont les propositions seraient du genre descriptif, constatif, neutre. Dans ce premier cas, j'aurais alors nommé l'opération qui consiste à "ne pas mêler les genres." Je l'aurais désignée de façon neutre, sans l'évaluer, sans la recommander ou déconseiller, surtout sans y obliger personne. Sans prétendre faire la loi ou en faire acte de loi, j'aurais seulement rassemblé, dans un énoncé fragmentaire, le sens d'une pratique, d'un acte ou d'un événement, comme vous voudrez: ce qui se passe parfois quand cela revient à "ne pas mêler les genres." Toujours dans le même cas, dans l'hypothèse du même type, du même mode, du même genre—ou du même ordre—quand j'ai dit "je ne mêlerai pas les genres," vous aurez pu entendre la description anticipée, je ne dis pas la prescription, la désignation descriptive disant à l'avance ce qui va se passer, le prévoyant sur le mode ou dans le genre constatif, à savoir que, cela se passera ainsi, je ne mêlerai pas les genres. Le temps du futur décrit alors ce qui va sans doute avoir lieu, comme vous pourrez le constater, mais il ne constitue pas pour moi un engagement. Ce n'est pas une promesse que je vous fais ni un ordre que je me donne, une loi à laquelle je décide de me soumettre. Le futur ici ne donne pas le temps d'un "speech act" performatif du type de la promesse ou de l'ordre.

Mais une autre hypothèse, un autre type d'écoute et une autre interprétation n'auraient pas été moins légitimes. Vous pouviez entendre "ne pas mêler les genres" comme un ordre bref. Vous pouviez y entendre résonner le rappel elliptique mais d'autant plus autoritaire à la loi d'un "il faut" ou "il ne faut pas" dont chacun sait qu'il habite le concept ou constitue la valeur de *genre*. Dès qu'on entend le mot "genre," dès qu'il paraît, dès qu'on tente de le penser, une limite se dessine. Et quand une limite vient à s'assigner, la norme et l'interdit ne se font pas attendre: "il faut," "il ne faut pas," dit le "genre," le mot "genre," la figure, la voix ou la loi du genre. Et cela peut se dire du genre en tous genres, qu'il s'agisse d'une détermination générique ou générale de ce qu'on appelle la "nature" ou la *physis* (par exemple un genre vivant ou le genre humain, un genre de ce qui est en général) ou qu'il s'agisse d'une typologie dite non-naturelle et relevant d'ordres ou de lois qu'on a cru, à un moment donné, opposer à la *physis* selon les valeurs de *tekhnè*, de *thesis*, de *nomos* (par exemple un genre artistique, poétique ou littéraire). Mais toute l'énigme du genre se tient peut-être au plus près de cette limite entre les deux genres du genre qui ne sont ni séparables ni inséparables, couple irrégulier de l'un sans l'autre dont chacun se cite régulièrement à comparaître dans la figure de l'autre, disant simultanément et indiscernablement "je" et "nous," moi le genre, nous les genres, sans qu'on puisse s'arrêter à penser que le "je" est une espèce du genre "nous." Car qui nous fera croire que nous, nous deux par exemple, formions un genre ou lui appartenions? Ainsi, dès que du genre s'annonce, il faut respecter une norme, il ne faut pas franchir une ligne limitrophe, il ne faut pas risquer l'impureté, l'anomalie ou la monstruosité. Et il en va ainsi dans tous les cas, que cette loi du genre soit ou non interprétée comme une détermination voire une destination de la *physis*, et quelle que soit la portée qu'on accorde à la *physis*. Si un genre est ce qu'il est ou s'il doit être ce qu'il est destiné à être en son *telos*, alors "ne pas mêler les genres," on ne doit pas mêler les genres, on se doit de ne pas mêler les genres. Plus rigoureusement, les genres doivent ne pas se mêler. Et s'il leur arrive de se mêler, par accident ou par transgression, par erreur ou par faute, alors cela doit confirmer, puisqu'on parle alors de "mélange," la pureté essentielle de leur identité. Cette pureté appartient à l'axiome typique, c'est une loi de la loi du genre, qu'elle soit ou non, comme on croit pouvoir dire, "naturelle." Cette position normative et cette évaluation sont inscrites et prescrites à même la "chose même," si on peut ainsi nommer quelque chose du genre "genre." Dès lors, la deuxième phrase à la première personne, "je ne mêlerai pas les genres," vous pouviez la recevoir comme un serment d'obéissance, la réponse docile à l'injonction venue de la loi du genre. Au lieu d'une description constative, vous entendriez une promesse, une parole donnée, cet engagement respectueux : je vous promets que je ne mêlerai pas les genres et qu'ainsi, fidèle à mon engagement, je serai fidèle à la loi du genre puisqu'elle m'invite et m'engage d'avance, d'elle-même, à ne pas mêler les genres. En répondant à l'appel impérieux de la loi, je m'engagerais à prendre ma responsabilité.

A moins que, plus qu'un engagement, il ne s'agisse là d'une gageure, d'un défi, d'un pari impossible. Et si c'était impossible, de ne pas mêler les genres? Et s'il y avait, logée au coeur de la loi même, une loi d'impureté ou un principe de contamination? Et si la condition de possibilité de la loi était l'apriori d'une contre-loi, un axiome d'impossibilité qui en affolerait le sens, l'ordre et la raison?

Je venais à l'instant de proposer une alternative entre deux interprétations. Ce n'était pas, vous vous en doutez, pour m'arrêter. La ligne ou le trait qui semblaient séparer les deux corpus d'interprétation sont *aussitôt* affectés d'une perturbation essentielle que je vous laisse pour l'instant nommer ou qualifier de toutes les façons que vous voudrez : division interne du trait, impureté, corruption, contamination, décomposition, perversion, déformation, cancérisation même, prolifération généreuse ou dégénérescence. Toutes ces "anomalies" perturbantes sont engendrées, c'est leur loi commune, le sort ou le ressort qu'elles partagent, par de la *répétition*. On pourrait dire par de la *citation* ou par du *ré-cit* pourvu que l'usage restreint de ces deux mots ne vienne pas précisément nous rappeler à l'ordre du genre strict. Une citation au sens strict implique toute sorte de conventions, de précautions et de protocoles contextuels dans le mode de réitération, de signes codés comme les guillemets ou d'autres artifices typographiques quand la citation est écrite. Il en va sans doute de même pour le récit comme forme, mode ou genre du discours, voire, j'y reviendrai, comme type littéraire. Et pourtant cet usage *stricto sensu* des mots *citation* et *récit*, la loi qui le protège est d'avance et intimement menacée par une contre-loi qui la constitue, la rend possible, la conditionne et se rend donc par là inabordable et indébordable, incontournable pour des raisons de bords auprès desquelles nous viendrons échouer tout à l'heure. La loi et la contre-loi se citent à comparaître et se récitent l'une l'autre en ce procès. On n'aurait à s'inquiéter de rien si l'on était rigoureusement assuré de pouvoir discerner en toute rigueur entre citation et une non-citation, un récit et un non-récit, une répétition dans la forme de l'un ou de l'autre.

Je n'entreprendrai pas de démontrer, considérant que c'est toujours possible, pourquoi vous n'aurez pas pu décider tout à l'heure si les phrases par lesquelles j'ai ouvert cette communication et marqué ce contexte étaient ou non des répétitions de type citationnel; ni si elles étaient ou non du type performatif; ni surtout si elles étaient toutes deux, ensemble, et chaque fois ensemble, ceci ou cela. Car il n'a peut-être pas échappé à tout le monde que d'une répétition à l'autre le rapport a sans doute changé entre les deux énoncés initiaux. La ponctuation s'est légèrement modifiée, autant que le contenu de la deuxième proposition indépendante. Ce déplacement à peine apparent pouvait rendre en principe indépendantes l'une de l'autre les options interprétatives qui auraient pu vous tenter à l'égard de l'une ou de l'autre, de l'une et de l'autre de ces deux sentences. S'ensuivrait une très riche combinatoire de possibilités que, pour ne pas déborder mon temps de parole et par respect pour la loi du genre et du colloque je m'abstiendrai de déployer. Je présume simplement un certain rapport entre ce qui vient à peine de se passer et l'origine de la littérature, aussi bien que son aborigine ou son avortement, pour citer l'un de nos hôtes, Philippe Lacoue-Labarthe.

M'autorisant provisoirement de cette présomption, je ferme l'angle d'une prise de vue, je me limite à une sorte d'espèce du genre "genre." Je m'en tiendrai à ce genre de genre dont on suppose généralement et toujours un peu vite qu'il n'appartient pas à la nature, à la *physis*, mais à la *tekhnè*, aux arts et plus étroitement encore à la poésie, plus spécialement à la littérature. Mais je m'autorise du même coup à penser qu'à me limiter ainsi je n'exclus rien, du moins en principe et en droit, les rapports n'étant plus ici d'extension, d'individu exemplaire à espèce, d'espèce à genre, ou de genre de genre à genre en général, mais, comme on verra, tout autres. Il y va en effet de l'exemplarité avec toute l'*énigme* —autrement dit, comme l'indique le mot d'énigme, le récit—qui travaille la logique de l'exemple.

Avant d'en venir à l'épreuve d'un certain exemple, je tenterai de formuler, de manière aussi elliptique, économique et formelle que possible, ce que j'appellerai la loi de la loi du genre. C'est précisément un principe de contamination, une loi d'impureté, une économie du parasite. Dans le code de la théorie des ensembles, si je m'y transportais au moins par figure, je parlerais d'une sorte de participation sans appartenance. Le trait qui marque l'appartenance s'y divise immanquablement, la bordure de l'ensemble vient à former par invagination une poche interne plus grande que tout, les conséquences de cette division et de ce débordement restant aussi singulières qu'illimitables.

Pour le montrer, je m'en tiendrai aux plus pauvres généralités mais je voudrais autant que possible justifier cette indigence ou cet ascétisme initial. Par exemple je ne m'engagerai pas dans le passionnant débat de poétique sur la théorie et l'histoire de la théorie des genres, sur l'histoire critique du concept de genre de Platon à nos jours. D'abord parce que nous disposons maintenant de travaux remarquables et récemment fort enrichis, qu'il s'agisse du matériau ou des analyses critiques. Je pense en particulier aux publications de *Poétique*, à son numéro intitulé *Genres* (32) et à son ouverture par l'essai de Genette, *Genres, "types," modes*. D'un autre point de vue, *L'absolu littéraire* aura fait événement à cet égard et tout ce que je risquerai ici se situera peut-être aussi comme une modeste annotation dans les marges de ce grand livre dont je suppose constamment la lecture. Je pourrais aussi justifier mon abstention ou mon abstinence au regard du luxe ou de l'ivresse terminologique comme de l'exubérance taxinomique auxquels, de manière non fortuite, ont donné lieu les débats de ce genre. Je me sens tout à fait impuissant à dominer cette prolifération—et non seulement pour des raisons de temps. J'invoquerai plutôx *deux motifs* principiels pour justifier que je m'en tienne ici à de pauvres généralités préliminaires au bord de cette problématique.

A quoi se rapportent, pour l'essentiel, ces deux motifs? Dans sa phase la plus récente, et cela s'illustre surtout des propositions de Genette, l'axe le plus critique a conduit à relire toute l'histoire de la théorie des genres en y repérant—et il faut bien dire, malgré la dénégation initiale, en y corrigeant—deux types de méconnaissance ou de confusion. D'une part, et ce sera le premier motif de mon abstention, en prêtant à Platon et à Aristote ce qui ne leur revenait pas ou qu'ils auraient même refusé, on a certes déformé, rappelle Genette, mais on a déformé presque toujours en *naturalisant*. Selon un procès classique on a considéré comme naturelles des structures ou des formes typiques dont l'histoire est aussi peu naturelle que possible, mais longue au contraire, complexe, hétérogène. On les a traitées comme naturelles, compte tenu de toute la gamme sémantique de ce mot difficile, et vous savez comme elle est ouverte, puisqu'elle va jusqu'à l'expression de "langue naturelle" là ou tout le monde s'entend à n'opposer langue naturelle qu'à langue formelle ou artificielle sans impliquer par là que la dite langue naturelle soit une simple production physique ou biologique. Genette insiste beaucoup sur cette naturalisation des genres: "L'histoire de la théorie des genres est toute marquée de ces schémas fascinants qui *informent et déforment la réalité* [je souligne] souvent hétéroclite du champ littéraire et prétendent découvrir un "système" naturel là où ils construisent une symétrie factice à grand renfort de fausses fenêtres" (p. 408). Dans ce qu'elle a de plus efficace et de plus légitime, cette lecture critique de l'histoire (et) de la théorie des genres fait ainsi fonds sur une opposition entre nature et histoire, et plus généralement, comme le signale—l'allusion à une construction artificielle (". . . là où ils construisent une symétrie factice . . ."), sur une opposition entre la nature et la série de tous ses autres. Une telle opposition semble aller de soi, elle n'est jamais questionnée dans cette mise en perspective critique. Si même elle l'avait été, fort discrètement, dans un passage qui m'aurait échappé, il est sûr que cette suspicion peu visible aura été sans effet sur l'organisation générale de la problématique. Cela ne limite pas l'intérêt ou la fécondité d'une lecture comme celle de Genette. Mais la place reste ouverte à des questions préliminaires sur ses présuppositions, à des questions sur les bords où elle commence à s'amarrer ou à s'arriver. C'est la forme de ces bords qui me retiendra. Il ne s'agira pas ici de ces présupposés généraux dont le nombre est toujours ouvert et indéterminable pour quelque interprétation critique que ce soit. Mais plus strictement du rapport de la nature à l'histoire, de la nature à ses autres *quand il y va précisément du genre.*

Considérons le concept le plus général de genre, dans le trait ou le prédicat minimal qui le constitue en permanence à travers toute la variété de ses types et tous les régimes de son histoire: il se fend et se défend de toute son énergie contre une opposition simple et survenue de la nature et de l'histoire, comme de la nature et de tous ses autres (*tekhnè, nomos, thesis,* puis *esprit, société, liberté, histoire,* etc.). Entre la *physis* et ses autres, le *genos* situe certainement l'un des lieux privilégiés du procès et y concentre à n'en pas douter la plus grande obscurité. On n'a pas besoin de mobiliser l'étymologie pour cela et on peut aussi bien entendre *genos* comme naissance, et naissance autant comme puissance généreuse de l'engendrement ou de la génération—*physis* précisément—que comme race, appartenance familiale, de généalogie classificatoire ou de classe, de classe d'âge (génération) ou de classe sociale; rien d'étonnant à ce que, dans la nature et dans l'art, le genre, concept par essence classificatoire et généalogico-taxonomique, engendre lui-même tant de vertiges classificatoires quand il s'agit de le classer lui-même et le situer, dans un ensemble, le principe ou l'instrument classificatoire. Comme la classe elle-même, le principe du genre est inclassable, il sonne le glas du glas, autrement dit du classicum, de ce qui permet d'appeler (*calare*) les ordres et de ranger les multiplicités dans une nomenclature. *Genos* indique donc le lieu, le moment ou jamais de la méditation la plus nécessaire sur le "pli"—qui n'est pas plus historique que naturel au sens classique de ces deux termes—qui rapporte le *phuein* à lui-même à travers des autres qui ne lui reviennent peut-être plus selon la logique décidante, critique, oppositionnelle, voire dialectique qui aura fait époque mais selon le trait d'un tout autre contrat. En droit, cette méditation est un préalable absolu sans lequel une mise en perspective historique aura toujours du mal à se légitimer. Par exemple, l'époque romantique, cette puissante figure accusée dans le procès instruit par Genette (puisqu'elle aurait réinterprété le système des modes en système des genres) n'est plus une simple époque et ne peut plus être inscrite comme un moment ou une étape situable dans le trajet d'une "histoire" dont le concept nous serait assuré. Le romantisme, si quelque chose de tel se laisse ainsi identifier, c'est aussi la répétition générale de tous les plis qui en eux-mêmes rapportent, accouplent, divisent aussi la *physis* ou le *genos* à travers le genre, tous les genres du genre, le mélange du genre qui est "plus qu'un genre," l'excès de genre, l'excès du genre par rapport à lui-même, son débordement, son rassemblement général à la fois et sa dissolution.[1] Un tel "moment" n'est plus un simple moment *dans* l'histoire et la théorie des genres littéraires. Le traiter ainsi ce serait même s'exposer encore à rester tributaire—d'où l'étrange logique—de quelque chose qui a aussi constitué un des motifs romantiques, à savoir la mise en ordre téléologique de l'histoire; le romantisme obéit simultanément à la logique naturalisante et à la logique historisante; et on pourra toujours démontrer qu'on ne s'est pas délivré de l'héritage romantique, quand même on le voudrait et à supposer qu'une telle délivrance ait le moindre intérêt, tant qu'on veut encore rappeler au souci historique et à la vérité de la production historique contre les abus ou les confusions naturalisantes. Ce débat on pouvait tenter de le montrer, reste aussi partie ou effet de romantisme.

Un deuxième motif me retient sur le seuil ou sur les bords d'une éventuelle problématique du genre (comme) histoire et théorie de l'histoire et de la théorie des genres—un autre genre en somme. C'est qu'il m'est pour l'instant impossible de décider—impossible pour des raisons que je ne crois pas accidentelles et c'est précisément ce qui m'importe—si le texte peut-être exemplaire dont je vous proposerai tout à l'heure l'épreuve se prête ou non à la distinction entre *mode* et *genre*. Or vous le savez, Genette démontre la nécessité rigoureuse de cette distinction; et le chef d'accusation dans son réquisitoire, c'est "la confusion entre modes et genres" (p. 417). Là encore les charges les plus graves pèsent sur le romantisme, même si "la réinterprétation romantique du système des modes en système de genres n'est ni en fait ni en droit l'épilogue de cette longue histoire" (p. 415). Cette confusion aurait, selon Genette, encouragé ou servi la naturalisation des genres en projetant sur eux un "privilège de naturalité qui était *légitimement* . . . celui des trois modes . . ." (p. 421). Du coup, cette naturalisation "constitue ces archigenres en types idéaux ou naturels qu'ils ne sont pas et ne peuvent être: il n'y a pas d'archigenres qui échapperaient totalement à l'historicité *tout en conservant une définition générique*. Il y a des modes, exemple: le récit. Il y a des genres, exemple: le roman; la relation des genres aux modes est complexe, et sans doute n'est-elle pas, comme le suggère Aristote, de simple inclusion."

Si je tiens à rester en-deçà de la démonstration de Genette, ce n'est pas seulement en raison de cette assurance vite prise sur la distinction entre nature et histoire, c'est aussi à cause de ce qu'elle implique quant au mode, à la distinction entre mode et genre. La définition du mode y comporte ceci de singulier et d'intéressant, vous le savez, qu'elle reste, selon Genette, purement formelle. Le rapport à un contenu n'y garde aucune pertinence. Ce n'est pas le cas du genre. Le critère générique et le critère modal, dit Genette, sont "absolument hétérogènes": "chaque genre se définissait essentiellement par une spécification de contenu que rien ne prescrivait dans la définition du mode . . ." (p. 417). Ce recours à l'opposition de la forme et du contenu, cette distinction entre mode et genre, je ne crois pas qu'on ait à les contester, et mon propos n'est pas de récuser quoi que ce soit dans la démonstration de Genette. On peut seulement se demander ce que présuppose la légitimité de cette démonstration. On doit aussi se demander jusqu'à quel point elle peut nous aider à lire tel ou tel texte quand il se comporte de telle ou telle façon au regard du mode et du genre et quand il semble écrit non pas sagement dans leurs limites mais à leur sujet et afin de perturber l'ordre de ces limites. Par exemple les limites de ce mode que serait, selon Genette, le récit ("il y a des modes, exemple: le récit"). Or le texte (peut-être) exemplaire auquel j'en viendrai tout à l'heure, je ne me hâterai pas de dire que c'est un "récit," vous le comprendrez vite. Le "récit" n'y est pas seulement un mode, et un mode pratiqué ou mis à l'épreuve comme impossible, c'est aussi le nom d'un thème, le contenu thématique non-thématisable de quelque chose d'une forme textuelle qui a *à voir* avec un point de vue sur le genre bien que peut-être elle ne relève d'aucun genre; et peut-être même plus de la littérature si s'épuisant autour de modalisations sans genre elle confirmait cette autre proposition de Genette: "les genres sont des catégories proprement littéraires/ ou esthétiques/, les modes sont des catégories qui relèvent de la linguistique, ou plus exactment d'une anthropologie de l'expression verbale" (p. 418). De façon très singulière, le texte très bref dont je parlerai dans un instant fait du récit et de l'impossibilité du récit son thème, son thème ou son contenu impossibles, à la fois inaccessible, indéterminable, interminable et intarissable; et il fait du mot "récit," sous une certaine forme, son titre sans titre, la mention sans mention de son genre. Ce texte, j'essaierai de le montrer, semble donc fait, entre autres choses, pour *se jouer* de toutes les catégories tranquilles de la théorie et de l'histoire des genres, pour inquiéter leurs assurances

taxonomiques, la distribution de leurs classes et les appellations con-
trôlables de leurs nomenclatures classiques. Texte destiné, du même
coup, à faire comparaître ces classes en instruisant leur procès, en
procédant au procès de la loi du genre. Car si le code judiciaire s'est si
souvent imposé à moi depuis tout à l'heure pour parler de cette affaire,
c'était pour introduire à ce texte (peut-être) exemplaire et parce que,
j'en suis convaincu, il y va du droit et de la loi en tout cela.

Telles étaient les deux raisons de principe pour lesquelles je me
tiendrai sur le bord liminaire de l'histoire (et) de la théorie des genres.
Voici maintenant, très vite, la loi de *débordement*, de participation sans
appartenance, de contamination, etc., que j'annonçais tout à l'heure.
Elle va vous paraître pauvre et même d'une stupéfiante abstraction.
Elle ne concerne en particulier ni les genres, ni les types, ni les modes
ni aucune forme dans l'acception stricte de son concept. Je ne sais donc
pas nommer le champ ou l'objet soumis à cette loi. C'est peut-être le
champ sans limite d'une textualité générale. Je peux prendre chacun
des mots de la série (genre, type, mode, forme) et décider qu'il vaudra
pour tous les autres (tous les genres de genres, types, modes, formes;
tous les types de types, genres, modes, formes; tous les modes de modes,
genres, types ou formes; toutes les formes de formes, etc.) Le trait
commun à ces classes de classes, c'est justement la récurrence identifiable d'un trait commun auquel on reconnaît, devrait reconnaître,
l'appartenance à la classe. Il doit y avoir un trait auquel se fier pour
décider que tel événement textuel, telle "oeuvre" relève de telle classe
(genre, type, mode, forme, etc.). Et il doit donc y avoir un code per-
mettant de juger, grâce à ce trait, de l'appartenance à une classe. Par
exemple, axiome très pauvre mais par là même peu contestable, si un
genre existe (disons le roman puisque personne ne semble lui contester
la qualité de genre), un code doit fournir un trait identifiable et donc
identique à lui-même qui autorise à décider, à arrêter que tel texte
appartient à tel genre ou relève de tel genre. De même, en dehors de la
littérature ou des arts, si on tient à classer, on doit se référer à un ensemble de traits identifiables et codables pour décider que ceci ou cela,
telle chose ou tel événement appartient à tel ensemble ou à telle classe.
Cela paraît trivial. En tant que marque, un tel trait distinctif est toujours
a priori remarquable. Il est toujours possible qu'un ensemble, j'appelle
ça un texte, pour des raisons essentielles, qu'il soit écrit ou oral, remarque en lui-même ce trait distinctif. Cela peut se produire dans des
textes qui ne se donnent pas à un moment donné pour littéraires ou
poétiques. Une plaidoirie ou la tribune libre d'un journal peut rappeler
par une marque, même si ce n'est pas une mention explicite, "voilà,
j'appartiens, comme chacun peut le remarquer, à ce type de texte qu'on
appelle plaidoirie ou article de journal du genre tribune libre." C'est
toujours possible. Cela ne les constitue pas *ipso facto* en "littérature,"

encore que cette possibilité, toujours ouverte et donc toujours remarquable, situe peut-être la possibilité du devenir-littérature de tout texte. Cela ne m'intéresse pas pour l'instant. Ce qui m'intéresse, c'est que, toujours possible pour tout texte, pour tout corpus de traces, cette remarque est absolument nécessaire et constitutive dans ce qu'on appelle l'art, la poésie ou la littérature. Elle signe l'irruption de la *tekhnè*, qui ne se fait jamais attendre. C'est la question axiomatique que je soumets à votre discusion: peut-on identifier une oeuvre d'art, quelle qu'elle soit et singulièrement une oeuvre d'art discursive, qui ne porte la marque d'un genre et qui ne la signale, remarque ou donne à remarquer de quelque façon? Je précise deux points à ce sujet. 1. Il peut s'agir de plusieurs genres, d'un mélange de genres ou du genre total, du genre "genre" ou du genre poétique ou littéraire comme genre des genres. Cette re-marque peut prendre un très grand nombre de formes et relever elle-même de types très divers. Ce n'est pas forcément une "mention" du type de celles qu'on lit sous le titre de certains livres (roman, récit, théâtre). La remarque d'appartenance ne passe pas forcément par la conscience de l'auteur ou du lecteur, bien qu'elle le fasse souvent. Elle peut aussi contredire cette conscience ou faire mentir la "mention" explicite, la rendre fausse, inadéquate ou ironique selon toutes sortes de figures surdéterminantes. Enfin ce trait de remarque n'est pas forcément un thème ni une composante thématique de l'oeuvre, bien que très souvent, et même avant ce qu'on appelle la "modernité," on ait fait un thème abondamment traité et joué de cette appartenance à un ou à plusieurs genres, comme de tous les traits qui marquent cette appartenance. Si je ne m'abuse pas en disant qu'un tel trait est remarquable en tout corpus esthétique, poétique ou littéraire, alors voici le paradoxe, voici l'ironie (qui ne se réduit pas à une conscience ou à une attitude): ce trait supplémentaire et distinctif, marque de l'appartenance ou de l'inclusion, ne relève, lui, d'aucun genre et d'aucune classe. Le re-marque d'appartenance n'appartient pas. Elle appartient sans appartenir et le "sans" qui rapporte l'appartenance à la non-appartenance ne paraît que le temps sans temps d'un clin d'oeil. Le clin d'oeil ferme, mais à peine, un instant entre les instants, et ce qu'il ferme c'est bien l'oeil, la vue, le jour. Mais sans le répit ou l'intervalle du clin d'oeil rien ne se donnerait à voir du jour. Pour la formuler de la manière la plus pauvre, la plus simple mais la plus apodictique, l'hypothèse que je soumets à votre discussion serait la suivante: un texte ne saurait appartenir à aucun genre. Tout texte participe d'un ou de plusieurs genres, il n'y a pas de texte sans genre, il y a toujours du genre et des genres mais cette participation n'est jamais une appartenance. Et cela non pas à cause d'un débordement de richesse ou de productivité libre, anarchique et inclassable, mais à cause du *trait* de participation lui-même, de l'effet de code et de la marque générique. En se marquant de genre, un texte se démarque.

Si la remarque d'appartenance appartient sans appartenir participe sans appartenir, la mention de genre ne fait pas simplement partie du corpus. Prenons l'exemple de la mention "roman." Elle doit être marquée d'une manière ou d'une autre même si ce n'est pas sous la forme explicite de la mention sous-titrante et même si elle est trompeuse ou ironique. Cette mention n'est pas romanesque, elle ne fait pas, de part en part, partie du corpus qu'elle désigne. Elle ne lui est pas non plus simplement étrangère. Mais ce topos singulier situe dans l'oeuvre et hors d'elle, à sa bordure, une inclusion et une exclusion au regard du genre en général, d'une classe identifiable en général. Il rassemble le corpus et du même coup, du même clin d'oeil il l'empêche de se fermer, de s'identifier à lui-même. Cet axiome de non-fermeture ou d'incomplétude croise en lui la condition de possibilité et la condition d'impossibilité d'une taxonomie. Cette inclusion et cette exclusion ne restent pas extérieures l'une par rapport à l'autre, elles ne s'excluent pas, mais elles ne sont pas davantage immanentes ou identiques l'une à l'autre. Elles ne font ni une ni deux. Elles forment ce que j'appellerai la *clause de genre*, clause disant à la fois l'énoncé juridique, la mention faisant droit et texte de loi, mais aussi la fermeture, la clôture qui s'exclut de ce qu'elle inclut (on pourrait parler aussi sans clin d'oeil d'une écluse de genre.) La clause ou l'écluse du genre déclasse ce qu'elle permet de classer. Elle sonne le glas de la généalogie ou de la généricité auxquelles elle donne pourtant le jour. Mettant à mort cela même qu'elle engendre, elle forme une étrange figure, une forme sans forme, elle reste à peu près invisible, elle ne voit pas le jour ou ne se donne pas le jour. Sans elle il n'y a ni genre ni littérature mais dès qu'il y a ce clin d'oeil, cette clause ou cette écluse de genre, à l'instant même où s'y entament un genre ou une littérature, la dégénérescence aura commencé, la fin commence.

La fin commence, c'est une citation. Peut-être une citation. Je l'aurais prélevée dans ce texte qui me paraît se donner en exemple, comme un exemple de cette figure infigurable de clusion.

Ce dont j'essaierai de vous parler maintenant, je ne l'appellerai pas de son nom de genre ou de mode. Je ne dirai pas ce drame, cette épopée, ce roman, cette nouvelle ou ce récit, surtout pas ce récit. Tous ces noms de genre ou de mode seraient aussi bien et aussi mal supportés par ce qui n'est pas même tout à fait un livre et qui fut publié en 1973 sous la forme éditoriale d'une plaquette de 32 pages sous le titre *La Folie du jour*. Nom d'auteur: Maurice Blanchot. Pour en parler, j'appellerai cette chose La Folie du jour, de son nom propre, celui qu'elle porte à l'état civil et sous lequel on est en droit de l'identifier et de la classer depuis cette date au dépôt légal à la Bibliothèque Nationale. De *La*

Folie du jour on peut faire un nombre non-fini de lectures. J'en ai tenté quelques-unes et le ferai encore ailleurs d'un autre point de vue. Le *topos* de la vue, de cécité et du *point-de-vue* y est d'ailleurs inscrit et traversé selon une sorte de révolution permanente qui engendre ou donne virtuellement le jour à des points de vue, des tours, des versions et réversions dont la somme reste nécessairement non-dénombrable et le compte-rendu impossible. Les prélèvements, rationalisations, sommations que je devrai fatalement proposer relèveront donc d'une violence injustifiable. Une sélectivité brutale et impitoyablement appauvrissante s'imposeront à moi, à nous, au nom d'une loi dont *La Folie du jour* à son tour aura déjà fait le procès, prévoyant jusqu'à la scène quasipolicière à laquelle le souci de compétence nous contraint peut-être.

Qu'est-ce que je vais demander à *La Folie du jour*? De répondre, de témoigner, de dire ce qu'elle a à dire quant à la loi du genre ou à la loi du mode, plus précisément quant à la loi du récit dont on vient de nous rappeler qu'il est ceci et non cela, un mode et non un genre.

Sur la couverture, sous le titre, aucune mention de genre. En ce lieu très singulier qui n'appartient ni au titre, ni au sous-titre ni même simplement au corpus de l'oeuvre, l'auteur n'a pas inscrit, comme il l'a fait plus d'une fois ailleurs, la mention "récit" ou "roman," peut-être (mais peut-être seulement) en les subsumant tous deux à tort, dirait Genette, sous la catégorie unique de genre. De cette mention qui figure ailleurs et paraît ici absente je dirai seulement deux mots.

1. D'une part elle n'engage à rien. Ni le lecteur ni le critique, ni l'auteur ne sont tenus de croire que le texte précédé de cette mention est bien conforme à la définition stricte, normale, normée ou normative du genre, à la loi du genre ou du mode. La confusion, l'ironie, le passage conventionnel à une autre définition (au nom de quoi l'interdire?), la recherche d'un effet supplémentaire peuvent pousser à intituler *roman* ou *récit* ce qui en vérité ou selon la vérité d'hier ne seraient ni l'un ni l'autre. *A fortiori* si les mots *récit, roman, ciné-roman théâtre complet* ou que sais-je, *littérature*, ne sont plus à la place conventionnelle de la mention de genre mais, comme cela est arrivé et arrivera encore (tout a l'heure) à la place et dans la fonction du titre même, du nom propre de l'oeuvre.

2. Il est arrivé plus d'une fois à Blanchot de modifier la mention de genre d'une version à l'autre ou d'une édition à l'autre. Faute de pouvoir aborder ici toutes les portées de ce problème, je citerai seulement l'exemple de la mention "récit" effacée d'une version à l'autre de *L'arrêt de mort* en même temps qu'un certain épilogue se trouvait retranché à la suite du double récit, si on peut dire, qui constitue ce livre. Cet effacement de "récit" reste, il laisse une trace inscrite et archivée, un effet de relief supplémentaire dont le compte n'est pas facile. Je ne peux pas m'y arrêter ici, pas plus qu'à la distribution très attentive et

différenciée des mentions "récit" et "roman" d'une oeuvre narrative à l'autre, pas plus qu'à la question de savoir si Blanchot y distinguait la mention de genre et la mention de mode, pas plus qu'à tout le discours de Blanchot sur la différence entre la voix narratrice et la voix narrative qui, elle, à coup sûr, est autre chose qu'un mode. Je signale seulement ceci: au moment même où paraît la première version de *L'arrêt de mort* portant la mention "récit" la première version de *La Folie du jour* est publiée avec un autre titre dont je parlerai plus tard.

La Folie du jour ne porte donc aucune mention de genre ou de mode. Mais le mot "récit" apparaît au moins quatre fois dans les deux dernières pages, et pour nommer le thème, le sens ou l'histoire, le contenu ou une partie du contenu de *La Folie du jour*, en tout cas son procès et son enjeu décisifs. C'est un récit sans thème et sans cause qui lui viennent du dehors; il est pourtant sans intériorité. C'est le récit d'un récit impossible dont la "production" fait arriver ce qui arrive, ou ce qui reste plutôt, mais qui ne le relate pas, ne s'y rapporte pas comme à un référent extérieur, même si tout lui reste étranger, hors bord. Je peux d'autant moins raconter l'histoire de *La Folie du jour* qu'il y va justement de la possibilité et de l'impossibilité de raconter une histoire. Toutefois, pour faire le plus de clarté possible, au nom du jour, c'est-à-dire, on le verra, au nom de la loi, je m'en vais prendre le risque calculé de mettre à plat le déroulement ou l'enroulement de ce texte, sa révolution permanente dont le tour est fait pour défier toute mise à plat. Voici: celui qui dit "je"—et qui finalement nous "dit," dit à ses inquisiteurs qu'il n'arrive pas à se constituer en narrateur (au sens non-nécessairement littéraire du terme), qu'il n'arrive pas à s'identifier assez à lui-même, à se garder en mémoire pour rassembler l'histoire et le récit qu'on exige de lui, que les représentants de la société et de la loi requièrent de lui—celui qui dit "je" (n'arrive pas à dire "je") semble raconter, après s'être présenté sur un mode qui défie toute norme de la présentation de soi, ce qui lui est arrivé, ou plutôt ce qui a failli lui arriver: il a failli perdre la vue à la suite d'un événement traumatique et probablement d'une agression. Je dis "probablement" parce que toute *La Folie du jour* fait trembler de façon discrète mais terriblement efficiente toutes les assurances sur lesquelles on construit tant de discours, la valeur d'événement d'abord, de réalité, fiction, d'apparaître, etc., le tout s'emportant dans la polysémie disséminale et folle du "jour," du mot "jour" que là non plus je ne peux pas considérer. Ayant failli perdre la vue, recueilli dans une sorte d'institution médico-sociale, il est sous le regard des médecins, livré à l'autorité de ces spécialistes qui sont aussi des représentants de la loi, des médecins légistes qui exigent de lui, et d'abord, semble-t-il, dans son propre intérêt, qu'il témoigne de ce qui lui serait arrivé afin que justice lui soit rendue. Son récit fidèle des événements devrait faire droit à la loi. La loi exige un récit.

Prononcé quatre fois dans les trois derniers paragraphes de *La Folie du jour*, le mot "récit" ne semble pas désigner un genre littéraire mais un certain type ou mode de discours. C'est en effet l'apparence. Tout semble en effet se passer comme si le récit—la question ou plutôt la demande de récit, la réponse et la non-réponse à la demande—se trouvait mis en scène et figurait l'un des thèmes, objets, enjeux d'un texte plus ample, *La Folie du jour* dont le genre serait, lui, d'un autre ordre et en tous cas déborderait le récit de toute sa généralité comme de toute sa généricité. Le récit, lui, ne couvrirait pas cette généralité générique du corpus littéraire nommé *La Folie du jour*. Or nous serions déjà invités à ne pas trop nous fier à cette apparence et inquiétés dans notre assurance par une allusion que "je" fait à un moment donné : celui qui dit "je," qui n'est pas forcément un narrateur et pas nécessairement le même toujours, note que les représentants de la loi, ceux qui lui demandent un récit au nom de la loi le considèrent et le traitent, dans son identité personnelle et civile, non seulement comme un homme "instruit" (et un homme instruit, lui disent-ils souvent, doit pouvoir parler et raconter, c'est un sujet compétent qui doit savoir rassembler une histoire en disant "je" et comment les choses lui sont arrivées "au juste") mais aussi comme un écrivain. C'est un écrivain et un lecteur, un animal de "bibliothèques," le lecteur de ce récit. Ce n'est pas une raison suffisante mais en tous cas un premier indice pour nous inciter à penser que le récit requis ne reste pas simplement étranger à la littérature et même à un genre littéraire. Mais ne nous contentons pas de ce soupçon. Considérons la possibilité de l'inclusion d'une structure modale dans un corpus plus vaste, plus général, qu'il soit ou non littéraire et qu'il relève ou non d'un genre. Une telle inclusion pose des problèmes de bord, de ligne de bordure et de débordement qui vont pas sans pli.

Quel pli? Selon quel pli et quelle figure de pli?

Voici les trois derniers paragraphes, ils sont de longueur inégale et le dernier tient à peu près sur une ligne :

On m'avait demandé : Racontez-nous comment les choses se sont passées "au juste." —Un récit? Je commençai : Je ne suis ni savant ni ignorant. J'ai connu des joies. C'est trop peu dire. Je leur racontai l'histoire tout entière qu'ils écoutaient, me semble-t-il, avec intérêt, du moins au début. Mais la fin fut pour eux une commune surprise. "Après ce commencement," disaient-ils, "vous en viendrez aux faits." Comment cela! le récit était terminé.

Je dus reconnaître que je n'étais pas capable de former un récit avec ces événements. J'avais perdu le sens de l'histoire, cela arrive dans bien des maladies. Mais cette explication ne les rendit que plus exigeants. Je remarquai alors pour la première fois qu'ils étaient deux, que cette entorse à la méthode traditionnelle, quoique s'expliquant par le fait que l'un était un technicien de la vue, l'autre un spécialiste des maladies mentales, donnait constamment à notre conversation le caractère d'un interrogatoire autoritaire, surveillé et contrôlé par une règle stricte. Ni l'un ni l'autre, certes, n'était le commissaire de police. Mais étant deux, à cause de cela ils étaient trois, et ce troisième restait fermement convaincu, j'en suis sûr, qu'un écrivain, un homme qui parle et raisonne avec distinction, est toujours capable de raconter des faits dont il se souvient.

Un récit? Non, pas de récit, plus jamais.

Dans le premier des trois paragraphes que je viens de citer, ce qu'il dit commencer après le mot "récit" suivi d'un point d'interrogation ("Un récit?" —sous-entendu: ils veulent un récit, est-ce un récit qu'ils exigent donc? "Je commençai. . ."), ce n'est rien d'autre que la première ligne de la première page de *La Folie du jour*. Ce sont les mêmes mots, dans le même ordre, mais ce n'est pas une citation au sens strict puisque, sans guillemets, cela commence ou recommence un quasi-récit qui de nouveau engendrera toute la séquence comprenant ce nouveau départ, etc. Ainsi ce qui vient après le mot "récit" et son point d'interrogation, ce qui entame le commencement de récit extorqué par les représentants de la loi, ces premiers mots ("Je ne suis ni savant ni ignorant . . .") marquent un effondrement impensable, irreprésentable, insituable dans l'ordre linéaire d'une succession, dans une séquentialité spatiale ou temporelle, dans une topologique ou une chronologique objectivables. On voit, sans voir, on lit l'effondrement du bord supérieur ou du bord initial de *La Folie du jour* déroulée selon l'ordre "normal," celui que règlent la loi commune, la convention éditoriale, le droit positif, le régime de la compétence dans notre culture logo-alphabétique, etc. Tout à coup ce bord supérieur ou initial, ce qu'on appelle la première ligne d'un livre, vient faire une poche à l'intérieur du corpus. Il vient prendre la forme d'une *invagination* par laquelle le trait de la première ligne, la "borderline" si vous voulez, se divise en restant la même et traverse le corpus que pourtant elle borde. Le "récit" qu'il dit commencer à la fin, sur réquisition légale, n'est autre que celui qui a commencé depuis le début de *La Folie du jour* et dans lequel, donc, il en vient à dire qu'il commence, etc. Et c'est sans commencement ni fin, sans contenu et sans bord. Il n'y a que du contenu sans bord, et il n'y a que du bord sans contenu. L'inclusion (ou l'occlusion, l'invagination inocclusive) est interminable, c'est une analyse du récit qui ne peut que tourner en rond, inarrêtable, inénarrable et insatiablement ressassante—mais terrible pour ceux qui au nom de la loi requièrent que l'ordre règne dans le récit et qui veulent savoir, avec toute la compétence requise, comment ça se passe "au juste." Car si "je" ou "il" continuait à raconter ce qu'il a raconté, il n'en finirait pas de revenir à ce point et de recommencer à commencer, c'est-à-dire à recommencer par une fin qui précède le début. Et du point de vue de l'espace-temps objectif, le point où il s'arrête est absolument inassignable ("Je leur racontai l'histoire tout entière . . .") car il n'y a pas d'histoire "tout entière" que celle qui s'interrompt ainsi.

A cette "première" invagination du bord supérieur va, si on peut dire, répondre, en la croisant, une invagination du bord inférieur. La "dernière ligne" reprend la question posée *avant* le "je commençai" (Un récit?) et dit la résolution ou la promesse, l'engagement de ne plus faire de récit. Comme s'il en avait déjà fait un! Et pourtant, oui (oui et non), il y a eu récit. Le dernier mot, donc: "Un récit? Non, pas de récit, plus jamais." Il était impossible de décider si l'événement raconté et l'événement du récit même ont eu lieu. Impossible de décider s'il y a eu récit puisque celui qui arrive à peine à dire "je" et à se constituer en narrateur raconte qu'il n'aura pas pu raconter— et quoi, au juste? eh bien tout, jusqu'à la demande de récit, etc.; et si la décision assurée, garantie, est impossible, c'est aussi bien qu'il n'y a plus qu'à décider sans garde-fou, sans bord, à s'engager, à performer, à parier, à laisser sa chance à la chance. Il est aussi impossible de décider si la promesse "Non, pas de récit, plus jamais," fait ou non partie du récit. Elle fait légalement partie de *La Folie du jour* mais non nécessairement du récit ou du simulacre de récit. Son trait se divise encore en un bord interne et un bord externe. Il répète—sans citer—la question apparement posée plus haut (Un récit?) dont on peut dire, dans cette révolution permanente de l'ordre, qu'elle la suit, la double ou la réitère d'avance. Alors se forme ici une autre bouche ou une outre boucle invaginante. Cette fois, c'est le bord inférieur qui s'empoche pour rentrer dans le corpus et pour remonter en deçà de la ligne d'invagination de la ligne supérieure ou initiale. Cela dessinerait une double invagination chiasmatique des bords:

    A. "Je ne suis ni savant ni ignorant . . ."
    B. "Un récit? Je commençai:
    A'. "Je ne suis ni savant ni ignorant . . ."
    B'. "Un récit? Non, pas de récit, plus jamais."

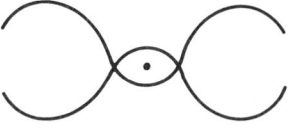

. . . "Je commençai"

Il est donc impossible de décider s'il y a eu événement, récit, récit d'événement ou événement de récit. Impossible d'arrêter les lignes de bordure simples de ce corpus, de cette ellipse qui s'annulle sans cesse dans sa propre expansion. Il est donc difficile, pour se replier sur cette conséquence poétique, de parler ici en toute rigueur d'un récit comme mode déterminé inclus dans un corpus plus général ou simplement rapporté, dans sa détermination, à d'autres modes ou tout simplement à autre chose que lui-même. Tout est récit et rien ne l'est, la sortie hors du récit reste dans le récit sur un mode non-inclusif et cette structure est si peu dialectique qu'elle inscrit la dialectique dans l'ellipse du récit.

Jacques Derrida

Tout est récit, rien ne l'est, et le rapport de ces deux propositions, l'étrange conjonction du récit au sans-récit, nous ne saurons pas si elle appartient à l'ordre du récit. Que se passe-t'il quand le bord fait une phrase?

Devant ce type de difficultés—dont nous ne pouvons ici déployer les conséquences ou les implications—on peut être tenté de recourir au droit et à la loi qui règle les corpus publiés. On peut être tenté d'argumenter ainsi: tous ces insolubles problèmes de délimitation se posent "à l'intérieur" d'un livre classé comme ouvrage de littérature ou de fiction littéraire. Selon ces normes juridiques, ce livre a un commencement et une fin qui ne laissent place à aucune indécision. Ce livre a un commencement et une fin déterminables, un titre, un auteur, un éditeur, il s'appelle *La Folie du jour*, voici son premier mot, sur cette page-ci que je montre du doigt, voici son point final, parfaitement situable dans l'espace objectif, etc. Et toutes les transgressions sophistiqués, toutes les subversions infinitésimales qui vous fascinent ne sont possibles que dans cet enclos dont elles ont d'ailleurs un besoin essentiel pour se produire. De plus, à l'intérieur de cet espace normé, poursuivrait-on, le mot "récit" ne nomme pas une opération ou un genre littéraire mais un mode discursif courant, quels que soient les redoutables problèmes de structure, de bordure, de théorie des ensembles de tout et de partie, etc., qu'il pose dans ce corpus dit littéraire.

Tout cela est vrai. Mais dans sa pertinence même, cette objection ne peut convaincre—et par exemple sauver la détermination modale du récit—qu'en se référant à des normes juridiques extra-littéraires, et même extra-linguistiques. L'objection fait appel à la loi et rappelle que la subversion de La folie du jour a besoin de la loi pour se produire. En quoi l'objection reproduit et accomplit la démonstration mise en scène dans *La Folie du jour*: le récit mandé, commandé par la loi mais aussi, on va le voir, le récit commandant la loi, la requérant et la produisant à son tour. Bref toute la scène critique de la compétence dans laquelle nous sommes engagés est *partie* de *La Folie du jour*, tout et partie, tout est partie.

Tout ne fait que commencer. J'aurais pu commencer par ce qui ressemble au commencement absolu, dans l'ordre juridico-historique de cette publication. Ce qu'on appelle légèrement la première version de *La Folie du jour* n'était pas un livre. Publiée dans la revue *Empédocle* (2, mai 1949), elle avait un autre titre et même plusieurs autres titres. Sur la couverture de la revue, la voici, on lit:

Maurice Blanchot
Un récit?

Le point d'interrogation disparaît ensuite par deux fois. D'abord quand le titre est reproduit dans le Sommaire à l'intérieur de la revue:

La Loi du genre

Maurice Blanchot
Un récit

puis au dessus de la première ligne:

Un récit
par
Maurice Blanchot

Pourriez-vous décider si ces titres antérieurs et archivés sont un seul titre, si ce sont les titres du même texte, si ce sont les titres du récit (comme mode d'ailleurs impraticable dans le livre) ou le titre d'un genre? Même si, dans ce dernier cas, il y avait confusion, une telle confusion pose des questions qui se trouvent d'ailleurs mises en oeuvre par *La Folie du jour*. Cette mise en oeuvre permet de dénaturaliser ou de déconstituer et l'opposition nature/histoire et l'opposition mode/genre.

A quoi se réfèrent les mots d' "Un récit" dans leurs multiples occurences et leurs ponctuations diverses? Comment y joue la référence? Dans l'un des cas, le point d'interrogation peut *aussi* remarquer en supplément, la nécessité de toutes ces questions, comme le caractère insolvable de l'indécision: est-ce là un récit? Est-ce un récit que j'intitule? demande le titre en intitulant. Est-ce un récit qu'ils demandent? A quel titre? Est-ce un récit comme mode discursif ou comme opération littéraire, voire comme genre littéraire ou fiction littéraire sur le thème du mode et du genre? De même, le titre peut prélever, comme fait une métonymie, un fragment du récit sans récit (à savoir les mots "un récit" avec et sans point d'interrogation) mais un tel prélèvement itératif n'est pas citationnel et le titre garanti par la loi mais aussi faisant loi garde une structure référentielle radicalement autre que celle des autres occurrences des "mêmes" mots dans le texte. Etc, etc. Qu'il s'agisse de titre, de référence, de mode et de genre, il y va toujours du rapport à la loi. L'énorme matrice de toutes ces questions forme la puissance thématique non-thématisable d'un simulacre de récit: c'est cela même que raconte sans le dire, que dit sans le raconter, cette oeuvre d'écriture intarissable.

Récit de récit sans récit, récit sans bord, récit dont tout l'espace visible n'est que bordure de soi sans soi, consistant en bord sans contenu, sans bordure générique ou modale, telle est la loi de cet événement textuel, de ce texte qui dit aussi la loi, la sienne et celle de l'autre comme lecteur, de ce texte qui, disant la loi, s'impose aussi comme texte de loi, texte de la loi. La loi du genre de ce texte singulier, c'est la loi, la figure de la loi qui sera aussi le centre invisible, le thème sans thème de *La Folie du jour* ou, je peux maintenant le dire d' *"Un récit?"*

Mais cette loi, comme loi du genre, ne commande pas seulement au genre entendu comme catégorie de l'art ou de la littérature. La loi

Jacques Derrida

du genre y commande aussi, et aussi paradoxalement, aussi impossible-
ment, à ce qui entraîne le genre dans l'engendrement, les générations,
la généalogie, la dégénérescence. Vous l'avez assez vu s'annoncer, déjà,
avec toutes les figures de cet auto-engendrement dégénérescent d'un
récit, avec cette figure de la loi qui, comme le jour qu'elle est, défie
l'opposition entre la loi de la nature et la loi de l'histoire symbolique.
Ce qui vient d'être remarqué de la double invagination chiasmatique
des bords suffit à exclure que toutes ces complications soient de pure
forme, et formalisables à l'extérieur du contenu. La question du genre
littéraire n'est pas une question formelle : elle traverse de part en part
le motif de la loi en général, de la génération, au sens naturel et symbolique, de la naissance, au sens naturel et symbolique, de la différence
de génération, de la différence sexuelle entre le genre masculin et le
genre féminin, de l'hymen entre les deux, d'un rapport sans rapport
entre les deux, d'une identité et d'une différence entre le féminin et le
masculin. Le mot d'*hymen* ne fait pas seulement signe vers la logique
paradoxale qui s'inscrit sans se formaliser sous ce nom ; le mot d'hymen
rappelle aussi tout ce que nous disent Philippe Lacoue-Labarthe et Jean-
Luc Nancy, dans *L'Absolu littéraire* (p. 276 notamment) du rapport
entre le genre (*Gattung*) et le mariage, comme de toute la série *gattieren*
(mélanger), *gatten* (s'unir), *Gatte/Gattin* (époux/épouse), etc.

Une fois articulée avec tout le discours de Blanchot quant au neutre,
la question la plus elliptique serait la suivante : qu'en irait-il d'un genre
neutre? Et d'un genre dont la neutralité ne serait pas négative (ni . . .
ni), ni dialectique, mais affirmative, et doublement affirmative (ou . . .
ou)?

Là encore, faute de temps mais aussi pour des raisons plus essentielles qui tiennent à la structure du texte, je devrai prélever quelques
fragments abstraits. Cela n'ira pas sans supplément de violence et de
souffrance.

Premier mot et mot impossible de *La Folie du jour*, "je" se présente
comme moi, un homme. La loi grammaticale ne laisse à ce sujet aucun
doute. La première phrase, au masculin ("Je ne suis ni savant ni ignorant") ne dit rien qu'une double négation au regard du savoir (ni . . .
ni). Elle n'a donc rien d'une présentation de soi. Mais la double négation
donne le passage à une double affirmation (oui, oui) qui se lie ou
s'allie à elle-même. Faisant alliance ou hymen avec elle-même, cette
double affirmation sans limite dit un *oui* sans mesure, excessif, immense :
et à la vie et à la mort.

Je ne suis ni savant ni ignorant. J'ai connu des joies. C'est trop peu dire;
je vis, et cette vie me fait le plaisir le plus grand. Alors, la mort? Quand je
mourrai (peut-être tout à l'heure), je connaîtrai un plaisir immense. Je ne
parle pas de l'avant-goût de la mort qui est fade et souvent désagréable.

Souffrir est abrutissant. Mais telle est la vérité remarquable dont je suis sur: j'éprouve à vivre un plaisir sans limite et j'aurai à mourir une satisfaction sans limite.

Or sept paragraphes plus loin la chance et la probabilité d'une telle affirmation (double et donc sans limite) est accordée à la femme. Elle revient à la femme. Plutôt: non pas à la femme ou même au féminin, au genre féminin, à la généralité du genre féminin mais— c'est pourquoi j'ai parlé de chance et de probabilité—"presque toujours" à des femmes. Ce sont "presque toujours" des femmes qui disent oui, oui. A la vie à la mort. Ce "presque toujours" évite de traiter le féminin comme une puissance générale générique, il fait sa part à l'événement, à la performance, à l'aléa, à la rencontre. Et c'est bien depuis l'expérience aléatoire de la rencontre que "je" parle ici. Dans le passage que je vais citer, l'expression "les hommes" intervient une fois, la seconde, pour nommer le genre sexuel, la différence sexuelle (*aner, vir*—mais la différence sexuelle ne passe pas entre une espèce et un genre), une autre fois, la première, de façon indécise pour nommer ou bien le genre humain (nommé d'ailleurs "espèce" dans le texte) ou bien la différence sexuelle.

Les hommes voudraient échapper à la mort, bizarre *espèce*. Et quelques-uns crient, mourir, mourir, parce qu'ils voudraient échapper à la vie. "Quelle vie, je me tue, je me rends." Cela est pitoyable et étrange, c'est une erreur.
J'ai pourtant rencontré des *êtres* qui n'ont jamais dit à la vie, tais-toi, et jamais à la mort, va-t-en. Presque toujours des femmes, de belles créatures. Les hommes, la terreur les assiège. . . (Je souligne)

Que s'est-il passé, déjà, dans ces sept paragraphes? Presque toujours des femmes, de belles créatures, dit "je." Il se trouve, rencontre, chance, affirmation de la chance, que cela n'arrive pas toujours. Il n'y a pas ici de loi naturelle ou symbolique, loi universelle ou loi d'un genre. Presque toujours, seulement, presque toujours des femmes, (virgule d'apposition) de belles créatures. Dans sa logique très calculée la virgule d'apposition laisse ouverte la possibilité de penser que ces femmes ne sont pas belles et puis, d'autre part, comme ça se trouve, capables de dire oui, oui à la vie à la mort, de ne pas dire tais-toi, va-t-en à la vie à la mort. La virgule d'apposition nous laisse penser qu'elles sont belles, femmes et belles, ces créatures, en tant qu'elles affirment et la vie et la mort. La beauté, la beauté féminine de ces "êtres" aurait ainsi partie liée avec cette double affirmation.

Or moi-même, qui ne "suis ni savant ni ignorant," "j'éprouve à vivre un plaisir sans limite et j'aurai à mourir une satisfaction sans limite." Dans cette présomption aléatoire qui lie l'affirmation presque toujours à des femmes, et belles, il est donc plus que probable que, pour autant que je dise oui, oui, je sois femme, et belle. Le sexe grammatical (ou aussi bien anatomique, en tous cas le sexe soumis à la loi de l'objectivité), le genre masculin est alors par l'affirmation affecté d'une dérive aléatoire qui peut toujours le faire autre. Il y aurait là une sorte d'accouplement secret, un hymen irrégulier, un couple irrégulier car rien de cela ne peut être réglé par une loi objective, naturelle ou civile. Le "presque toujours" est la marque de cet hymen secret et irrégulier, de cet accouplement qui est aussi peut-être mélange des genres. Les genres passent l'un dans l'autre. Et on ne nous interdira pas de croire qu'entre ce mélange des genres comme folie de la différence sexuelle et le mélange des genres littéraires il y ait quelque rapport.

"Je" garde donc la chance d'être femme ou de changer de sexe. La trans-sexualité lui permet, de façon plus que métaphorique et trans-férentielle, d'engendrer. Il peut donner naissance, et cela se marque entre beaucoup d'autres signes que je ne peux pas relever ici, au fait que, à plusieurs reprises, il "donne le jour." Dans la rhétorique de *La Folie du jour*, l'expression idiomatique "donner le jour" est partie prenante d'un jeu polysémique et disséminal très puissant que je ne tenterai pas de rassembler ici. J'en retiens seulement le sens courant et dominant dans le sentiment linguistique: donner le jour, c'est donner naissance, verbe dont le sujet est presque toujours maternel, c'est-à-dire générale-ment féminin. Au centre, tout près d'un centre invisible, une scène primitive aurait pu, si nous en avions eu le temps, nous rappeler au *point de vue* de *La Folie du jour* et d'*Une Scène primitive*. C'est ce qui s'appelle une "courte scène."

"Je" donne le jour. A quoi? Eh bien précisément à la loi, ou plus strictement, pour commencer, aux représentants de la loi, à ceux qui détiennent l'autorité (entendons aussi l'autorité de l'auteur, le droit d'auteur) du simple fait d'avoir droit de regard, droit de voir, droit d'avoir tout sous les yeux. Cette panoptique, cette synopse, ils ne demandent rien d'autre, mais rien de moins. Or voici le paradoxe essent-iel: d'où tiennent-ils, et de qui, ce pouvoir, leur pouvoir-voir qui leur permet de disposer de "moi"? Eh bien de "moi," du sujet plutôt qui leur est assujetti. C'est le "je" sans "je" de la voix narrative, le je "dépouillé" de lui-même, celui qui n'a pas lieu, c'est lui qui leur donne le jour, qui engendre ces hommes de loi en leur donnant à voir ce qui les regarde et ne devrait pas les regarder:

J'aimais assez les médecins, je ne me sentais pas diminué par leurs doutes. L'ennui, c'est que leur autorité grandissait d'heure en heure. On ne s'en aperçoit pas, mais ce sont des rois. Ouvrant mes chambres, ils disaient: Tout ce qui est là nous appartient. Ils se jetaient sur mes rognures de pensée: Ceci est à nous. Ils interpellaient mon histoire: Parle, et elle se mettait à leur service. En hâte je me dépouillais de moi-même. Je leur distribuais mon sang, mon intimité, je leur prêtais l'univers, je leur donnais le jour. Sous leurs yeux en rien étonnés, je devenais une goutte d'eau, une tache d'encre.

Je me réduisais à eux-mêmes, je passais tout entier sous leur vue, et quand enfin, n'ayant plus présente que ma parfaite nullité et n'ayant plus rien à voir, ils cessaient aussi de me voir, très irrités, ils se levaient en criant: Eh bien, où êtes-vous? Ou vous cachez-vous? Se cacher est interdit, c'est une faute, etc.

La loi, le jour. On croit pouvoir en général opposer la loi à l'affirmation et singulièrement à l'affirmation illimitée, à l'immensité du oui, oui. La loi, nous la figurons souvent comme l'instance de la limite interdictrice, de l'obligation liante, la négativité d'une ligne de bord à ne pas franchir. Or le trait le plus fort et le plus divisé de *La Folie du jour* ou d'*Un récit?*, c'est celui qui rapporte la naissance de la loi, sa généalogie, son engendrement, sa génération ou son genre, le genre même de la loi, au procès de la double affirmation. La démesure du *oui, oui* n'est pas étrangère à la genèse de la loi (ni à la genèse tout court, car il s'agit aussi, cela se montrerait facilement, d'un récit de la Genèse "à la lumière de sept jours" [p. 20]). La double affirmation n'est pas étrangère au genre et au génie de la loi. Pas d'affirmation, et surtout pas d'affirmation *double* sans qu'une loi voie le jour et que le jour se fasse droit. Telle est la folie du jour, tel est un récit dans sa vérité "remarquable," dans sa vérité sans vérité.

Or le féminin, genre presque généralement affirmateur, c'est aussi le genre de cette figure de la loi, non pas de ses représentants mais de la loi elle-même qui tout au long d'un récit fait couple avec moi, avec le "je" de la voix narrative.

La loi est au féminin.

Elle n'est pas femme (c'est seulement une figure, une "silhouette," et non un représentant de la loi) mais elle est au féminin, déclinée au féminin; mais non pas seulement comme genre grammatical dans ma langue (ailleurs, Blanchot aura joué de ce genre pour *la* parole et *la* pensée). Non, elle est décrite comme "élément féminin," ce qui ne signifie pas personne féminine. Et le "je" affirmateur, la voix narrative qui aura donné le jour aux représentants de la loi, se dit séduit par la loi, séduit sexuellement, la loi lui plaît: "La vérité, c'est qu'elle me plaisait. Elle était dans ce milieu surpeuplé d'hommes le seul élément féminin. Elle m'avait une fois fait toucher son genou: une bizarre impression. Je le lui avais déclaré: Je ne suis pas homme à me contenter d'un genou. Sa réponse: ce serait dégoûtant!" Elle lui plaît et il voudrait ne pas se contenter du genou qu'elle lui "fait toucher," ce contact du genou, comme me le faisait remarquer un étudiant et ami, Pierre-François Berger, pouvant bien rappeler la contiguïté, dans le mot, et la flexion d'un je/nous, d'un couple je/nous dont nous reparlerons tout à l'heure.

L'élément féminin de la loi a donc toujours attiré: moi, je, il, nous.

Jacques Derrida

La loi attire: "La loi m'attirait . . . Pour la tenter, j'appelai doucement la loi: "Approche, que je te voie face à face." (Je voulais un instant, la prendre à part.) Impudent appel, qu'aurais-je fait si elle avait répondu?"

Il est peut-être assujetti à la loi mais il ne fuit pas devant elle, il n'est pas intimidé, il veut séduire la loi à laquelle il donne naissance (il y a là soupçon d'inceste) et surtout, c'est un des traits les plus forts et les plus singuliers de cette scène, il fait peur à la loi. Il n'inquiète pas seulement les représentants de la loi, les hommes de loi que sont les médecins légistes et les "psy"-qui exigent de lui sans l'obtenir un récit organisé, un témoignage orienté par le sens de l'histoire, ordonné par la raison et par l'unité d'un je pense ou d'une aperception originairement synthétique accompagnant toutes les représentations. Comme ici le "je" ne s'accompagne pas toujours, il fait peur aux hommes de loi, il les persécute radicalement et à sa manière en leur dérobant sans lutter la vérité qu'ils demandent et sans laquelle ils ne sont rien. Mais il ne fait pas seulement peur aux hommes de loi, il fait peur à la loi, on dirait à la loi elle-même si elle ne restait ici une silhouette et un effet de récit. Et de surcroît cette loi à laquel le "je" fait peur n'est autre que "moi," que le "je," effet de son désir, enfant de son affirmation, du genre "je" enfermé dans un couple spéculaire avec "moi." Ils sont inséparables (je/nous et genou, je/toi et je/toit) et elle le lui dit, encore une fois comme la vérité: "La vérité, c'est que nous ne pouvons plus nous séparer. Je te suivrai partout, je vivrai sous ton toit, nous aurons le même sommeil." La loi, dont la silhouette se tient derrière ses représentants, nous la voyons effrayée par "moi," par "lui," elle s'incline et décline à *je/nous* devant "moi," devant lui, ses genoux marquant peut-être l'articulation du pas, la flexion du couple et de la différence sexuelle mais aussi la contiguité sans contact de l'hymen et le "mélange des genres."

Derrière leur dos, j'apercevais la silhouette de la loi. Non pas la loi que l'on connaît, qui est rigoureuse et peu agréable: celle-ci était autre. Loin de tomber sous sa menace c'est moi qui semblais l'effrayer. A la croire, mon regard était la foudre et mes mains des occasions de périr. En outre, elle m'attribuait ridiculement tous les pouvoirs, elle se déclarait perpétuellement à mes genoux. Mais elle ne me laissait rien demander et quand elle m'avait reconnu le droit d'être en tous lieux, cela signifiait que je n'avais de place nulle part (c'est ainsi qu'ailleurs Blanchot désigne le non-lieu et la mobilité atopique ou hypertopique de la voix narrative). Quand elle me mettait au-dessus des autorités, cela voulait dire: vous n'êtes autorisés à rien.

A quoi joue la loi, une loi de ce genre? A quoi joue-t-elle quand elle fait toucher son genou? Car si *La Folie du jour* se joue de la loi, joue la loi, joue avec la loi, c'est qu'aussi la loi joue. La loi, dans son élément féminin, c'est une silhouette qui joue. A quoi? A naître, à naître comme personne. Elle joue sa génération et son genre, elle joue sa nature et son histoire, et elle se joue d'un récit. En se jouant elle récite; et elle naît de celui-là même, on peut dire de celle-là même, la voix narrative, *lui, elle, je, nous,* le genre neutre qui s'y assujettit alors même qu'il lui donne le jour, qui se laisse attirer par la loi et qui la fuit, qu'elle fuit et qu'elle aime, etc. Elle se laisse mettre en mouvement, elle se laisse citer par lui quand au milieu de son jeu elle vient à dire, selon un idiome que sa polysémie disséminale emporte à l'abîme, "je vois le jour":

Voici un de ses jeux (Il vient de rappeler qu'elle lui "avait une fois fait toucher son genou"). Elle me montrait une portion de l'espace, entre le haut de la fenêtre et le plafond: "Vous êtes là," disait-elle. Je regardais ce point avec intensité. "Y êtes-vous?" Je la regardais avec toute ma puissance. "Eh bien?" Je sentais bondir les cicatrices de mon regard, ma vue devenait une plaie, ma tête un trou, un taureau éventré. Soudain, elle s'écriait: "Ah, je vois le jour, ah, Dieu," etc. Je protestais que ce jeu me fatiguait énormément, mais elle était insatiable de ma gloire.

Voir le jour, pour la loi, c'est sa folie, ce qu'elle aime à la folie comme la gloire l'illustration ensoleillée, le jour de l'écrivain, de l'auteur qui dit "je" et qui donne le jour à la loi. Il dit qu'elle est insatiable de sa gloire à lui, lui qui est aussi l'auteur de la loi à laquelle il se soumet, lui qui l'engendre, lui sa mère qui ne sait plus dire "je" et garder la mémoire. Je suis la mère de la loi, voilà la folie de ma fille. C'est aussi la folie du jour, car le jour, le mot "jour" en son abîme disséminal, c'est la loi, la loi de la loi. La folie de ma fille, c'est de vouloir naître— comme personne. Alors qu'elle resta "silhouette," ombre, profil, double, jamais vue de face, il lui avait dit, à la loi, pour "la tenter": "Approche, que je te voie face à face."

Telle serait la "vérité remarquable," celle qui ouvre la folie du jour—et qui plaît, comme la loi, comme la folie, à qui dit "je" ou je/nous. Soyons attentifs à cette syntaxe de la vérité. Elle, la loi, dit: "La vérité, c'est que nous ne pouvons plus nous séparer. Je te suivrai partout, je vivrai sous ton toit . . ." Lui: "La vérité, c'est qu'elle me plaisait . . . ," elle, la loi, mais aussi, c'est toujours le thème principal de ces phrases, la vérité. On ne peut pas la penser sans la folie de la loi.

Je me suis laissé commander par la loi de notre colloque, par la convention de notre sujet, à savoir le genre, la loi du genre. Cette loi, articulée comme un je/nous plus ou moins autonome dans ses mouvements, nous assignait des places et des limites. Le procès que j'ai pu tenter de faire à cette loi, c'est encore elle qui le réglait pour la confirmation de sa propre gloire. Mais c'est aussi la nôtre qu'elle désire insatiablement. Soumis au sujet de notre colloque, comme à sa loi, j'ai criblé "Un récit," *La Folie du jour*. J'ai isolé un type, sinon un genre, de lecture dans une série innombrable de trajets ou de courses possibles. Le principe générateur de ces courses, commencements et recommencements en tous sens, je l'ai indiqué: d'un certain point de vue. Ailleurs, selon d'autres sujets, d'autres colloques, d'autres je/nous rassemblés en un lieu, j'aurais pu, j'ai pu suivre d'autres trajets.

Je ne pourrais pas rassembler néanmoins, ce serait une folie, quelque conclusion pour le rapport de ce colloque. Je ne pourrais pas dire ce qui s'est passé au juste dans cette scène, dans mon discours ou mon récit. Ce qui fut peut-être évident, le temps d'un clin d'oeil, c'est une folie de la loi—et donc de l'ordre, de la raison, du sens, du jour: "Mais souvent (dit "je") je mourais sans rien dire. A la longue, je fus convaincu que je voyais face à face la folie du jour; telle était la vérité: la lumière devenait folle, la clarté avait perdu tout bon sens; elle m'assaillait déraisonnablement, sans règle, sans but. Cette découverte, fut un coup de dent à travers ma vie." Je suis femme, et belle, ma fille la loi est folle de moi. Je spécule sur ma fille. Ma fille est folle de moi, c'est la loi.

La loi est folle, elle est folle de "moi." Et à travers la folie de ce jour, ça me regarde. Voilà, cela aura été mon auto-portrait du genre.

La loi est folle. La loi est folie, la folie, mais la folie n'est pas le prédicat de la loi. Il n'y a pas de folie sans la loi, on ne peut penser la folie que depuis la folie, par rapport à la loi. C'est la loi, c'est une folie, la loi.

Il y a là un trait général: la folie de la loi folle de moi, le jour amoureux fou de moi, la silhouette de ma fille folle de moi, sa mère, etc., etc. Mais de ce trait général, *Un récit?* sans récit portant et déportant ses titres, *La Folie du jour*, n'est pas du tout exemplaire. Pas du tout. Ce n'est pas l'exemple d'un tout général ou générique. Pas du tout. Du tout—qui commence par finir et n'en finit pas de commencer à partir de soi, du tout qui reste au bord sans bord de lui-même, du tout plus grand et plus petit que tout et rien, *Un récit?* n'aura pas été exemplaire. Plutôt contre-exemplaire de tout.

Depuis toujours le genre en tous genres a pu jouer le rôle de principe d'ordre: ressemblance, analogie, identité et différence, classification taxonomique, ordonnancement et arbre généalogique, ordre de la raison, ordre des raisons, sens du sens, vérité de la vérité, lumière naturelle et sens de l'histoire. Or l'épreuve d'*Un récit?* a mis au jour la folie du genre. Elle (lui) a donné le jour au sens le plus éblouissant, le plus aveuglant du mot. Et dans l'écriture d'*Un récit?*, dans la littérature, pratiquant satiriquement tous les genres, les buvant mais ne se laissant jamais saturer par un catalogue des genres, elle s'est mise à y faire tourner la *rose des genres* de Petersen comme un soleil fou. Et elle ne le fait pas seulement *dans* la littérature puisqu'en dérobant les bords qui séparent mode et genre, elle a aussi débordé *et* divisé les limites entre la littérature et ses autres.

Voilà, c'est tout, c'est seulement ce que, ici, à genoux, "je," disent-ils, au bord de la littérature, voit. La loi en somme. Ce que "je" voit et que "je" dit que je vois en un récit où je/nous somme—

NOTE

1. A cet égard, la note 2 (p. 271) de *L'Absolu littéraire* me paraît disons, un peu trop juste dans sa rigoureuse et honnête prudence.

THE LAW OF GENRE

Genres are not to be mixed.

I will not mix genres.

I repeat: genres are not to be mixed. I will not mix them.

Now suppose I let these utterances resonate all by themselves.

Suppose: I abandon them to their fate, I set free their random virtualities and turn them over to my audience—or rather, to *your* audience, to your auditory grasp, to whatever mobility they retain and you bestow upon them to engender effects of all kinds without my having to stand behind them.

I merely said, and then repeated: genres are not to be mixed; I will not mix them.

As long as I release these utterances (which others might call speech acts) in a form yet scarcely determined, given the open context out of which I have just let them be grasped from "my" language—as long as I do this, you may find it difficult to choose among several interpretative options. They are legion, as I could demonstrate. They form an open and essentially unpredictable series. But you may be tempted by *at least* two types of audience, two modes of interpretation, or, if you prefer to give these words more of a chance, then you may be tempted by two different genres of hypothesis. Which ones?

On the one hand, it could be a matter of a fragmentary discourse whose propositions would be of the descriptive, constative, and neutral genre. In such a case, I would have named the operation which con- sists of "genres are not to be mixed." I would have designated this operation in a neutral fashion without evaluating it, without recommending or advising against it, certainly without binding anyone to it. Without claiming to lay down the law or to make this an act of law, I merely would have summoned up, in a fragmentary utterance, the sense of a practice, an act or event, as you wish: which is what sometimes happens when we revert to "genres are not to be mixed." With reference to the same case, and to a hypothesis of the same type, same mode, same genre—or same order: when I said, "I will not mix genres," you may have discerned a foreshadowing description—I am not saying a prescription—the descriptive designation telling in advance what will transpire, predicting it in the constative mode or genre, i.e. it will happen thus, I will not mix genres. The future tense describes, then, what will surely take place, as you yourselves can judge; but for my part it does not constitute a commitment. I am not making you a promise here, nor am I issuing myself an order or invoking the authority of some law to which I am resolved to submit myself. In this case, the future tense does not set the time of a performative speech act of a promising or ordering type.

But another hypothesis, another type of audience, and another interpretation would have been no less legitimate. "Genres are not to be mixed" could strike you as a sharp order. You might have heard it resound the elliptical but all the more authoritarian summons to a law of "do" or "do not" which, as everyone knows, occupies the concept or constitutes the value of *genre*. As soon as the word "genre" is sounded, as soon as it is heard, as soon as one attempts to conceive it, a limit is drawn. And when a limit is established, norms and interdictions are not far behind: "Do," "Do not" says "genre," the word "genre," the figure, the voice, or the law of genre. And this can be said of genre in all genres, be it a question of a generic or a general determination of what one calls "nature" or *physis* (for example, a biological *genre* in the sense of *gender*, or the human *genre*, a genre of all that is in general), or be it a question of a typology designated as non-natural and depending on laws or orders which were once held to be opposed to *physis* according to those values associated with *technè, thesis, nomos* (for example, an artistic, poetic or literary genre). But the whole enigma of genre springs perhaps most closely from within this limit between the two genres of genre which, neither separable nor inseparable, form an odd couple of one without the other in which each evenly serves the other a citation to appear in the figure of the other, simultaneously and indiscernibly saying "I" and "we," me the genre, we genres, without it being possible to think that the "I" is a species of the genre "we." For who would have us believe that we, we two for example, would form a genre or belong to one? Thus, as soon as genre announces itself, one must respect a norm, one must not cross a line of demarcation, one must not risk impurity, anomaly or monstrosity. And so it goes in all cases, whether or not this law of genre be interpreted as a determination or perhaps even as a destination of *physis*, and regardless of the weight or range imputed to *physis*. If a genre is what it is, or if it is supposed to be what it is destined to be by virtue of its *telos*, then "genres are not to be mixed"; one should not mix genres, one owes it to oneself not to get mixed up in mixing genres. Or, more rigorously, genres should not intermix. And if it should happen that they do intermix, by accident or through transgression, by mistake or through a lapse, then this should confirm, since, after all, we are speaking of "mixing," the essential purity of their identity. This purity belongs to the typical axiom: it is a law of the law of genre, whether or not the law is, as one feels justified in saying, "natural." This normative position and this evaluation are inscribed and prescribed even at the threshold of the "thing itself," if something of the genre "genre" can be so named. And so it follows that you might have taken the second sentence in the first person, "I will not mix genres," as a vow of obedience, as a docile response to the injunction emanating from the law of genre. In place of a constative description, you would then hear a promise, an oath; you would grasp the following respectful commitment: I promise you that I will not mix genres, and, through this act of pledging utter faithfulness to my commitment, I will be faithful to the law of genre, since, by its very nature, the law invites and commits me in advance not to mix genres. By publishing my response to the imperious call of the law, I would correspondingly commit myself to be responsible.

Unless, of course, I were actually implicated in a wager, a challenge, an impossible bet—in short, a situation that would exceed the matter of merely engaging a commitment from me. And suppose for a moment that it were impossible not to mix genres. What if there were, lodged within the heart of the law itself, a law of impurity or a principle of contamination? And suppose the condition for the possibility of the law were the *a priori* of a counter-law, an axiom of impossibility that would confound its sense, order and reason?

I have just proposed an alternative between two interpretations. I did not do so, as you can imagine, in order to check myself. The line or trait that seemed to separate the two bodies of interpretation is affected *straight away* by an essential disruption that, for the time being, I shall let you name or qualify in any way you care to: as internal division of the trait, impurity, corruption, contamination, decomposition, perversion, deformation, even cancerization, generous proliferation or degenerescence. All these disruptive "anomalies" are engendered—and this is their common law, the lot or site they share—by *repetition*. One might even say by citation or re-citation (*ré-cit*), provided that the restricted use of these two words is not a call to strict generic order. A citation in the strict sense implies all sorts of contextual conventions, precautions and protocols in the mode of reiteration, of coded signs such as quotation marks or other typographical devices used for writing a citation. The same holds no doubt for the *récit* as a form, mode, or genre of discourse, even—and I shall return to this—as a literary type. And yet the law that protects the usage, in *stricto sensu*, of the words *citation* and *récit*, is threatened intimately and in advance by a counter-law that constitutes this very law, renders it possible, conditions it and thereby renders it impossible—for reasons of edges on which we shall run aground in just a moment—to edge through, to edge away from or to hedge around the counter-law itself. The law and the counter-law serve each other, citations summoning each other to appear, and each re-cites the other in this proceeding (*procès*). There would be no cause for concern if one were rigorously assured of being able to distinguish with rigor between a citation and a non-citation, a *récit* and a non-*récit* or a repetition within the form of one or the other.

I shall not undertake to demonstrate, assuming it is still possible, why you were unable to decide whether the sentences with which I opened this presentation and marked this context were or were not repetitions of a citational type; or whether they were or were not of the performative type; or certainly whether they were, both of them, together—and each time together—the one or the other. For perhaps someone has noticed that, from one repetition to the next, a change had insinuated itself into the relationship between the two initial utterances. The punctuation had been slightly modified, as had the content of the second independent clause. This barely noticeable shift could theoretically have created a mutual independency between the interpretative alternatives that might have tempted you to opt for one or the other, or for one *and* the other of these two sentences. A particularly rich combinatory of possibilities would thus ensue, which, in order not to exceed my time-limit and out of respect for the law of genre and of the audience, I shall abstain from recounting. I am simply going to assume a certain relationship between what has just now happened and the origin of literature, as well as its aborigine or its abortion, to quote Philippe Lacoue-Labarthe.

Provisionally claiming for myself the authority of such an assumption, I shall let our field of vision contract as I limit myself to a sort of species of the genre "genre." I shall focus on this genre of genre which is generally supposed, and always a bit too rashly, not to be part of nature, of *physis*, but rather of *technè*, of the arts, still more narrowly of poetry, and most particularly of literature. But at the same time, I take the liberty to think that, while limiting myself thus, I exclude nothing, at least in principle and *de jure*—the relationships here no longer being those of extension, from exemplary individual to species, from species to genre as genus or from the genre of genre to genre in general; rather as we shall see, these relationships are a whole order apart. What is at stake, in effect, is exemplarity and its whole *enigma*— in other words, as the word enigma indicates, exemplarity and the *récit* which works through the logic of the example.

Before going about putting a certain example to the test, I shall attempt to formulate, in a manner as elliptical, economical, and formal as possible, what I shall call the law of the law of genre. It is precisely a principle of contamination, a law of impurity, a parasitical economy. In the code of set theories, if I may use it at least figuratively, I would speak of a sort of participation without belonging—a taking part in without being part of, without having membership in a set. The trait that marks membership inevitably divides, the boundary of the set comes to form, by invagination, an internal pocket larger than the whole; and the outcome of this division and of this abounding remains as singular as it is limitless.

To demonstrate this, I shall hold to the leanest generalities. But I should like to justify this initial indigence or asceticism as well as possible. For example, I shall not enter into the passionate debate brought forth by poetics on the theory and the history of genre-theory, on the critical history of the concept of genre from Plato to the present. My stance is motivated by these considerations: in the first place, we now have at our disposal some remarkable, and, of late, handsomely enriched works dealing either with primary texts or critical analyses. I am thinking especially of the journal *Poétique*, of its issue entitled "Genres" (32) and of Genette's opening essay, "Genres, 'Types,' Modes." From yet another point of view, *L'Absolu littéraire* (*The Literary Absolute*) has already created quite a stir in this context, and everything that I shall risk here should perhaps resolve itself in a modest annotation on the margins of this magistral work which I assume some of you have already read. I could further justify my abstention or my abstinence here simply by acknowledging the terminological luxury or rapture as well as the taxonomic exuberance which debates of this kind, in a manner by no means fortuitous, have sparked: I feel completely powerless to contain this fertile proliferation—and not only because of time-constraints. I shall put forth, instead, *two* principal *motives*, hoping thereby to justify my keeping to scant preliminary generalities at the edge of this problematic.

To what do these two motives essentially relate? In its most recent phase—and this much is certainly clear in Genette's propositions —the most advanced critical axis has led to a rereading of the entire history of genre-theory. This rereading has been inspired by the perception—and it must be said, despite the initial denial, by the correction—of two types of misconstruing or confusion. On the one hand, and this will be the first motive or ground for my abstention, Plato and Aristotle have been subjected to considerable deformation, as Genette reminds us, insofar as they have been viewed in terms alien to their thinking, and even in terms that they themselves would have rejected; but this deformation has usually taken on the form of *naturalization*. Following a classical precedent, one has deemed natural structures or typical forms whose history is hardly natural, but rather, quite to the contrary, complex and heterogeneous. These forms have been treated as natural —and let us bear in mind the entire semantic scale of this difficult word whose span is so far-ranging and open-ended that it extends as far as the expression "natural language," by which term everyone agrees tactitly to oppose natural language only to a formal or artificial language without thereby implying that this natural language is a simple physical or biological production. Genette insists at length on this naturalization of genres: "The history of genre-theory is strewn with these fascinating outlines that *inform and deform reality*, a reality often heterogenous to the literary field, and that claim to discover a natural 'system' wherein they construct a factitious symmetry heavily reinforced by fake windows" (italics added, p. 408). In its most efficacious and legitimate aspect, this critical reading of the history (and) of genre-theory is based on an opposition between nature and history, and, more generally—as the allusion to an artificial construct indicates (". . . wherein they construct a factitious symmetry. . . .")—on an opposition between nature and what can be called the series of all its others. Such an opposition seems to go without saying; placed within this critical perspective, it is never questioned. Even if it has been tucked away discretely in some passage that has escaped my attention, this barely visible suspicion clearly had no effect on the general organization of the problematic. This does not diminish the relevance or fecundity of a reading such as Genette's. But a place remains open for some preliminary questions concerning his presuppositions, for some questions concerning the boundaries where it begins to take hold or take place. The form of these boundaries will contain me, and rein me in. These general propositions whose number is always open and indeterminable for whatever critical interpretation will not be dealt with here. What however seems to me to require more urgent attention is the relationship of nature to history, of nature to its others, *precisely when genre is on the line.*

Let us consider the most general concept of genre, from the minimal trait or predicate delineating it permanently through the modulations of its types and the regimens of its history: it rends and defends itself by mustering all its energy against a simple opposition that arises from nature and from history, as from nature and the vast lineage of its others (*technè*, *nomos*, *thesis*, then *spirit*, *society*, *freedom*, *history*, etc.). Between *physis* and its others, *genos* certainly situates one of the privileged scenes of the process, and, no doubt, sheds the greatest obscurity on it. One need not mobilize etymology to this end and could just as well equate *genos* with birth, and birth in turn with the generous force of engenderment or generation—*physis*, in fact—as with race, familial membership, classificatory genealogy or class, age class (generation) or social class; it comes as no surprise that, in nature and art, genre, a concept that is esssentially classificatory and genealogico-taxonomic, itself engenders so many classificatory vertigines when it goes about classifying itself and situating the classificatory princple or instrument within a set. As with the class itself, the principle of genre is unclassifiable, it tolls the knell of the knell [*glas*], in other words of classicum, of what permits one to call out (*calare*) orders and to order the manifold within a nomenclature. *Genos* thus indicates the place, the now or never of the most necessary meditation on the "fold" which is no more historical than natural in the classical sense of these two words, and which turns *phyein* over to itself across others that perhaps no longer relate to it according to that epoch-making logic which was decisory, critical, oppositional, even dialectical, but rather according to the trait of a contract entirely other. *De jure*, this meditation acts as an absolute prerequisite without which any historical perspectivizing will always be difficult to legitimate. For example, the romantic era—this powerful figure indicted by Genette (since it attempted to reinterpret the system of modes as a system of genres)—is no longer a simple era and can no longer be inscribed as a moment or a stage placeable within the trajectory of a "history" whose concept we could be certain of. Romanticism, if something of the sort can be thus identified, is also the general repetition of all the folds that in themselves gather, couple, divide *physis* as well as *genos* through the genre, and through all the genres of genre, through the mixing of genre that is "more than a genre," through the excess of genre in relation to itself, as to its abounding movement and its general assemblage which coincides, too, with its dissolution.[1] Such a "moment" is no longer a simple moment *in* the history and theory of literary genres. To treat it thus would in effect implicate one as tributary—whence the strange logic— of something that has in itself constituted a certain romantic motif, namely, the teleological ordering of history. Romanticism simultaneously obeys naturalizing and historicizing logic, and it can be shown easily enough that we have not yet been delivered from the romantic heritage —even though we might wish it so and assuming that such a deliverance would be of compelling interest to us—as long as we persist in drawing attention to historical concerns and the truth of historical production in order to militate against abuses or confusions of naturalization. The debate, it could be argued, remains itself a part or effect of romanticism.

A second motive detains me at the threshold or on the edge of a possible problematic of genre (as) history and theory of history and of genre-theory—another genre, in fact. For the moment, I find it impossible to decide—impossible for reasons that I do not take to be accidental, and this, precisely, is what matters to me—I find it impossible to decide whether the possibly exemplary text which I intend to put to the test does or does not lend itself to the distinction drawn between *mode* and *genre*. Now, as you may recall, Genette demonstrates the stringent necessity of this distinction; and he rests his case on "the confusion of modes and genres" (p. 417). This implies a serious charge against romanticism, even though "the romantic reinterpretation of the system of modes as a system of genres is neither *de facto* nor *de jure* the epilogue to this long history" (p. 415). This confusion, according to Genette, has aided and abetted the naturalization of genres by projecting onto them the "privilege of naturalness, which was *legitimately* . . . that of three modes . . . " (p. 421). Suddenly, this naturalization "makes these arch-genres into ideal or natural types which they neither are nor can be: there are no arch-genres that can totally escape historicity *while preserving a generic definition*. There are modes, for example: the *récit*. There are genres, for example: the novel; the relation of genres to modes is complex and, perhaps not, as Aristotle suggests, one of simple inclusion."

If I am inclined to poise myself on *this* side of Genette's argument, it is not only because of his ready acceptance of the distinction between nature and history, but also because of its implications with regard to mode and to the distinction between mode and genre. Genette's definition of mode contains this singular and interesting characteristic: it remains, in contradistinction to genre, purely formal. Reference to a content has no pertinence. This is not the case with genre. The generic criterion and the modal criterion, Genette says, are absolutely heterogenous: "each genre defined itself essentially by a specification of content which was not prescribed by the definition of mode . . ." (p. 417). I do not believe that this recourse to the opposition of form and content, this distinction between mode and genre, need be contested, and my purpose is not to challenge isolated aspects of Genette's argument. One might just question the presuppositions for the legitimacy of such an argument. One might also question the extent to which his argument can help us read a given text when it behaves in a given way with regard to mode and genre, especially when the text does not seem to be written sensibly within their limits, but rather about the very subject of those limits, and with the aim of disrupting their order. The limits, for instance, of that mode which would be, according to

Genette, the *récit* ("there are modes, for example: the *récit*"). Of the (possibly) exemplary text which I shall address shortly, I shall not hasten to add that it is a "*récit*," and you will soon understand why. In this text, the *récit* is not only a mode, and a mode put into practice or put to the test because it is deemed impossible; it is also the name of a theme. It is the nonthematizable thematic content of something of a textual form that *assumes* a point of view with respect to the genre, even though it perhaps does not come under the heading of any genre—and perhaps no longer even under the heading of literature, if it indeed wears itself out around genre-less modalizations, it would confirm one of Genette's propositions: "Genres are, properly speaking, literary/or aesthetic/ categories; modes are categories that pertain to linguistics or, more precisely, to an anthropology of verbal expression" (p. 418).

In a very singular manner, the very short text which I will discuss presently makes the *récit* and the impossibility of the *récit* its theme, its impossible theme or content at once inaccessible, indeterminable, interminable and inexhaustible; and it makes the word "*récit*," under the aegis of a certain form, its titleless title, the mentionless mention of its genre. This text, as I shall try to demonstrate, seems to be made, among other things, *to make light* of all the tranquil categories of genre-theory and history in order to upset their taxonomic certainties, the distribution of their classes, and the presumed stability of their classical nomenclatures. It is a text destined, at the same time, to summon up these classes by conducting their proceeding, by proceeding from the proceeding to the law of genre. For if the juridical code has frequently thrust itself upon me in order to hear this case, it has done so to call as witness a (possibly) exemplary text, and because I am convinced copious rights are bound up in all of this: the law itself is at stake.

These are the two principal reasons why I shall keep to the liminal edge of (the) history (and) of genre-theory. Here now, very quickly, is the law of abounding, of *excess*, the law of participation without membership, of contamination, etc., which I mentioned earlier. It will seem meager to you, and even of staggering abstractness. It does not particularly concern either genres, or types, or modes or any form in the strict sense of its concept. I therefore do not know under what title the field or object submitted to this law should be placed. It is perhaps the limitless field of general textuality. I can take each word of the series (genre, type, mode, form) and decide that it will hold for all the others (all genres of genres, types, modes, forms; all types of types, genres, modes, forms; all forms of forms, etc.). The trait common to these classes of classes is precisely the identifiable recurrence of a common trait by which one recognizes, or should recognize, a membership in a class. There should be a trait upon which one could rely in order to decide that a given textual event, a given "work," corresponds to a given class (genre, type, mode, form, etc.). And there should be a code enabling one to decide questions of class-membership on the basis of this trait. For example—a very humble axiom, but, by the same token, hardly contestable—if a genre exists (let us say the novel, since no one seems to contest its generic quality), then a code should provide an identifiable trait and one which is identical to itself, authorizing us to determine, to adjudicate whether a given text belongs to this genre or perhaps to that genre. Likewise, outside of literature or art, if one is bent on classifying, one should consult a set of identifiable and codifiable traits to determine whether this or that, such a thing or such an event belongs to this set or that class. This may seem trivial. Such a distinctive trait *qua* mark is however always *a priori* remarkable. It is always possible that a set—I have compelling reasons for calling this a text, whether it be written or oral—re-marks on this distinctive trait within itself. This can occur in texts that do not, at a given moment, assert themselves to be literary or poetic. A defense speech or newspaper editorial can indicate by means of a mark, even if it is not explicitly designated as such, "Violà! I belong, as anyone may remark, to the type of text called a defense speech or an article of the genre newspaper-editorial." The possibility is always there. This does not constitute a text *ipso facto* as "literature," even though such a possibility, always left open and therefore eternally remarkable, situates perhaps in every text the possibility of its becoming literature. But this does not interest me at the moment. What interests me is that this re-mark—ever possible for every text, for every corpus of traces—is absolutely necessary for and constitutive of what we call art, poetry or literature. It underwrites the eruption of *technè*, which is never long in coming. I submit this axiomatic question for your consideration: can one identify a work of art, of whatever sort, but especially a work of discursive art, if it does not bear the mark of a genre, if it does not signal or mention it or make it remarkable in any way? Let me clarify two points on this subject. First, it is possible to have several genres, an intermixing of genres or a total genre, the genre "genre" or the poetic or literary genre as genre of genres. Second, this re-mark can take on a great number of forms and can itself pertain to highly diverse types. It need not be a designation or "mention" of the type found beneath the title of certain books (novel, *récit*, drama). The remark of belonging need not pass through the consciousness of the author or the reader, although it often does so. It can also refute this consciousness or render the explicit "mention" mendacious, false, inadequate or ironic according to all sorts of overdetermined figures. Finally, this remarking-trait need be neither a theme nor a thematic component of the work—although of course this instance of belonging to one or several genres, not to mention all the traits that mark this belonging, often have been treated as theme, even before the advent of what we call "modernism." If I am not mistaken in saying that such a trait is remarkable, that is, noticeable, in every aesthetic, poetic or literary corpus, then consider this paradox, consider the irony (which is irreducible to a consciousness or an attitude): this supplementary and distinctive trait, a mark of belonging or inclusion, does not properly pertain to any genre or class. The re-mark of belonging does not belong. It belongs without belonging, and the "without" (or the suffix "-less") which relates belonging to non-belonging appears only in the timeless time of the blink of an eye [*Augenblick*]. The eyelid closes, but barely, an instant among instants, and what it closes is verily the eye, the view, the light of day. But without such respite, nothing would come to light. To formulate it in the scantiest manner—the simplest but most apodictic—I submit for your consideration the following hypothesis: a text cannot belong to no genre, it cannot be without or less a genre. Every text participates in one or several genres, there is no genreless text; there is always a genre and genres, yet such participation never amounts to belonging. And not because of an abundant overflowing or a free, anarchic and unclassifiable productivity, but because of the *trait* of participation itself, because of the effect of the code and of the generic mark. Making genre its mark, a text demarcates itself. If remarks of belonging belong without belonging, participate without belonging, then genre-designations cannot be simply part of the corpus. Let us take the designation "novel" as an example. This should be marked in one way or another, even if it does not appear, as it often does in French and German texts, in the explicit form of a subtitled designation, and even if it proves deceptive or ironic. This designation is not novelistic; it does not, in whole or in part, take part in the corpus whose denomination it nonetheless imparts. Nor is it simply extraneous to the corpus. But this sigular topos places within and without the work, along its boundary, an inclusion and exclusion with regard to genre in general, as to an identifiable class in general. It gathers together the corpus and, at the same time, in the same blinking of an eye, keeps it from closing, from identifying itself with itself. This axiom of non-closure or non-fulfillment enfolds within itself the condition for the possibility and the impossibility of taxonomy. This inclusion and this exclusion do not remain exterior to one another; they do not exclude each other. But neither are they immanent or identical to each other. They are neither one nor two. They form what I shall call the *genre-clause*, a clause stating at once the juridical utterance, the precedent-making designation and the law-text, but also the closure, the closing that excludes itself from what it includes (one could also speak of a floodgate ["*écluse*"] of genre). The clause or floodgate of genre declasses what it allows to be classed. It tolls the knell of genealogy or of genericity, which it however also brings forth to the light of day. Putting to death the very thing that it engenders, it cuts a strange figure; a formless form, it remains nearly invisible, it neither sees the day nor brings itself to light. Without it, neither genre nor literature come to light, but as soon as there is this blinking of an eye, this clause or this floodgate of genre, at the very moment that a genre or a literature is broached, at that very moment, degenerescence has begun, the end begins.

The end begins, this is a citation. Maybe a citation. I might have taken it from that text which seems to me to bring itself forth as an example, as an example of this unfigurable figure of clusion.

What I shall try to convey to you now will not be called by its generic or modal name. I shall not say this drama, this epic, this novel, this novella or this *récit*, certainly not this *récit*. All of these generic or modal names would be equally valid or equally invalid for something which is not even quite a book, but which was published in 1973 in the editorial form of a small volume of thirty-two pages. It bears the title *La Folie du jour* (approximately: The Madness of the Day). The author's name: Maurice Blanchot. In order to speak about it, I shall call this thing La Folie du jour, its given name which it bears legally and which gives us the right, as of its publication date, to identify and classify it in our copyright records at the Bibliothèque Nationale. One could fashion a non-finite number of readings from *La Folie du jour*. I have attempted a few myself, and shall do so again elsewhere, from another point of view. The *topos* of view, sight, blindness, *point of view* is, moreover, inscribed and traversed in *La Folie du jour* according to a sort of permanent revolution that engenders and virtually brings to the light of day points of view, twists, versions and reversions of which the sum remains necessarily uncountable and the account, impossible. The deductions, rationalizations, and warnings that I must inevitably propose will arise, then, from an act of unjustifiable violence. A brutal and mercilessly depleting selectivity will obtrude upon me, upon us, in the name of a law that *La Folie du jour* has, in its turn, already reviewed, and with the foresight that a certain kind of police brutality is perhaps an inevitable accomplice to our concern for professional competence.

What will I ask of *La Folie du jour*? To answer, to testify, to say what it has to say with respect to the law of mode or the law of genre, and more precisely, with respect to the law of the *récit*, which, as we have just been reminded, is a mode and not a genre.

On the cover, below the title, we find no mention of genre. In this most peculiar place that belongs neither to the title nor to the subtitle, nor even simply to the corpus of the work, the author did not affix, although he has often done so elsewhere, the designation *"récit"* or "novel," maybe (but only maybe) by erroneously subsuming both of them, Genette would say, under the unique category of the genre. About this designation which figures elsewhere and which appears to be absent here, I shall say only two things.

1. On the one hand it commits one to nothing. Neither reader nor critic nor author are bound to believe that the text preceded by this designation conforms readily to the strict, normal, normed or normative definition of the genre, to the law of the genre or of the mode. Confusion, irony, the shift in conventions toward a new definition (in what name should it be prohibited?), the search for a supplementary effect, any of these things could prompt one to entitle as *novel* or *récit* what in truth or according to yesterday's truth would be neither one nor the other. All the more so if the words *récit, novel, ciné-roman, complete dramatic works* or, for all I know, *literature* are no longer in the place which conventionally mentions genre but, as has happened and will happen again (shortly), they are found to be holding the position and function of the title itself, of the work's given name.

2. Blanchot has often had occasion to modify the genre-designation from one version of his work to the next, or from one edition to the next. Since I am unable to cover the entire spectrum of this problem, I shall simply cite the example of the *"récit-"* designation effaced between one version and the next of *Death Sentence* (trans. Lydia Davis, Barrytown, New York: Station Hill, 1978) at the same time as a certain epilogue is removed from the end of a double *récit* which, in a manner of speaking, constitutes this book. This effacement of *"récit,"* leaving a trace that, in-scribed and filed away, remains as an effect of supplementary relief which is not easily accounted for in all of its facets. I cannot arrest the course of my lecture here, no more than I can pause to consider the very scrupulous and minutely differentiated distribution of the designations *"récit"* and "novel" from one narrative work to the next, no more than I can question whether Blanchot distinguished the genre and mode designations, no more than I can discuss Blanchot's entire discourse on the difference between the narratorial voice and the narrative voice which is, to be sure, something other than a mode. I would point out only one thing: at the very moment the first version of *Death Sentence* appears, bearing mention as it does of *"récit,"* the first version of *La Folie du jour* is published with another title about which I shall momentarily speak.

La Folie du jour, then, makes no mention of genre or mode. But the word *"récit"* appears at least four times in the last two pages in order to name the theme of *La Folie du jour*, its sense or its story, its content or part of its content—in any case, its decisive proceedings and stakes. It is a *récit* without a theme and without a cause entering from the outside; yet it is without interiority. It is the *récit* of an impossible *récit* whose "production" occasions what happens, or rather, what remains, but which does not relate it, nor relate to it as to an outside reference, even if everything remains foreign to it and out of bounds. It is even less feasible for me to relate to you the story of *La Folie du jour* which is staked precisely on the possibility and the impossibility of relating a story. Nonetheless, in order to create the greatest possible clarity, in the name of daylight itself, that is to say (as will become clear), in the name of the law, I shall take the calculated risk of flattening out the unfolding or coiling up of this text, its permanent revolution whose rounds are made to recoil from any kind of flattening. And this is why the one who says "I," and the one after all who speaks to us, who "recites" for us, this one who says "I" tells his inquisitors that he cannot manage to constitute himself as narrator (in the sense of the term that is not necessarily literary), and tells them that he cannot manage to identify with himself sufficiently, or to remember himself well enough to gather the story and *récit* that are demanded of him—which the representatives of society and the law require of him. The one who says "I" (who does not manage to say "I") seems to relate what has happened to him, or rather, what has nearly happened to him after presenting himself in a mode that defies all norms of self-presentation: he nearly lost his sight (his facility for *viewing*) following a traumatic event—probably an assault. I say "probably" because *La Folie du jour* wholly upsets, in a discrete but terribly efficient manner, all the certainties upon which so much of discourse is constructed: the value of an event, first of all, of reality, of fiction, of appearance and so on, all this being carried away by the disseminal and mad polysemy of "day," of the word "day," which, once again I cannot dwell upon here. Having nearly lost his sight (*"vue"*), having been taken in by a kind of medico-social institution, he now resides under the watchful eye of doctors, handed over to the authority of these specialists who are representatives of the law as well, legist doctors who demand that he testify—and in his own interest, or so it seems at first—about what happened to him so that remedial justice may be dispensed. His faithful *récit*—(but let me borrow for the sake of simplicity, and because it conforms fairly well to this context, the English word "account")—hence, his faithful account of events should render justice unto the law. The law demands a narrative account.

Pronounced four times in the last three pages of *La Folie du jour*, the word "account" does not seem to designate a literary genre, but rather a certain type or mode of discourse. That is, in effect, the appearance of it. Everything seems to happen as if the account—the question of or rather the demand for the account, the response and the non-response to the demand—found itself staged and figured as one of the themes, objects, stakes in a more bountiful text, *La Folie du jour*, whose genre would be of another order and would in any case overstep the boundaries of the account with all of its generality and all its genericity. The account itself would of course not cover this generic generality of the literary corpus named *La Folie du jour*. Now we might already feel inclined to consider this appearance suspect, and we might be jolted from our certainties by an allusion that "I" will make: the one who says "I," who is not by force of necessity a narrator, nor necessarily always the same, notes that the representatives of the law, those who demand of him an account in the name of the law, consider and treat him, in his personal and civil identity, not only as an "educated" man— and an educated man, they often tell him, ought to be able to speak and recount; as a competent subject, he ought to be able to know how to piece together a story by saying "I" and "exactly" how things happened to him—they regard him not only as an "educated" man, but also as a writer. He is writer and reader, a creature of "libraries," *the* reader of this account. This is not sufficient cause, but it is, in any case, a first clue and one whose impact incites us to think that the required account does not simply remain in an extraneous relationship to literature or even to a literary genre. Lest we not be content with this suspicion, let us weigh the possibility of the inclusion of a modal structure within a vaster, more general corpus, whether literary or not and whether or not related to the genre. Such an inclusion raises questions concerning edge, borderline, boundary, and abounding which do not arise without a fold.

What sort of a fold? According to which fold and which figure of enfoldment?

Here are the three final paragraphs; they are of unequal length, with the last of these comprising approximately one line:

They demanded: Tell us "exactly" how things happened.—An account? I began: I am neither learned nor ignorant. I have known some joy. This is saying too little. I related the story in its entirety, to which they listened, it seems, with great interest—at least initially. But the end was a surprise for them all. "After that beginning," they said "you should proceed to the facts." How so? The account was over.

I should have realized that I was incapable of composing an account of these events. I had lost the sense of the story; this happens in a good many illnesses. But this explanation only made them more demanding. Then I remarked, for the first time, that they were two and that this infringement on their traditional method—even though it can be explained away by the fact that one of them was an eye doctor, the other a specialist in mental illnesses—increasingly gave our conversation the character of an authoritarian interrogation, overseen and controlled by a strict set of rules. To be sure, neither of them was the chief of police. But being two, due to that, they were three, and this third one remained firmly convinced, I am sure, that a writer, a man who speaks and reasons with distinction, is always capable of recounting the facts which he remembers.

An account? No, no account, nevermore.

In the first of the three paragraphs that I have just cited, he claims that something is to begin after the word "account" punctuated by a question mark (An account?—herein implied: they want an account, is it then an account that they want? "I began . . . "). This something is nothing other than the first line on the first page of La Folie du jour. These are the same words, in the same order, but this is not a citation in the strict sense for, stripped of quotation marks, these words commence or recommence a quasi-account that will engender anew the entire sequence comprising this new point of departure. In this way, the first words ("I am neither learned nor ignorant . . .") that come after the word "account" and its question mark, that broach the beginning of the account extorted by the law's representatives—these first words mark a collapse that is unthinkable, irrepresentable, unsituable within a linear order of succession, within a spatial or temporal sequentiality, within an objectifiable topology or chronology. One sees, without seeing, one reads the crumbling of an upper boundary or of the the initial edge in La Folie du jour, uncoiled according to the "normal" order, the one regulated by common law, editorial convention, positive law, the regime of competency in our logo-alphabetical culture, etc. Suddenly, this upper or initial boundary, which is commonly called the first line of a book, is forming a pocket inside the corpus. It is taking the form of an *invagination* through which the trait of the first line, the borderline, splits while remaining the same and traverses yet also bounds the corpus. The "account" which he claims is beginning at the end, and by legal requisition, is none other than the one that has begun from the beginning of La Folie du jour and in which, therefore, he gets around to saying that he begins, etc. And it is without beginning, or end, without content and without edge. There is only content without edge—without boundary or frame—and there is only edge without content. The inclusion (or occlusion, inocclusive invagination) is interminable, it is an analysis of the account that can only turn in circles in an unarrestable, inenarrable and insatiably recurring manner—but one terrible for those who, in the name of the law, require that order reign in the account, for those who want to know, with all the required competence, "exactly" how this happens. For if "I" or "he" continued to tell what he has told, he would end up endlessly returning to this point and beginning again to begin, that is to say, to begin with an end that precedes the beginning. And from the viewpoint of objective space and time, the point at which he stops is absolutely unascertainable ("I have told them the entire story . . . "), for there is no "entire" story except for the one that interrupts itself in this way.

A lower edge of invagination will, if one can say so, respond to this "first" invagination of the upper edge by intersecting it. The "final line" resumes the question posed *before* the "I began" (An account?) and bespeaks a resolution or promises it, tells of the commitment made no longer to give an account. As if he had already given one! And yet, yes (yes and no), an account has taken place. Hence the last word: "An account? No, no account, nevermore." It has been impossible to decide whether the recounted event and the event of the account itself ever took place. Impossible to decide whether there was an account, for the one who barely manages to say "I" and to constitute himself as narrator recounts that he has not been able to recount—but what, exactly? Well, everything, including the demand for an account. And if an assured and guaranteed decision is impossible, this is because there is nothing more to be done than to commit oneself, to perform, to wager, to allow chance its chance—to make a decision that is essentially edgeless, bordering perhaps only on madness.

Yet another impossible decision follows, one which involves the promise "No, no account, nevermore": Is this promise a part of or apart from the account? Legally speaking, it is party to *La Folie du jour*, but not necessarily to the account or to the simulacrum of the account. Its trait splits again into an internal and external edge. It repeats—without citing—the question apparently posed above (An account?) of which it can be said that, in this permanent revolution of order, it follows, doubles or reiterates it in advance. Thus another lip or invaginating loop takes shape here. This time the lower edge creates a pocket in order to come back into the corpus and to rise again on this side of the upper or initial line's line of invagination. This would form a double chiasmatic invagination of edges:

A. "I am neither learned nor ignorant . . ."
B. "An account? I began":
A'. "I am neither learned nor ignorant . . ."
B'. "An account? No, no account, nevermore . . ."

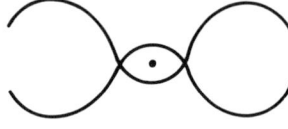

"I began . . ."

It is thus impossible to decide whether an event, account, account of event or event of accounting took place. Impossible to settle upon the simple borderlines of this corpus, of this ellipse unremittingly repealing itself within its own expansion. When we fall back on the poetic consequences enfolded within this dilemma, we find that it becomes difficult indeed to speak here with conviction about an account as a determined mode included within a more general corpus or one simply related, in its determination, to other modes, or, quite simply, to something other than itself. All is account and nothing is; the account's outgate remains within the account in a non-inclusive mode, and this structure is itself related so remotely to a dialectical structure that it even inscribes dialectics in the account's ellipse. All is account, nothing is: and we shall not know whether the relationship between these two propositions—the strange conjunction of the account and the accountless—belongs to the account itself. What indeed happens when the edge pronounces a sentence?

Faced with this type of difficulty—the consequences or implications of which cannot be deployed here—one might be tempted to take recourse in the law or the rights which govern published texts. One might be tempted to argue as follows: all these insoluble problems of delimitation are raised "on the inside" of a book classified as a work of literature or literary fiction. Pursuant to these juridical norms, this book has a beginning and an end that leave no opening for indecision. This book has a determinable beginning and end, a title, an author, a publisher, its distinctive denomination is *La Folie du jour*. At this place, where I am pointing, on this page, right here, you can see its first word; here, its final period, perfectly situable in objective space. And all the sophisticated transgressions, all the infinitesimal subversions that may captivate you are not possible except within this enclosure for which these transgressions and subversions moreover maintain an essential need in order to take place. Furthermore, on the inside of this normed space, the word "account" does not name a literary operation or genre, but a current mode of discourse, and it does so regardless of the formidable problems of structure, edge, set theory, the part and whole, etc., that it raises in this "literary" corpus.

That is all well and good. But in its very relevance, this objection cannot be sustained—for example, it cannot save the modal determination of the account—except by referring to extra-literary and even extra-linguistic juridical norms. The objection appeals to the law and calls to mind the fact that the subversion of La Folie du jour needs the law in order to take place. Whereby the objection reproduces and accomplishes its staging within *La Folie du jour*: the account, mandated and prescribed by law but also, as we shall see, commanding, requiring, and producing law in turn. In short, the whole critical scene of competence in which we are engaged is *party* to and *part* of *La Folie du jour*, in whole and in part, the whole is a part.

The whole does nothing but begin. I could have begun with what

Jacques Derrida

resembles the absolute beginning, with the juridico-historical order of this publication. What has been lightly termed the first version of *La Folie du jour* was not a book. Published in the journal *Empédocle* (May 2, 1949), it bore another title—indeed, several other titles. On the journal's cover, here it is, one reads:

Maurice Blanchot
Un récit?
(*An Account?*)

Later, the question mark disappears twice. First, when the title is reproduced within the journal in the table of contents:

Maurice Blanchot
Un récit
(*An Account*),

then below the first line:

Un récit	(*An Account*
par	by
Maurice Blanchot	M.B.)

Could you tell whether these titles, written earlier and filed away in the archives, make up a single title, titles of the same text, titles of the account (which of course figures as an impracticable mode in the book), or the title of a genre? Even if the latter were to cause some confusion, it would be of the sort that releases questions already implemented and enacted by *La Folie du jour*. This enactment enables in turn the denaturalization and deconstitution of the oppositions nature/ history and mode/genre.

Now let us turn to some of these questions. First, to what could the words "An Account" refer in their manifold occurrences and diverse punctuations? And precisely how does reference function here? In one case, the question mark can *also* serve as a supplementary remark indicating the necessity of all these questions as the insolvent character of indecision: is this an account? Is it an account that I entitle? asks the title in entitling. Is it an account that they want? What entitles them? Is it an account as discursive mode or as literary operation, or perhaps even as literary genre whose theme would be mode or genre? Likewise, the title could excerpt, as does a metonymy, a fragment of the account without an account (to wit, the words "an account" with and without a question mark), but such an iterative excepting is not citational. For the title, guaranteed and protected by law but also making law, retains a referential structure which differs radically from the one underlying other occurrences of the "same" words in the text. Whatever the issue—title, reference, or mode and genre—the case before us always involves the law and, in particular, the relations formed around and to law. All the questions which we have just addressed can be traced to an enormous matrix that generates the non-thematizable thematic power of a simulated account: it is this inexhaustible writing which recounts without telling, and which speaks without recounting.

Account of an accountless account, an account without edge or boundary, account all of whose visible space is but some border of itself without "self," consisting of the framing edge without content, without modal or generic boundaries—such is the law of this textual event, of this text that also speaks the law, its own and that of the other as reader of this text which, speaking the law, also imposes itself as a law text, as the text of the law. What is, then, the law of the genre of this singular text? It is law, it is the figure of the law which will also be the invisible center, the themeless theme of *La Folie du jour*, or, as I am now entitled to say, of "An Account?"

But this law, as law of genre, is not exclusively binding on the genre *qua* category of art and literature. But, paradoxically, and just as impossibly, the law of genre also has a controlling influence and is binding on that which draws the genre into engendering, generations, genealogy, and degenerescence. You have already witnessed its approach often enough, with all the figures of this degenerescent self-engendering of an account, with this figure of the law which, like the day that it is, challenges the opposition between the law of nature and the law of symbolic history. The remarks that have just been made on the double chiasmatic invagination of edges should suffice to exclude any notion linking all these complications to pure form or one suggesting that they could be formalized outside the content. The question of the literary genre is not a formal one: it covers the motif of the law in general, of generation in the natural and symbolic senses, of birth in the natural and symbolic senses, of the generation difference, sexual difference between the feminine and masculine genre/gender, of the hymen between the two, of a relationless relation between the two, of an identity and difference between the feminine and masculine. The word *"hymen"* tells us several things. It not only points towards a paradoxical logic that is inscribed without however being formalized under this name. It should, in the first place, serve to remind the Anglo-American reader that, in French, the semantic scale of *genre* is much larger and more expansive than in English, and thus always includes within its reach the gender. Additionally, and with respect to the "hymen," let us not forget everything that Philippe Lacoue-Labarthe and Jean-Luc Nancy tell us in *L'Absolu littéraire* (especially on p. 276) about the relationship between genre (*Gattung*) and marriage, as well as about the intricate bonds of serial connections begotten by *gattieren* (to mix, to classify), *gatten* (to couple), *Gatte/Gattin* (husband/wife), and so forth.

Jacques Derrida

Once articulated within the precinct of Blanchot's entire discourse on the neuter, the most elliptical question would inevitably have to assume this form: what about a neutral genre/gender? Or one whose neutrality would not be *negative* (neither . . . nor), nor dialectical, but affirmative, and doubly affirmative (or . . . or)?

Here again, due to time-limitations but also to more essential reasons concerning the structure of the text, I shall have to excerpt some abstract fragments. This will not occur without a supplement of violence and pain.

As first word and surely most impossible word of *La Folie du jour*, "I" presents itself as self (*moi*), me, a man. Grammatical law leaves no doubt about this subject. The first sentence, phrased in French in the masculine ("Je ne suis ni savant ni ignorant" and not "je ne suis ni savante ni ignorante") says, with regard to knowledge, nothing but a double negation (neither . . . nor). Thus, no glint of self-presentation. But the double negation gives passage to a double affirmation (yes, yes) that enters into alignment or alliance with itself. Forging an alliance or marriage-bond ("hymen") with itself, this boundless double affirmation utters a measureless, excessive, immense *yes*: both to life and to death:

I am neither learned nor ignorant. I have known some joy. This is saying too little: I am living, and this life gives me the greatest pleasure. And death? When I die (perhaps soon), I shall know an immense pleasure. I am not speaking of the foretaste of death, which is bland and often disagreeable. Suffering is debilitating. But this is the remarkable truth of which I am sure: I feel a boundless pleasure in living and shall be boundlessly content to die.

Now, seven paragraphs further along, the chance and probability of such an affirmation (one that is double and therefore boundless, limitless) is granted to woman. It returns to woman. Rather, not to woman or even to the feminine, to the female genre/gender, or to the generality of the feminine genre but—and this is why I spoke of chance and probability—"usually" to women. It is "usually" women who say yes, yes. To life to death. This "usually" avoids treating the feminine as a general and generic force; it makes an opening for the event, the performance, the uncertain contingencies, the encounter. And it is indeed from the contingent experience of the encounter that "I" will speak here. In the passage that I am about to cite, the expression "men" occurs twice. The second occurence names the sexual genre, the sexual difference (*aner, vir*—but sexual difference does not occur between a species and a genre); in the first occurrence, "men" comes into play in an indecisive manner in order to name either the genre of human beings (the *genre humain*, named "species" in the text) or sexual difference:

Men would like to escape death, bizarre *species* that they are. And some cry out, "die, die," because they would like to escape life. "What a life! I'll kill myself, I'll surrender!" This is pitiful and strange; it is in error.

But I have encountered *beings* who never told life to be quiet or death to go away—usually women, beautiful creatures. As for men, terror besieges them. . . . (italics added)

What has thus far transpired in these seven paragraphs? Usually women, beautiful creatures, relates "I." As it happens, encounter, chance, affirmation of chance do not always manage to happen. There is no natural or symbolic law, universal law, or law of a genre/gender here. Only usually, usually women, (comma of apposition) beautiful creatures. Through its highly calculated logic, the comma of apposition leaves open the possibility of thinking that these women are not beautiful and then, on the other hand, as it happens, capable of saying yes, yes to life to death, of not saying be quiet, go away to life to death. The comma of apposition lets us think that they are beautiful, women and beauties, these creatures, insofar as they affirm both life and death. Beauty, the feminine beauty of these "beings," would be bound up with this double affirmation.

Now I myself, who "am neither learned nor ignorant," "I feel a boundless pleasure in living and shall be boundlessly content to die." In this random claim that links affirmation usually to women, beautiful ones, it is then more than probable that, as long as I say yes, yes, I am a woman and beautiful. *I am a woman, and beautiful.* Grammatical sex (or anatomical as well, in any case, sex submitted to the law of objectivity): the masculine genre is thus affected by the affirmation through a random drift that could always render it other. A sort of secret coupling would take place here, forming an odd marriage ("hymen"), an odd couple, for none of this can be regulated by objective, natural, or civil law. The "usually" is a mark of this secret and odd hymen, of this coupling that is also perhaps a mixing of genres. The genres pass into each other. And we will not be barred from thinking that this mixing of genres, viewed in light of the madness of sexual difference, may bear some relation to the mixing of literary genres.

"I," then, can keep alive the chance of being a fe-male or of changing sex. His transsexuality permits him, in a more than metaphorical and transferential way, to engender. He can give birth, and many other signs which I cannot mention here bear this out, among other things the fact that on several occasions he "brings something forth to the light of day." In the rhetoric of *La Folie du jour*, the idiomatic expression "to bring forth to the light of day" ("donner le jour") is one of the players in an exceedingly powerful polysemic and disseminal game that I shall not attempt to reproduce here. I only retain its standard and dominant meaning which the spirit of linguistics gives it: *donner le jour* is to give birth—a verb whose subject is usually maternal, that is to say, generally female. At the center, closely hugging an invisible center, a primal scene could have alerted us, if we had had the time, to the *point of view* of *La Folie du jour* and to *A Primal Scene.* This is also called a "short scene."

"I" can bring forth to light, can give birth. To what? Well, precisely to law or more exactly, to begin with, to the representatives of law, to those who wield authority—and let us also understand by this the authority of the author, the rights of authorship—simply by virtue of possessing an overseer's right, the right to see, the right to have everything in sight. This panoptic, and this synopsis demand nothing else, but nothing less. Now herein lies the essential paradox: from where and from whom do they derive this power, this right-to-sight that permits them to have "me" at their disposal? Well, from "me," rather, from the subject who is subjected to them. It is the "I"-less "I" of the narrative voice, the "I" "stripped" of itself, the one that does not take place, it is he who brings them to light, who engenders these lawmen in giving them insight into what regards them and what should not regard them.

I liked the doctors well enough. I did not feel belittled by their doubts. The bother was that their authority grew with every hour. One isn't initially aware of it, but these men are kings. Showing me my rooms they said: Everything here belongs to us. They threw themselves upon the parings of my mind: This is ours. They interpellated my story: Speak! and it placed itself at their service. In haste, I stripped myself of myself. I distributed my blood, my privacy among them, I offered them the universe, I brought them forth to the light of day. Under their unblinking gaze, I became a water drop, an ink blot. I was shrinking into them, I was held entirely in their view and when, finally, I no longer had anything but my perfect nullity present and no longer had anything to see, they, too, ceased to see me, most annoyed, they rose, shouting: Well, where are you? Where are you hiding? Hiding is prohibited, it is a misdeed, etc.

Law, day. One believes it generally possible to oppose law to affirmation, and particularly to unlimited affirmation, to the immensity of yes, yes. Law—we often figure it as an instance of the interdictory limit, of the binding obligation, as the negativity of a boundary not to be crossed. Now the mightiest and most divided trait of *La Folie du jour* or of "An Account?" is the one relating birth to law, its genealogy, engenderment, generation or genre—and here I ask you once more to be especially aware of gender—the one joining the very *genre* of the law to the process of the double affirmation. The excessiveness of *yes, yes* is no stranger to the genesis of law (nor to Genesis, as could be easily shown, for it also concerns an account of Genesis "in the light of seven days" [p. 20]). The double affirmation is not foreign to the genre, genius or spirit of the law. No affirmation, and certainly no *double* affirmation without the law sighting the light of day and the daylight becoming law. Such is the madness of the day, such is an account in its "remarkable" truth, in its truthless truth.

Now the feminine, or generally affrmative gender/genre, is also the genre of this figure of law, not of its representatives, but of the law herself who, throughout an account, forms a couple with me, with the "I" of the narrative voice.

The law is in the feminine.

She is not a woman (it is only a figure, a "silhouette," and not a representative of the law) but she, *la loi*, is in the feminine, declined in the feminine; but not only as a grammatical gender/genre in my language (elsewhere Blanchot brought this genre into play for speech ["*la* parole"] and for thought ["*la* pensée"]). No, she is described as a "female element," which does not signify a female person. And the affirmative "I," the narrative voice, who has brought forth the representatives of the law to the light of day, claims to find the law seductive—sexually seductive. The law appeals to him: "The truth is that she appealed to me. In this milieu overpopulated with men, she was the only female element. One time she had me touch her knee: a bizarre impression. I declared to her: I am not the kind of man who contents himself with a knee. Her response: that would be revolting!" She pleases him and he would not like to content himself with the knee that she "had (him) touch." This contact with the knee (*genou*), as my student and friend Pierre-François Berger brought to my notice, recalls the inflectional contiguity of the I and the we, the *je* and the *nous*, of an I/we couple of whom we shall speak again in a moment.

The law's female element has thus always appealed to: me, I, he, we. The law appeals: "The law appealed to me . . . In order to tempt her, I called softly to the law: 'Approach, so I can see you face to face' (I wanted to take her aside for a moment). Impudent appeal; what would I have done had she responded?"

He is perhaps subjected to law, but he neither attempts to escape her, nor does he shrink before her: he wishes to seduce the law to whom he gives birth (there is a hint of incest in this) and especially— this is one of the most striking and singular traits of this scene—he inspires fear in the law. He not only troubles the representatives of the law, the lawmen who are the legist doctors and the "psy-" who demand of him, but are unable to obtain, an organized account, a testimony oriented by a sense of history or his history, ordained and ordered by reason, and by the unity of an I think, or of an originally synthetic apperception accompanying all representations. That the "I" here does not always accompany itself is by no means borne lightly by the lawmen; in fact, he alarms thus the lawmen, he radically persecutes them, and, in his manner, he conceals from them without altercation

Jacques Derrida

the truth they demand and without which they are nothing. But he
not only alarms the lawmen, he alarms the law; one would be tempted to
say the law herself, if she did not remain here a silhouette and an
effect of the account. And what is more, this law whom the "I" frightens
is none other than "me," than the "I," effect of his desire, child of his
affirmation, of the genre "I" clasped in a specular couple with "me."
They are inseparable (*je/nous* and *genou, je/toi—je/toit*), and so she
tells him, once more, as truth: "The truth is that we can no longer be
separated. I shall follow you everywhere, I shall dwell under your roof
(*toit*), we shall have the same sleep." We see the law, whose silhouette
stands behind her representatives, frightened by "me," by "him"; she
is inclined towards and declined by *je/nous*, I/we, in front of "me," in
front of him, her knees marking perhaps the articulation of a gait, the
flexion of the couple and sexual difference, but also the contiguity without contact of the hymen and the "mixing of genres."

Behind their backs, I perceived the silhouette of the law. Not the familiar
law, who is strict and not terribly agreeable: this one was different. Far
from falling prey to her menace, I was the one who seemed to frighten her.
According to her, my glance was lightning and my hands, grounds on which
to perish. Moreover, she ridiculously attributed to me all kinds of power,
she declared herself perpetually to be kneeling before me. But she let me
demand nothing, and when she granted me the right to be in all places,
that meant that I hadn't a place anywhere (Elsewhere Blanchot designates
the non-place and the atopical or hypertopical mobility of the narrative voice
in this way.) When she placed me above the authorities, that meant: you
are authorized to do nothing.

What game is the law, a law of this genre, playing? What is she
playing up to when she has her knee touched? For if *La Folie du jour*
plays down the law, plays at law, plays with law, it is also because the
law herself plays. The law, in its female element, is a silhouette that
plays. At what? At being . . . born, at being born like anybody and no
body. She plays upon her generation and displays her genre, she plays
out her nature and her history, and she makes a plaything of an account. In mock-playing herself she takes into account the account:
she recites; and her birth is accountable to the account, the *récit*, one
could even say to her, (to la voix . . .) the narrative voice, *him, her, I,
we*, the neuter genre that subjects and merges itself while giving birth
to her, who lets himself be captivated by the law and escapes her,
whom she escapes and whom she loves. She lets herself be put in motion, she lets herself be cited by him when, in the midst of her game,
she says, pursuing an idiom that her disseminal polysemy conveys to
the abyss, "I see day":

Here is one of her games (He has just recalled that she "once had [him]
touch her knee"). She showed me a section of the space between the top of

the window and the ceiling: "You are there," she said. I looked at this point with intensity. "Are you there?" I looked at it with all my power. "Well?" I felt the scars of my gaze leap, my sight became a wound, my head, a gap, a gutted bull. Suddenly she cried out: "Oh! I see day! Oh God!" etc. I protested that this game tired me enormously, but she was insatiable for my glory.

For the law to see the day, is her madness, is what she loves madly like the glory, the emblazed illustration, the day of the writer, of the author who says "I," and who brings forth law to the light of day. He says that she is insaturable, insatiable for his glory—he, who is, too, author of the law to which he submits himself, he, who engenders her, he, her mother who no longer knows how to say "I" or to keep memory intact. I am the mother of law, behold my daughter's madness. It is also the Madness of the Day, for day, the word "day" in its disseminal abyss, is law, the law of the law. My daughter's madness is to want to be born—like anybody, whereas she remains a nobody, a "silhouette," a shadow, a profile, her face never in view. He had said to her, to the law, in order to "tempt her": "Approach, so I can see you face to face."

Such would be the "remarkable truth" that clears an opening for the madness of day—and that appeals, like law, like madness, to the one who says "I" or I/we. Let us be attentive to this syntax of truth. She, the law, says: "The truth is that we can no longer be separated. I shall follow you everywhere, I shall live under your roof . . ." He: "The truth is that she appealed to me . . . ," she, law, but also—and this is always the principal theme of these sentences—she, *la vérité*, truth. One cannot conceive truth without the madness of the law .

I have let myself be commanded by the law of our encounter, by the convention of our subject, notably the genre, the law of genre. This law, articulated as an I/we which is more or less autonomous in its movements, assigned us places and limits. Even though I have launched an appeal against this law, it was she who turned my appeal into a confirmation of her own glory. But she also desires ours insatiably. Submitting myself to the subject of our colloquium, as well as to its law, I sifted "An Account," *La Folie du jour*. I isolated a type, if not a genre, of reading from an infinite series of trajectories or possible courses. I have pointed out the generative principle of these courses, beginnings, and new beginnings in every sense: but from a certain point of view.

Jacques Derrida

Elsewhere—in accordance with other subjects, other colloquia and lectures, other I/we drawn together in one place—other trajectories could have, and have, come to light.

Nonetheless, it would be folly to draw any sort of general conclusion here. I could not say what exactly has happened in this scene, nor in my discourse or my account. What was perhaps seen, in the blink of time's eye, is a madness of law—and, therefore, of order, reason, sense and meaning, of day: "But often," (said "I") "I was dying without saying a thing. In time, I became convinced that I was seeing the madness of day face to face; such was the truth: light became mad, clarity took leave of her senses; she assailed me unreasonably, without a set of rules, without a goal. This discovery was like jaws clutching at my life." I am woman, and beautiful; my daughter, the law, is mad about me. I speculate on my daughter. My daughter is mad about me; this is law.

The law is mad, she is mad about "me." And across the madness of this day, I keep this in sight. There, this will have been my self-portrait of the genre.

The law is mad. The law is mad, is madness; but madness is not the predicate of law. There is no madness without the law; madness cannot be conceived before its relation to law. Madness is law, the law is a madness. There is a general trait here: the madness of the law mad for me, the day madly in love with me, the silhouette of my daughter mad about me, her mother, etc., etc. But La Folie du jour, An (accountless) Account?, carrying and miscarrying its titles, is not at all exemplary of this general trait. Not at all, not wholly. This is not an example of a general or generic whole. The whole, which begins by finishing and never finishes beginning apart from itself, the whole that stays at the edgeless boundary of itself, the whole greater and less than a whole and nothing, An Account? will not have been exemplary. Rather, with regard to the whole, it will have been wholly counter-exemplary.

The genre has always in all genres been able to play the role of order's principle: resemblance, analogy, identity and difference, taxonomic classification, organization and genealogical tree, order of reason, order of reasons, sense of sense, truth of truth, natural light and sense of history. Now, the test of An Account? brought to light the madness of genre. Madness has given birth to, thrown light on the genre in the most dazzling, most blinding sense of the word. And in the writing of An Account?, in literature, satirically practicing all genres, imbibing them but never allowing herself to be saturated with a catalogue of genres, she, madness, has started spinning Peterson's genre-disc like a demented sun. And she does not only do so in literature, for in concealing the boundaries that sunder mode and genre, she has also inundated and divided the borders between literature and its others.

There, that is the whole of it, it is only what "I," so they say, here kneeling at the edge of literature, can see. In sum, the law. The law summoning: what "I" can sight and what "I" can say that I sight in this site of a recitation where I/we is.

Une traduction?
par
M

Translated by Avital Ronell

1. In this respect, the second footnote in *L'Absolu litteraire*, p. 271, seems to me, let us say, a bit too equitable in its rigorous and honest prudence.

Second voice: can you recall the Law, the feminine element that usually says yes, yes. To life to death. To writing to translating? A silhouette, she never shows her face. She is profiled by "je," but also by "J," tenth letter of the English alphabet, formerly a variant of "I" (and not just today, but already in the century of Descartes; it was then that "I" became "J"). Can you remember the "I" "je" "J" ("J." is I's signature) who claims not to be able to constitute himself as narrator—and not just in the literary sense, decrees a certain genre of legist doctors, J.D., Doctor of Law, philosopher meta-physician attending the Law?—
First voice: I . . . object.
Third voice: Jemand musste J. verleumdet haben, denn ohne dass er etwas Böses getan hätte, wurde er eines Morgens übersetzt.

WHY I WRITE SUCH GOOD TRANSLATOR'S NOTES

Since Derrida has himself sensitized us to the delicate issue of writing and difference, I might do well to point out at the outset that this version of "The Law of Genre" was originally intended solely for oral delivery. It was written in the hope of creating a plausible, though by no means conclusive, transposition of the internal rhyme and resonance contained within Derrida's essay. The Law, then, has not been fully transcribed, not yet, and it may even be destined to bear the constitutive mark of incompletion.

Whether intended to engage a live audience or the reflective consciousness silently withdrawn from life, the text before you, regardless of the type of reading it invites, solemnly holds itself in abeyence. It is neither itself nor its other: unable to make authoritative claims for its autonomy—for instituting *its own name*—it is also prohibited by an implicit limit from drawing too closely to its origin, to the ever engendering Urtext. Perhaps this hybrid form of non-identity might best be spoken about as the peculiar frame of mind or mood attending translation, one that inevitably arises from a certain will to violence and forgetfulness. Some might wish to call this a will to power, but a power, as you know, forcefully divested of mastery. To speak of power here is thus to ask that it be viewed in light of a series of essential displacements. Surely every translator of Derrida labors under a negative sign, for it is possible—and this possibility both inspires and exacerbates our entire enterprise—that we do not yet know quite how to translate Derrida. Indeed, the works of Derrida seem to be designed with the hidden intentionality of accomplishing, in a prefigurative manner, an ironic subversion of the very act that seeks to house them in another lanugage. And yet it must be said in all fairness that these works also seem to stand in perpetual anticipation of passing into the other language, at times even calling out explicitly to the translator. These calls, emanating as they do from within the mother text, issue a challenge; it is as if they wanted to ward off the future, and to protect themselves from the renovating acts of division and revision. But at the same time, the same calls imperiously demand the very performance of their "becoming-translation" (this is a citation—almost a citation). Ceaselessly testing the limits of his "own" language, Derrida necessarily, and, we can say, self-consciously, pushes the possibilities of translation to its limits. It therefore comes as no surprise that Derrida has devoted a good part of his lectures at Yale this Fall precisely to this impossible yet mandated activity called translation.

Now, for some reason, translation inevitably seeks to enter into an alliance with a certain language of desire. Spoken of and judged largely in terms of fidelity, the second text (which is, of course, in a sense, the first text since it is only after the "second" text has been produced that the first acquires its aura of originality) strives to remain in close proximity to the "original" of which it is the origin, etc. And the indwelling order of the double bind is well known. While earnestly attempting to demonstrate faithfulness to the (m)other tongue, one is secretly exchanging and renewing vows of constancy with the other language—which wins one the dubious distinction of double dissimulation. To bring this double bind to light, to break the illusion of the translation's separability or inseparability from its source—in short, to make palpable the tensions binding this specular couple, I have asked Derrida to let these two texts approach each other, if only asymptotically, by facing each other. This "face-off" aims to regenerate a major facet of the argument which Derrida advances in his discussion of *La Folie du jour*.

What do they tell us about themselves? The truth is that you can no longer separate these texts. And yet, I have already intimated that this pair is separated by an immense gulf of linguistic displacement, a willfull act of forgetfulness and, to complete the account, it has been deeply seared by a supplement of pain and violence which J.D. seems to know more intimately than I. Exiled even from the assured despair of Kafka's commentators, the disrepair of this pair, eternally coupled and divided over an abysmal boundary at once linking and sundering our languages (which are neither one nor two)—the ineluctable disrepair of this pair is perhaps, finally, the only text that you will have read.

But let me simply now recite, in a somewhat telegrammatic form, a few of the infidelities that have accrued to this translation. Those of you who are familiar with the French version will have noted that I have often had to sacrifice poetic resonance to philosophical clarity, although I cannot assert with conviction that these two aspects of the same discourse can be thus distinguished. In his discussion of the genre's participatory but non-belonging remark, Derrida would have liked to retain the "part" that you perceive in the word *appartenir* (to belong); "partake of" would have provided at least a partial solution here, but I found it to pose too many obstacles to the flow of his argument. The word "mention," on the other hand, properly belongs to our language and, in this context, hails from speech act theory which draws a distinction between mention and use. Curiously enough, this word seems to have found a more stable holding in the French, and I have substituted it with "designation" as in "genre-designation." The word *bord* lends the French version a certain continuity which I have had to disrupt by splintering it into several possible English equivalents: thus you will read "edge," "boundary," "border," "borderline" where Derrida has written *bord*. With the word *récit*, I have had to enter another area of linguistic turbulence, for English does not contain a term that would correspond exactly to the French, although "story," "narration" and "account" all capture the basic drift of the word. In keeping with the text, its acute sense of nuance and unfolding, I have decided to retain the *récit* until the time came to cross over to "account." Another moment of concentrated labor was occasioned by the law's wanting to "*naître comme personne*," for this phrase releases any number of possible interpretations: it lets us hear *naître* (to be born) as *n'être* (not to be), *personne* as a person and its opposite, namely, nobody. The law thus simultaneously wants to be born, wants to be, or does not want to be, like anybody, unlike anybody, a nobody, and so forth. Finally, let me simply draw your attention to another of these restless problems that refuses to be wrestled down to a solution, whose solution may in fact amount to its dissolution. In French, as I have tried to indicate in the body of the translation itself (for a translator's note should probably be banished from its conventional place, it should speak in the text, and in the absence of any defense speech), the word "genre" enjoys a suppleness and freedom of semantic movement that is vigorously constrained in the English. French can be considered far more maternal than English in the way it embraces, for instance, the shifting moods and (pardon the expression) modes of this word. In his mother tongue, Derrida's *genre* always appears to be abundantly housed and nurtured despite its duplicitous guises. The very same *genre* would be expelled, and rather swiftly (the italics already suggest a form of expulsion or at least of uneasy accomodation), from the English habitat as a deviant type, a loose and even transsexual figure. We recognize in *it* only the disfigured figure of a lost son. A genderless language, English by definition does not take well to the business of mixing with genders—it does not especially care to mix genres, certainly not with genres, nor with genus or other step-types (cf. *le genre humain*). Thus, for example, the rich ambiguities in which the Law (*la loi, elle*) indulges, spirals down to the law, "she," thereby losing its "itness" in the process—and Derrida, together with Blanchot, insists on the double designation of the law as a female element and as a silhouette approximating neutrality.

Two final words before this text folds. First, the reader may wish to consult a book which has recently appeared and which contains an essay by Derrida. To a certain extent that essay treats the "same" material as this one, but from a different point of view: *Deconstruction and Criticism* (Harold Bloom, et al., The Seabury Press: New York, 1979). Second, by way of indicating the disseminal process to which this text has been submitted, I should like now to coimplicate those who have contributed to the production of this translation. Their contributions range from a single word to the type of rephrasing that takes place when one stands Before the Law (this is a translation—maybe a translation—of *Vor dem Gesetz*, but it is perhaps only a prejudice that we live in one language).

Michel Beaujour, David Bisset, Jacques Derrida, Maurice Hamidi, Alfred MacAdam, Barbara MacAdam, Evelyn Ronell, Marc Selva, Roland Simon, William Strong, Allen Thiher, Samuel Weber, the eds., etc.

A translation? No, no translation, nevermore.   A.R.

APPENDIX
BULLETIN OF THE INTERNATIONAL COLLOQUIUM
ON GENRE

COLLOQUE   INTERNATIONAL

LE GENRE / DIE GATTUNG / GENRE

Université de Strasbourg

4 - 8 juillet 1979

UNIVERSITE DE STRASBOURG II

GROUPE DE RECHERCHES
SUR LES
THEORIES DU SIGNE ET DU TEXTE
25, rue du Maréchal Juin
67084 STRASBOURG CEDEX

Pour situer le colloque «LE GENRE»

Deux préoccupations ont été à l'origine de ce projet : d'une part, le souci de poursuivre une recherche sur le romantisme et à partir de lui, dans la mesure où ce moment de l'histoire littéraire et philosophique nous semble commander à beaucoup d'égards notre situation la plus actuelle. D'autre part, le désir d'exploiter, dans une telle recherche, les chances d'une confrontation entre des pays dont les expériences, tout en ayant largement communiqué entre elles dans cette histoire, n'en revêtent pas moins des caractères chaque fois bien particuliers (ce dont l'analyse pourrait ne pas être indifférente à la position même des questions).

Telle est au fond la double proposition que nous faisons. Son second aspect relève directement de la tenue du colloque lui-même, des échanges qui pourront s'y produire. Nous pensons toutefois qu'un certain temps pourra en outre y être spécialement réservé à l'analyse des situations nationales et de leurs rapports (cela aussi, on le sait, constitue un thème littéraire, théorique et politique du romantisme). — Quant au premier aspect, si nous voulions éviter une excessive dispersion des contributions, et de faire basculer cette rencontre, comme il arrive assez souvent, du colloque dans le collage, il était nécessaire de le spécifier.

Nous avons donc choisi la question du genre. Ou plutôt, nous a paru s'imposer cette interrogation : en quoi «le genre» nous fait-il, aujourd'hui, question ? Et nous devons rapidement nous en expliquer, puisque c'est à cette question que nous demandons réponse.

Zum Kolloquium : «Die Gattung»

Bezog diejenige geistige Strömung, die Strukturalismus genannt wird, ihre Einheit aus der Uberzeugung, daß die Sprache zum Gegenstand einer Wissenschaft gemacht werden konnte - der Semiotik - die ihrerseits den Geistes- und Sozialwissenschaften als Modell dienen sollte, so haben die Probleme, an denen der Strukturalismus gescheitert ist, zu einem veränderten Selbstverständnis innerhalb der Humanwissenschaften geführt. Vor allem ist der Anspruch, der vom Strukturalismus (aber nicht von ihm allein) erhoben worden ist, nämlich eine «Metasprache» konstruieren zu können, zunehmend als unhaltbar zurückgewiesen worden. Die Sprache wird heute weniger als begreifbarer Gegenstand betrachtet denn als ein höchst problematischer Vorgang, in den wir verstrickt, ja eingeschrieben sind. Das Bewußtsein dieser Verstrickung hat eine Abkehr von szentistischen Idealen und eine Zuwendung zu jenen Praktiken mit sich gebracht, welche die problematische und unausweichliche Dynamik der Sprache am radikalsten artikulieren : zur Philosophie und zur Literatur. Oder genauer : zu einer Neubestimmung ihrer wechselseitigen Beziehung.

Dieses erneute Interesse an der Beziehung von Literatur und Philosophie liegt dem Kolloquium : «Die Gattung» zugrunde. Denn die Gattungsfrage hat sich gerade zu jener Zeit entschieden gestellt, die sich ebenfalls der Beziehung von Dichtung und Philosophie besonders widmete : zur Zeit der Romantik nämlich, einer Epoche, die unsere Modernität viel tiefer bestimmt, als zumeist erkannt wird. Gerade diese Nachwirkung der Romantik bildet den gemeinsamen Ausgangspunkt eines Kolloquiums, das besonders darauf angelegt ist, die Vielseitigkeit dieser Wirkung je nach den verschiedenen Sprach-

Situating the Colloquium : «Genre»

If the intellectual movement known as Structuralism drew much of its unity from the conviction that language could be treated as an object of scientific study, of a semiotics that in turn would provide the humanities and the social sciences with a privileged model, the demise of this scientistic ideal and the demonstrated frailty of the notion of meta-language that it ultimately presupposed have led to an increasing awareness that language, far from constituting an object susceptible of exhaustive comprehension entails an enigmatic process upon which cognitive processes depend but with which they can never simply coincide. Hence, in recent years much of the interest previously directed at the discovery or elaboration of scientific models for humanistic research has shifted towards those forms of articulation that have historically engaged the enigmatic aspects of language in the most radical manner. Of these practices, the equivocal but dynamic interrelation of literature and philosophy has progressively emerged as a decisive area of investigation.

It is such developments that have determined the focus of this colloquium. For at no period of our literary and philosophical history, was the relation between the two modes of discourse - literature and philosophy - more at the center of interest than during romanticism. And this is but a symptom of the man-

Si «le genre» fait question, ce n'est certainement pas au sens d'une doctrine ou d'une théorie des genres — si l'on entend par là ce que l'histoire littéraire a déposé sous ces expressions (classification des genres, déduction empirique ou normalisation dogmatique de leurs divisions, etc.). Ce qui nous sollicite, c'est le passage du pluriel au singulier. C'est la singularisation du concept ou de la visée du genre. Et ce passage s'est effectué par le romantisme allemand.

A l'égard du genre, en effet, le romantisme a pratiqué un double geste : d'une part il dénonçait la validité des doctrines des genres en vigueur, et appelait de ses voeux une théorie des genres radicalement nouvelle ; d'autre part, il substituait à l'analyse par genres la problématique de l'unique Dichtung, c'est-à-dire non pas de la littérature «en général» mais d'une littérature générale, par-delà tous les genres. Les deux gestes se déploient sur le même fond : celui de la littérature constituée comme son propre absolu (et comme l'absolu de tout discours et de toute écriture). C'est-à-dire de l'oeuvre comme processus autonome, auto-institué et auto-réflexif, porteur des lois de sa production et de sa propre théorie. Le genre, dès lors, ce qu'on peut appeler le genre littéraire, c'est le genre de l'auto-génération.

Rigoureusement, il ne devrait plus s'agir d'un genre. Et pourtant, il s'agit aussi bien de l'essence même du genre, de la littérature s'engendrant comme genre — et dans ses divers genres. C'est alors que les deux gestes romantiques entretiennent un écart problématique. Tout se passe comme si, généralisée (et auto-générative), la littérature se visait toujours comme genre (comme spécification). D'où la question cruciale, latente dans toute l'élaboration d'Iéna : que pourrait être un genre général ?

bereichen, aus denen seine Teilnehmer stammen, zu artikulieren. Um aber zu gewährleisten, daß bei dieser Begegnung eingehende Auseinandersetzungen und wirkliche Diskussion zustandekommen, und daß man nicht - wie so oft bei solchen Anlässen - nur aneinander vorbeiredet, haben wir uns für eine Einschränkung und zugleich für eine Konkretisierung des Bereichs entschieden, vor allem indem wir die Gattungsfrage in den Vordergrund stellen, wie sie durch die Romantik - besonders die deutsche Romantik - verarbeitet worden ist. Ohne also die Diversität der verschiedenen Beiträge vorausnehmen zu wollen, scheint es uns zum Zwecke einer vorläufigen Orientierung nützlich anzuzeigen, wie sich uns das Problem innerhalb unserer vorbereitenden Arbeit dargestellt, oder genauer : aufgenötigt hat. Dabei dachten wir weniger an die traditionellen Gattungstheorien, sofern sie sich auf die Klassifizierung von Dichtarten, auf ihre empirische Deduktion, oder umgekehrt, auf ihre dogmatische Normierung beschränkt haben. Vielmehr geht es uns um den Übergang von der Mehrzahl zur Einzahl, von den Gattungen zu der Gattung : also um die Singularisierung des Gattungsbegriffs. Und dieser Übergang vollzieht sich in ausgezeichneter Weise in der deutschen Romantik.

Zwei Gesten zeigen sich in der romantischen Behandlung dieses Problems : einerseits hat sie die Gültigkeit der herkömmlichen Gattungslehre denunziert und zugleich eine neue Theorie gefordert; andererseits hat sie an die Stelle der gattungsmäßigen Analyse die Perspektive einer einheitlichen Dichtung gestellt ; d.h. sie hat nicht die Literatur «im allgemeinen» betrachten wollen, sondern den Begriff einer allgemeinen Dichtung, jenseits aller Einzelgattungen, einzuführen versucht. Diese zwei Gesten entfalteten sich auf einem gemeinsamen Hintergrund : dem der Dichtung, die sich als ihr eigenes Abso-

ner in which romanticism continues to determine our thinking and our concerns even today. To be sure, such determinations are as diverse as the different linguistic and cultural areas from which the participants in this colloquium will have come. One of its major purposes is precisely to provide a forum in which such differences can be elaborated, discussed and reflected, from a variety of perspectives. Nevertheless, in order to provide the minimal common ground that is necessary in order for effective interchange to take place, we propose to outline the manner in which the question of genre has posed, or rather imposed, itself in the course of our previous work.

If we have chosen the question of genre (or rather, if it has chosen us), it is not so much in the sense of traditional genre-theory, which has tended either to limit itself to the classification of genres, to their empirical deduction, or to the construction of normative, prescriptive systems. What has come to concern us is rather the transition from the plural to the singular, the singularization of the concept (or of what it implies). And this transition was effected most of all by German romanticism.

In regard to the question of genre, the practice of romanticism entailed a dual gesture : first, it denounced the traditional theory of genres and called for a radically new and different doctrine ; second, it replaced genre-analysis by the problem of a single, unified Dichtung : not by literature «in general», but by literature generalized beyond all individual genres. Both these gestures, however, were enacted à

Cette question distribue deux grands axes d'interrogation :

1) qu'est-ce donc que le genre, que la notion même de genre ? On ne peut, du coup, se passer d'interroger la formation de cette notion, par rapport aux sources dont elle se réclame — Platon et Aristote, chez qui il n'est peut-être en fait pas possible de retrouver un concept du «genre». — Dès lors, on ne peut pas non plus éviter de se demander de quel genre relève la théorie du genre, ou bien si cette question même est pertinente.

2) que signifie, au sein de l'opération généralisante et générative, la résurgence ou la résistance des genres au sens le plus traditionnel — et en tout cas multiple ? Cette question en contient à son tour plusieurs :

— que signifie l'oscillation permanente des romantiques entre plusieurs genres désignés comme «supports», ou comme «vérité», du genre : le roman, le poème, le théâtre, l'opéra, mais aussi parfois la philosophie, ou la messe ?

— que signifie la résorption toujours incomplète ou malaisée de toutes sortes de «petits» genres, ou de genres mal ou non classés : idylle, élégie, épigramme, etc., et le Witz, et la satire (le mélange des genres comme genre) ?

— que signifie l'entrée de la critique littéraire dans la littérature ? est-elle elle-même un genre ? de quelle manière ? genre de tous les genres, ou genre d'aucun genre ? générative ou dégénérée ?

lutum (als Absolutum aller Sprache wie aller Schrift) konstituiert. Die Dichtung wurde demnach als autonomes Werk konzipiert, das sich selbst erzeugt, reflektiert und die Gesetze der eigenen Produktion wie der eigenen Theorie in sich trägt. Damit wurde die Gattung - die zugleich die Gattung der Dichtung überhaupt genannt werden könnte - zur Gattung der Selbstbegattung, zum Genre der Selbstgeneration.

Streng genommen also dürfte es gar nicht mehr um eine Gattung handeln. Und dennoch geht es gerade um das Wesen der Gattung als Begattung, um eine Dichtung, die sich selbst erzeugt, und zwar zugleich als Gattung überhaupt, wie auch in und durch ihre verschiedenen Gattungen. Damit allerdings scheint alles daraufhinaus zu laufen, daß die verallgemeinerte, generalisierte und generalisierende Dichtung zugleich auf ihre Besonderung als Gattung abzielt. Daher läßt sich die entscheidende Frage, die latent in der gesamten Arbeit der Jenaer Romantik enthalten ist, so formulieren : Was wäre eine Gattung, ein Genre, der zugleich generell wäre ?

Diese Frage läßt sich in zwei Richtungen verfolgen :

1. Was bedeutet Gattung überhaupt ? Was trägt die Geschichte des Begriffs zu deren Verständnis bei ? Kann man die Antwort darauf den Quellen entnehmen, auf die sich diese Geschichte meistens beruft, auf Platon und Aristoteles ? Andererseits : steht wirklich außer Frage, daß diese über einen Gattungsbegriff verfügten (wie gemeinhin angenommen wird) ? Überhaupt : zu welcher Gattung gehört die Gattungstheorie selbst ?

against a common background : that of literature constituted as its own Absolute, (and as the Absolute of all discourse and of all writing). The literary work came to be considered as an autonomous process, self-instituting and self-reflexive, entailing the laws of its own production and of its own theory. Hence, genre, in the sense of the literary genre, became the genre of self-generation.

Rigorously speaking, this should no longer be a genre at all. And yet what is at stake is nothing less than the very essence of genre itself : that of literature engendering itself as genre, in and through its diverse genres. In this sense, however, the dual gesture of the romantics raises the following problem : in its generalized and self-generating movement, literature seems to imply its own specification. Thus, the crucial question arises : how can there be a genre which is also general ?

This question can be developed along two principal lines :

1. What does genre — its very notion — entail ? Can one ignore the historical formation of the concept, and in particular the origins usually attributed to that history : Plato and Aristotle ? On the other hand, is it as evident as has generally been supposed that Plato and Aristotle really entertained a concept of genre at all ? If not, to what genre would genre-theory itself belong (and is this question itself pertinent) ?

Tout pourrait aussi se rassembler sous une seule question, que notre modernité aborde peut-être à peine, et qui se formulerait ainsi :

«Pourquoi y a-t-il quelque chose et non pas rien ?» - par une transformation réglée selon le rapport même de la littérature et de la philosophie, cette célèbre demande s'énonce : pourquoi y a-t-il du genre, et non pas de la littérature générale ?

Comme on l'aura compris, il ne s'agit là que d'une proposition, destinée à situer le colloque, mais en aucune façon à lui imposer un cadre ni une ligne. Expliciter notre point de départ nous a paru le meilleur moyen de favoriser la discussion la plus large, sans exclure aucune déplacement ou remise en cause de notre question elle-même.

2. **In Bezug auf die generalisierende, generative Dynamik der Gattung, was bedeutet die Wieder kehr oder der Widerstand der Gattungen im herkömmlichen Sinne, d.h. als Mehrzahl ? Diese Frage enthält mehrere andere :**

a. **Was bedeutet das unablässige Schwanken der Romantiker in ihrer Auffassung über die verschiedenen Gattungen, die sie als Träger oder als Wahrheit der Gattung überhaupt bezeichnet haben : Roman, Gedicht, Theater, Oper ; aber auch manchmal Philosophie, oder gar die Messe ?**

b. **Was bedeutet die nie ganz gelungene, immer etwas beargwöhnte Assimilerung von allerlei «kleineren», schlecht oder gar nicht klassifizierten Gattungen : Idylle, Elegie, Epigramm usw., aber auch Witz, Satire (ist die Mischung von Gattungen selbst eine Gattung) ?**

c. **Was bedeutet der Eintritt der Literaturkritik in die Dichtung selbst ? Bildet damit auch sie eine neue Gattung ? Und wenn, auf welche Weise ? Handelt es sich um eine Gattung, die über alle anderen steht, oder um eine, worunter keine mehr fällt ? Ist dieses Genre generativ oder degenerativ ?**

Damit sollen nur einige der Fragen angeschnitten werden, die im Laufe des Kolloquiums entwickelt werden könnten. Es werden gewiß auch andere gestellt und diskutiert. Für uns aber läßt sich das bisher Beschriebene abschließend so zusammenfassen :

«Warum gibt es überhaupt etwas, und nicht vielmehr nichts ?» - - eine Frage, die das Moderne verfolt und sich in unserem Kontext vielleicht so umzuformulieren wäre : Warum gibt es die Gattung, und nicht Dichtung überhaupt ? Warum Genre, und nicht generalisierte Literatur ?

2. *Within the generalizing, generative process of genre, what is the significance of the resurgence or the resistance of genres, in the most traditional (i.e. multiple) sense ? This question in turn comports several others :*

a. *What is the meaning of the romantics' oscillation in designating different genres as being the supports or the truth of genre (in general) : the novel, the poem, the theater, the opera, but sometimes even philosophy, or the mass ?*

b. *What is the significance of the attempted but never entirely successful (or tranquil) assimilation of all kinds of «small» genres, or of those that are poorly classified, if at all : the idyll, the elegy, the epigramm etc., as well as the Witz, the satire (and is the mixing of genres itself a genre) ?*

c. *What does the entry of literary criticism into literature «proper» signify ? Does this itself constitute a new genre ? If so, in what way ? A genre of genres ? A genre of no genre ? One that is generative ? Degenerative ?*

These are, of course, just some of the questions that a colloquium on genre might wish to consider. There will doubtless be others, posed from other perspectives. And yet precisely to provide a possible common point-of-departure for the diversity we seek, we offer the following remark in conclusion as one that seems to condense much of what we have endeavored to describe :

«Why is there something, rather than nothing at all ?» — A question that haunts our modernity, and which, in the context just formulated, might be transformed to read : Why is there genre, rather than generalized Literature ?

Jean-Jacques Chartin, Strasbourg II - Philippe Lacoue-Labarthe, Strasbourg II Jean-Luc Nancy, Strasbourg II, Samuel Weber, The Johns Hopkins University

NOTES ON CONTRIBUTORS

MICHEL BEAUJOUR is professor of French literature at New York University where he is assistant director of the Institute of French Studies. His works include *Le Jeu de Rabelais*.

JACQUES DERRIDA teaches philosophy at the Ecole Normale Supérieure in Paris. He is best known for his theory and practice of "deconstruction," which he elaborates in such texts as *La Voix et le phénomène*, *La Dissémination*, and *Marges*. His more recent work has dealt with writers such as Genet and Hegel (*Glas*), Kant, Francis Ponge, and the theory of aesthetics (*La Vérité en peinture*). His text here published is part of a larger study of Maurice Blanchot.

MANFRED FRANK teaches German literature at the University of Düsseldorf. In addition to *Die unendliche Fahrt* he has published works on Schleiermacher, Schelling, and German Romanticism.

RODOLPHE GASCHE is associate professor of comparative literature at the State University of New York at Buffalo. He has recently published his second book, *System und Metaphorik in der Philosophie von Georges Bataille*, and is currently at work on a book-length study of Gaston Bachelard.

DENIS KAMBOUCHNER teaches philosophy at the University of Besançon. His article in this issue of *Glyph* is an early stage of a work in progress on literature as a symbolic activity.

FRIEDRICH KITTLER teaches German literature at the University of Freiburg in Breisgau. He has written extensively on Goethe and on German nineteenth-century literature. He is presently writing *Das Aufschreibesystem*.

PHILIPPE LACOUE-LABARTHE and JEAN-LUC NANCY teach philosophy at the University of Strasbourg. In addition to *L'Absolu littéraire*, they have collaborated on a work on Jacques Lacan, *Le Titre de la lettre*. Nancy has written on Kant (*Logodaedalus*), Hegel (*La Remarque speculative*), Plato, and Descartes. Lacoue-Labarthe has written on Höderlin, German Romanticism, Nietzsche, and Heidegger. He has recently published *Le Sujet de la philosophie*.

IRVING WOHLFARTH is an associate professor of comparative literature at the University of Oregon. He has published essays on Laclos, Baudelaire, and Benjamin, on whom he is currently completing two book-length studies.

NOTES ON TRANSLATORS

AVITAL RONELL teaches German at the University of Virginia. Her publications include *Poetics of Desire and Principles of Textuality in Kafka's Das Schloss*. She is currently working on a book, tentatively entitled *The Poetics of the Self-reflexive Text: Goethe, Hölderlin, and Kafka*, and on a study of Nietzsche.

EVELYN PERRY is a graduate student in Near Eastern Studies at The Johns Hopkins University where she is completing a Ph.D. in Egyptology.

LAWRENCE R. SCHEHR, who is currently preparing a dissertation on the nineteenth-century French novel, is a teaching fellow in the Department of Romance Languages at The Johns Hopkins University.

MICHAEL SCHWERIN is a graduate student in German literature at The Johns Hopkins University.

ROBERT VOLLRATH is a graduate student in the Department of Romance Languages at The Johns Hopkins University. He is completing a dissertation on Chateaubriand.

MARILYN WYATT is a graduate student in German and comparative literature at The Johns Hopkins University. She is preparing a dissertation on the problem of authorship in the eighteenth-century novel.